P9-EDQ-730

QUEBEC SOCIETY: TRADITION, MODERNITY, AND NATIONHOOD

The voice of Hubert Guindon has been outspoken on Quebec politics and society from the days of the Quiet Revolution to the defeat of the Parti Québécois and beyond. The essays in this collection constitute a comprehensive and insightful analysis of social and political change in Quebec since the Second World War.

The earlier essays focus on changes within the traditional culture and institutions. They argue the crucial role of the new middle classes in the modernization of the national movement in Quebec. Guindon makes a stinging critique of Canada's Official Languages Act and the federal bilingualism policy, describing it as an insult to English Canada and irrelevant to a modernizing Quebec. The essay on the referendum argues that the lesson to be gleaned from the defeat concerns the 'overinstitutionalization' of the national movement by the Parti Québécois which had the effect of demobilizing its supporters and facilitating the mobilization of its opponents with impunity.

The seventies ushered in what Guindon calls 'the politics of exaggeration,' a phenomenon born in the October crisis when both Trudeau and the terrorists indulged in exaggeration. The labour unions and the first Bourassa government adopted the same technique, with the common front strike and the jailing of the labour leaders. Exaggeration informed the conflict around language policy, as reflected in the Canadian Air Traffic Controllers strike and the introduction of Bill 22, which subjected pre–school-age children to language tests. The Parti Québécois engaged in exaggerations of its own when it rolled back the salaries of public service employees and later purged 'indépendantistes' from its ranks.

The collection concludes with an essay on the historical roots of Quebec nationalism, which suggests that party politics may be a liability for the national movement, and an epilogue outlines more effective alternatives to further the goal of independence.

HUBERT GUINDON is a professor in the department of sociology at Concordia University. He is co-editor, with D. Glenday and A. Turowetz, of *Modernization and the Canadian State*, and has written many articles.

ROBERTA HAMILTON is a professor in the department of sociology at Queen's University.

JOHN McMULLAN is associate professor and chairman of the department of sociology at St Mary's University.

HUBERT GUINDON

Quebec Society:
Tradition, Modernity,
and Nationhood

Edited and with an introduction by
Roberta Hamilton and John L. McMullan

UNIVERSITY OF TORONTO PRESS
Toronto Buffalo London

©University of Toronto Press 1988
Toronto Buffalo London
Printed in Canada

ISBN 0-8020-2645-1 (cloth)
ISBN 0-8020-6671-2 (paper)

Canadian Cataloguing in Publication Data

Guindon, Hubert
Quebec society

ISBN 0-8020-2645-1 (bound) ISBN 0-8020-6671-2 (pbk.)

1. Quebec (Province) – Politics and government –
1936–1960.* 2. Quebec (Province) – Politics and
government – 1960–   . 3. Quebec (Province) –
Social conditions – 1945–1960.* 4. Quebec (Province)–
Social conditions – 1960–   .* 5. Nationalism –
Quebec (Province). I. Hamilton, Roberta.
II. McMullan, John L., 1948–   . III. Title.

FC2925.G85 1988   971.4'04   c88-093720-3
F1053.2.G85 1988

61,466

This book has been published with the assistance of block grants
from the Canada Council and the Ontario Arts Council.

Contents

CAMROSE LUTHERAN COLLEGE
LIBRARY

Preface

The somewhat lengthy, indiscreet introduction written by two former students gives a clue about the unspoken assumption behind this book, an assumption shared by its publisher, author, and editors: namely that it is the first and last book expected from me. But perhaps I will surprise everyone – including myself.

The essays in this book span more than thirty years of my career in university teaching (1954–87). They were not written in order to have a political impact, which they obviously did not have. They were written essentially as an attempt to make sense for myself of the society in which I was living as it underwent the deep social and political changes that shaped my biography. While it was unpopular, for a time, to observe society in a detached manner, uninvolved in praxis or political action, by temperament more than principle and because of a radical distrust of all institutions, I always remained not above but outside of any world of social and political action, yet deeply interested in them as a concerned spectator.

My former students claim these essays had an impact on academia in English Canada but were ignored, if not systematically boycotted, in Quebec. It seems to upset them more than me. An academic impact stays academic and, while it is flattering to have some influence on those involved in the world of ideas, it is a much safer world, as Socrates learned to his detriment, than the world of politics. The world of ideas has this strange requirement, so perceptively described by Hannah Arendt, that in order to enter it you must shut yourself off from the social and political world of daily life. The academic life makes this possible, not probable, practically on a full-time basis. In fact, as those who are in it know, academia is often anything but a world of ideas: it is a world of politics, resource hunting, and self-glorification. So, one should not be shocked to discover pettiness, careerism, and pretension. When the growth of academia transformed it into a market-place, it lost the 'noblesse' of a bygone era in which it seemed, according to the myth, a world more 'noble' than the world of commerce.

What's nice about ageing is that one increasingly lives in a world of memories. What's even nicer is that one discovers that there are essentially two kinds of memories: fond and faint ones. Slights, boycotts, bitter conflicts, if one has a good disposition, eventually belong to the world of faint memories. They become events that have lost their sting, and the personal animosity once felt, dissipates. Fond memories for an academic seldom have to do with rectors, deans, or department heads. Sometimes they are tied to colleagues, but they are always bound up with students: students who fearfully enter the world of ideas, whose intellectual confidence has to be built up, and who, once developed, are eternally grateful to those who encouraged them to entertain that 'calling.'

My debt to my students is stupendous, and not only to the good ones. Because of their age, which is constant, they are very much searching for certitudes, but they are not ready to accept those that their parents and the worlds they were born into insist upon. Sociology as a discipline can validate both the quest and the doubt, the ambivalence and uneasiness they feel towards the world they confront. The class-room can be a wonderfully semiprivate space shared by a teacher and his or her students, where the former can with the complicity of the latter take exception with and be scathingly critical of the conduct of social affairs by the élites of the day. Young people's reckless disregard, not to say disrespect, for the world and life-styles so painstakingly constructed by their elders stems from the fact that the world they are entering is a given, that it is not theirs. Arendt calls this phenomenon 'natality': the challenge to the world-as-constructed by the new generations entering it. Teaching is usually defined as imparting acquired knowledge to the younger generation. Teaching as an intellectual production is quite exactly the opposite: challenging the world-as-constructed with the complicity of the younger generation.

There has been no lack of challenge to the world-as-constructed in Quebec over the last thirty years. The men and women of my generation were impatient and restless under the socio-political system and the world of tradition we entered in the post-war period. We espoused modernism with a vengeance, and the jaundiced view of the traditional society we constructed and propagated was not, in retrospect, an 'objective, detached, and scientific' analysis of reality. When tradition has lost its 'sacred' character, for many it becomes unbearable. As my essays progress over time they do become more mellow towards the Catholic church and its role in the development of the Québécois as a people. I do take increasingly strong exception with both right-wing and left-wing views, rampant in academic and business schools as well as in the professional and business world of upwardly mobile francophones, about the negative impact of the Catholic church on Quebec society's economic development.

I did not share in the socialist dream that inspired so many of the youth and intellectuals in the late sixties. The denunciation of the exploitation of capitalism was interspersed with a fascination with power and ideological closure. People fascinated with power should not be given it. Ideological closure is something I became immune to when I parted with dogmatic Catholicism. The new left successfully challenged the 'liberalism' of the fifties and early sixties to see themselves overtaken by the right-wing ideologists now triumphant in the eighties. Far from the socialist dream of equality, inequality is now taken as a fact to be personally avoided, not as a social situation to be politically corrected. A vitiated dream is still to be preferred to a ruthless and unscrupulous scramble for wealth. It is not coincidental, I would argue, that Conservative rule is so often associated with moral and political corruption historically rampant in the development of imperialism and increasingly apparent after eight years of triumphant conservatism in North America.

Over time, reluctantly and with increasing acrimony, I have taken a more jaundiced view of the role of the Canadian state in its dealings, then and now, with the people of Quebec. That it is in continuity with a vitiated beginning is increasingly clear to me. That no one in politics is willing or able squarely to face up to this is equally evident. It might be paradoxical, but the dream of independence for me is a sad but necessary conclusion. The youthful exuberance that marked its entrance in the world of party politics in mass society captivated the media and monopolized the centre stage of politics for a decade. The exuberance and media attention masked the dangerous underlying naïve belief in the myth that party politics could lead to independence. This naïvety has now vanished and, while the dream will no longer be in the public spotlight, it will be the quiet resolve of a sufficient number of Québécois to make equally unattainable the other dream of 'national unity.'

The Canadian political problem is one of the sad legacies our generation will have left unsolved for future generations. Over time, one hopes, political courage and wisdom will make it possible.

In conclusion, it is a pleasant duty for me to thank the people directly responsible for facilitating the production of this book: Roberta Hamilton and John McMullan who conceived the idea and, true to their character, actually carried it out. The other person, Virgil Duff, I do not know personally very well. First at Macmillan and now at the University of Toronto Press, he believed this book should exist. For that I am most grateful to him.

My final thanks is to the Thursday Club. It consisted of six academics and a former politician who met every other Thursday around a simple friendly dinner to discuss and support one another's intellectual pursuits. These gatherings stimulated those of us with writer's cramp occasionally to take up the pen after having dropped the fork. This book, in good measure, owes a lot to their pleasant company.

H.G.
October 1987
Montreal

Editors' Acknowledgments

The editors are very grateful to the following people: the Honourable Monique Bégin, Dr Jeannine Guindon, l'abbé Norbert Lacoste, M. Jean-Louis Martel, Professors John Jackson and Kurt Jonassohn of Concordia University, Professors Pierre Dandurand and Jean-Marie Rainville of the Université de Montréal, and Professor John Meisel of Queen's University. Roberta Hamilton wishes to acknowledge the support of the Advisory Research Committee of Queen's University, and the assistance of Carolyn Hider in preparing the typescript.

Editors' Introduction

Hubert Guindon has been our teacher, our mentor, and our friend, and we have come to love him in an extraordinary way. He has taught us, as he taught so many others, around his kitchen table at breakfast; over long, often liquid suppers; through ordinary conversation; and sometimes through passionate argument. He has let us teach him, too, though what we had to teach never looked quite the same after he had confronted it with his irony, experience, and humour.

Because we have had this kind of relationship with him, and most especially because whatever else he is, he is not an academic *comme les autres*, it is impossible to introduce his work without introducing him. As students and colleagues before and after us have discovered, Hubert Guindon, the sociologist, cannot be separated from Hubert Guindon, the person. The passions often ascribed to the emotional realm and the rationality said to be the province of the intellect are joined together in his work and in his life. The result has been passionate scholarship, which draws as much from his experiences living in society as it does from conscious intellectual pursuits. The result has been profound and persuasive, and goes a long way to explain both the influence of his work and the appeal he has for students of sociology throughout Canada and Quebec. 'How many of us write two articles in the 1960s, and for the next decade are invited across the country to talk about them?' was Concordia colleague John Jackson's answer to a question about Guindon's influence. Jackson continued, 'I have used that question to combat deans who measure quality by quantity because they don't know how to assess quality. Hubert was invited everywhere during that period, and all the time he was developing and trying out the "modernization" piece, which did not appear until 1977.'[1]

Clearly Guindon's influence does not stem from the cubic-foot-of-publications method of measuring influence. Few and far between, his published articles have usually been developed first as class lectures or public presentations. Committing them to paper was and continues to be an exhilarating but painful process. As his friend and colleague Kurt Jonassohn once said in response to a frustrated editor waiting for a promised article, 'It's the students' fault – they're not like they used to be. George Herbert Mead didn't write much – his students published his lecture notes. That's what Hubert's students should have done!'[2] Indeed, Guindon never submitted an article to a journal in the usual sense: they were always solicited following public presentations.

Guindon's chief contribution to sociology over the last twenty-five years has been to develop and disseminate interpretations of Quebec society for English Canada. For reasons that we will discuss, his influence in francophone Quebec has been more uneven and uncertain, often contained in pockets, and not fully realized until the 1980s. The coming of the Quiet Revolution, the growth of the state-employed middle class and its exclusion from the corridors of corporate power, the political nature of lower-class unrest, the role of the Church in the sponsoring of the Canadian confederation and in protecting the heritage of the French, the consequences of the demise of clerical power, the character of the Canadian confederation, the timing of the challenge to the legitimacy of the state created by that 'unequal union,'[3] the rise of neo-nationalism in the 1960s, the political opportunism and sociological naïvety of official bilingualism policies, the politics of the referendum, the rise and fall of the Parti Québécois: all this has been captured in Hubert Guindon's quest to understand his own society.

Given that the dramatic transformations in Quebec society often occupied the forefront of the Canadian stage in the last twenty-five years, his interpretations have been not only sociologically plausible, but politically satisfying. John Meisel, professor of politics at Queen's University, put it this way: 'English Canada – intellectual English Canada – was desperately trying to reach out to find out what was going on in Quebec and Hubert was wonderfully adept at that. Hubert was a messenger who wasn't shot for the message that he brought because he really was scholarly in the way that he portrayed events in Quebec.'

Hubert Guindon was a young professor at the University of Montreal when he delivered his first paper on Quebec society at the annual meetings of the Canadian Political Science Association in Kingston, in June 1960. It was a controversial paper. On the surface it was a qualified defence of the 'Chicago School's' interpretation of the folk society of Quebec. Horace Miner and Everett Hughes had published highly influential monographs on St Denis and Drummondville, respectively. Their work had been subjected to a critique by Philippe Garigue, while he was teaching during the mid-1950s at McGill University. By 1959 Garigue had been appointed dean of social sciences at the University of Montreal – Guindon's dean, in fact. Guindon rose to defend the 'Chicago School' against the Garigue indictment, launching an uncompromising attack on Garigue's thesis, and presenting an interpretation of the transition in Quebec society that went far beyond the terms of the Chicago School. The night before Guindon's presentation Everett Hughes suggested to his former student that he launch his career more quietly, more empirically, and in less global terms. Such all-encompassing analyses were for the well-established; the young should begin less pretentiously!

That paper – 'The Social Evolution of Quebec Reconsidered' – was published in *The Canadian Journal of Economics and Political Science* and established Hubert Guindon's reputation in English Canada. The Chicago School researchers argued that Quebec was in the midst of a transition from a traditional to an urban society that had occurred earlier in much of English America. In the 1930s Horace Miner had provided an ethnographic study of St Denis, 'a completely rural parish' which argued that until recently the outside urban, industrializing world had impinged very little on the economic, religious, political, social, and sexual practices of the residents of St Denis. With comparably little commotion, land passed quietly from generation to generation. In the urban setting of Cantonville (Drummondville) Everett Hughes substantiated Miner's findings: 'The current changes in French-Canadian life and problems are those of concurrent industrialization and urbanization, both brought about by expansion of the Anglo-American world. The completely rural parish described by Horace Miner in *St. Denis, a French-Canadian Parish* may be taken as the prototype of Quebec communities as yet scarcely affected by these changes.'[4]

Philippe Garigue was not impressed by these studies. Drawing on his study of St Justin he argued that French Canada, rural and urban, comprised an integral part of modern, industrialized society. By ignoring the rich urban history of Quebec, dating back to New France, the Chicago School contrived to find ruptures instead of continuities, distinctions instead of similarities. According to Garigue the French Canadians were a thoroughly 'modern' people in their ideas, practices, family life, and economic pursuits. Far from being tied to the land, they were an intensely

mobile people, fully responding to the economic imperatives of industrialized society. As Garigue put it, 'By focusing ... on the process of
integration it was found that rural French Canadians held beliefs they
shared with urban French Canadians, and that the pattern of social
institutions had prevented the rise of a specific rural culture ... French-
Canadian culture already had incorporated within itself all the elements
necessary for contemporary large scale urbanization, and as such did not
suffer major stress through change.'[5]

Guindon's response had been some years in the making. University of
Montreal professor Jean-Marie Rainville was his student during that
period and recalls that 'all the ideas of the "Social Evolution of Quebec
Reconsidered" – the basic categories of analysis – were present as early as
1956. The published text was an elaboration of these earlier papers, and it
was a project he was to build upon.' That paper drew upon historical
sources, the perspective and research of the Chicago School, and his own
field-work in St Denis. Although it was true that New France had been a
'rural trading society,' Garigue had failed to notice the devastating effects
of the Conquest on French society in America. Citing the recently
published work of Michel Brunet and Guy Frégault, Guindon argued that
the bourgeoisie had moved back to France (the decapitation thesis), and
the rest of the population had little choice but to withdraw to the
countryside. There, under the watchful gaze of the Catholic clergy, itself
duly impressed by the horrific effects of the French Revolution upon the
Church, the remaining people continued to reproduce a traditional, rural,
and religious life. Each generation provided the next with land and a
suitable ideology idealizing hard work, large families, and Catholic
religious practices – in contradistinction to the secular and materialist
life-style of its distant English conquerors.

But in his analysis of the French-Canadian élites, secular and religious,
and their attempts both to define the terms of the transition to industrial
capitalism and to retain power during the transition, Guindon went
beyond the terms of the Chicago School and Garigue. Here we see the
influence of C. Wright Mills, perhaps Guindon's only hero in sociology.
By looking at the behaviour of élites in these ways, Guindon showed for the
first, though not the last, time his impressive predictive skills. The Church
was realizing that the needs of the people – thrown onto the uncertain
and impersonal capitalist market-place as workers and consumers – had
far outstripped its administrative resources and abilities. In the process
its institutions became large scale; priests and nuns turned themselves
into bureaucrats, and eventually had to have recourse to state funding.

Guindon predicted that in this process the *meaning* of the religious life would be lost on its congregants: the Church would have won the battle for administrative control, but lost the war – its own legitimacy in the eyes of the population. As he put it, 'The [cherished] symbols may become hollow and meaningless for the population, and even for parts of the clergy. And not because of alien and foreign culture, but as a direct result of the clergy's own successful control of the whole society.'[6] In a recent interview we asked him if the signs of loss of faith were present when the prediction was made. 'No, it wasn't happening yet,' he replied, and in characteristic fashion continued, 'It was a threat! And it was prophetic in fact. It was through logic that I came to write that: there were no empirical signs. Because I go as far as saying that [the meaning would be lost] not just to the faithful but to the clerics themselves. It was a nice sort of thought!'[7] It was 'a nice sort of thought' because a key theme running through Guindon's reflections on society – both written and spoken – is the intolerance of authority that aspires beyond its social mandate, that cloaks itself in ostentation, that claims to offer much, but is transparently self-serving. As a sociologist he could see that the meaning of the religious life, for clergy and lay people alike, would unravel, as indeed it did, with dizzying speed, during the 1960s.

His stance towards authority affected not only his writing, informing his insights and style, but also his career as a sociologist and his differential impact in Quebec and English Canada. For in 'The Social Evolution of Quebec Reconsidered' he took on the interpretation not just of another social scientist, but of his dean, Philippe Garigue, whose appointment he had strongly opposed, and whose style of leadership and politics continued to distress him. A footnote in 'The Social Evolution' displays these intertwined concerns: 'Professor Garigue does not conceive of himself as a soldier in the army of science but rather as a field general. There is nothing particularly wrong in the ambition, for most social scientists cherish the same one secretly; but the common practice is not to voice it quite so openly and aggressively.'[8]

For a young, untenured professor those were bold words. His sister Dr Jeannine Guindon recalls that the original text was even tougher. '"Hubert," I said to him, "you can't say these things" – after all, you must remember, this was his dean!' But that, of course, was part of the problem, and requires some discussion of Hubert Guindon's stance towards authority, of how it affected his sociology, why it led him into opposition to Philippe Garigue and, ultimately, contributed to the reasons for his departure from the University of Montreal. For the debate with Garigue, as Professor Pierre Dandurand of the University of Montreal and a student of Guindon's at the time recalls, was vociferous and public: 'The principal reason Hubert left the University of Montreal was Garigue ... Garigue won the administrative battle.'

Guindon is a Franco-Ontarien, born in Bourget and raised in Apple Hill, the youngest child of Pascal and Josephine, small-business people. His five brothers and sisters máde professional careers: Fernand, a politician; Bernard, a priest; Jeannine, a psychologist; Ghislaine, a social worker; and Jean, a manager of part of the family business. Hubert was sent to boarding-school at ten, and because of his precocity (not just in academic subjects but also in music, winning competitions sponsored by the Ontario Conservatory of Music as a young boy, and later becoming the school organist) found himself with boys thirteen and fourteen. Guindon recalls, 'Even in boarding-school, I was rebellious. I was fighting Catholic Action, which I thought was a sort of fifth column: a hierarchy of holier people. We were all supposed to be becoming priests, but some were holier than others.' The despising of pretensions appeared early. Yet, he had his own kind of confidence:

There was a Sulpician priest from Montreal and we called him 'Bouboule.' He used to take on students one at a time and make them cry. I knew my turn would come, and it did. He called me 'Lammenais' – pride, the sin of pride. It was a compliment to me, and he was very upset when he saw he didn't have the desired effect. There was this sense of revolt from the time I was ten or eleven. Because I was bright and always came first there was a grudging respect from teachers – and from my peers, with whom I was not close. But I was thought to have *le mauvais esprit* by those in authority.

Why he went on at seventeen to Le Séminaire Universitaire of the University of Ottawa is a bit of a mystery. According to Jeannine, she and his other siblings were against it because 'we knew he didn't have the vocation.' They tried to rally their parents against the idea. But for Guindon what is surprising is not so much his going, but the manner of his leaving: 'I remember asking Ghislaine to tell our parents that I wouldn't be going back to the seminary, but I think I also told her that I wouldn't be practising [the faith]. And I felt that if they didn't accept it they wouldn't see me again. After all, this is 1949, and not a time when these things were accepted.'

Guindon's description of how he made the decision is somewhat jarring in a secular age, and provides moving testimony about the transition that would occur in Quebec – the transition that Garigue later argued only existed in the minds of the Chicago School researchers. 'I asked my closest friend, Robert Gay [now Superior General of the White Fathers in Rome], if I still had the faith. He consulted other people and he told me that I didn't. That came as a liberation in many ways.' On a lighter, but none the less true note, Guindon added, 'My recollection is that as I left the seminary I left the faith too. I think I thought that if I couldn't be a saint, I may as well not try at all!'

Perhaps because Guindon left the Church with little fanfare – and with silent acceptance rather than hostility from his family – he has not been among the Quebec intellectuals to celebrate the Church's demise. On the contrary, he analyses the role of the Church in Quebec in the years before the Quiet Revolution in a way that exposes the nature of the Anglo-French contract underlying the Canadian confederation, and that highlights the role of the Church in maintaining the language and culture of the French 'nation' in America. For him, current pretensions and abuses of power are more suitable targets for sociological rapiers. In his words, 'it takes little courage to kick dead horses. Never has this maxim been better illustrated than in the case of the Catholic church since its demise in Quebec society ... If verbal crucifixion produces purification, it can now indeed be called the Holy Roman Catholic church.'[9]

Guindon argues that much that has been written about the Church since the Quiet Revolution needs to be read with great circumspection. 'I accused the Church for a long time – maybe not more unfairly than those of my era, but I'm willing to say, there is more to the Church than what we wrote about it in the fifties.'

Guindon left the Church in 1949. After a year spent at the University of Montreal studying philosophy he went to the University of Chicago to study sociology. It was not an obvious choice for a French Canadian at that time – the only department in Quebec was at McGill University – but family connections played a role. Through his sister Jeannine, Hubert met Father Noel Mailloux, OP, the founder of the Department of Psychology at the University of Montreal. It was Father Mailloux who first introduced him to sociology, the summer after he left the seminary. Jeannine reports that Hubert had a predisposition towards sociology: 'What he liked was really to learn about the mores, the ways that people were living ... that was really his interest.' She continues, 'My brother could always see the whole picture – he could see the connections, way far ahead, and he expected others to see them; it was so *evident* for him. He already had those cognitive structures.'

Guindon reports a short walk with his father the same summer. 'Clearly he thought that there was no future in philosophy: what would I do? I mentioned sociology, which I had heard about from my sister through Father Mailloux – I did not know what the hell it was – and I mentioned law. My father couldn't stand the idea of law: he thought lawyers and judges were corrupt. So he said maybe I should think of sociology – of course, he didn't know what it was either!'

Whatever sociology turned out to be for Hubert Guindon in the ensuing three years at Chicago, and throughout his career, it was thoroughly informed by his earlier decision to quit the faith: 'What I fought against were closed ideological systems. I think that once I rejected the Church, that immunized me against Parsons and Marxism – both. Instead I had this idea of the importance of history, that it is our function – and this comes through Mills – to unmask, to make sense of our own society.' He added, 'I am Marxist in only one very important respect – at the epistemological level I've never believed in anything other than the historical specificity of the social sciences.'

The rejection of Grand Theory would not stand him in good stead in the faculty that Philippe Garigue was building – what l'abbé Norbert Lacoste describes as 'a formal, high-status institution with a less pragmatic and more abstract emphasis.' But there was more that Hubert Guindon took from his days in Chicago that would prove problematic in a changing department. Studying with Ernest W. Burgess ('the first Protestant saint I ever met'), William Fielding Ogburn, Herbert Blumer ('the greatest lecturer I ever heard'), Edward Shils, Lloyd Warner, and Everett Hughes ('he was a slave-driver – I just audited his course!') left him with a 'respect in sociology for those who went to the field.' That meant something quite specific for Guindon: 'you don't stay on your turf – you go to their turf, and, therefore, you can't call the shots or the rules of the game. That kind of field-work hardly exists.'

That kind of sociology takes a dim view of some of the stock-in-trade of most sociologists – attitude studies: 'What you got from Blumer was that you couldn't study attitudes divorced from situations. He hated those attitude studies'; questionnaires: 'I never believed that the questionnaire was an instrument to discover social reality, and I still don't. I think the tide is on my side – for a while!'; categories and quantification: 'I had Otis Dudley Duncan – we called him Otis Deadly Duncan. He was a demographer, a number cruncher. And then I took a course in Mass Media. I did a study of Irv Kupcinet's gossip column in *The Chicago Sun-Times*. I didn't think it was a very exciting paper, but I tried as best I could with categories and numbers. It was an "empirical" paper. Then the professor did me a favour and gave me my only C while I was at Chicago: it cured me for life. Never again would I enter into this counting game!'[10]

There was something else Guindon took away from his days in Chicago – not so much from the university but from the city. It did not affect directly his published work, but exerted enormous impact upon his teaching, his style, and the reputation for being almost 'mysterious' he gained among students and colleagues. That was a consolidation of his feelings about the bourgeoisie and the middle class, on the one hand, and a fascination and identification with those on the wrong side of the tracks – 'the humble people, the poor people, the simple people' – on the other.

Unlike most graduate students in those days at the University of Chicago, Guindon attended all his lectures – except for one quarter during a period of prolonged depression. That term he spent in West Madison, site of Chicago's skid row. 'I just started going there,' he recalls. 'People get to know your face; you don't need a formal introduction.' Nor did he need an introduction to attend criminal hearings in the court-house, located in the heart of skid row. Here he fostered his interest in the law-career option that he had never fully rejected and would put to good use later in both of his social worlds.

For everyone who knows Hubert Guindon knows that there are two social worlds, the academic world with colleagues, and especially students, and the other world, the *demi-monde* of the dispossessed and the underdog. This latter is not a world that he inhabits as a professional sociologist. Here there are friends, those who have shared their stories with him and with whom he has shared his time, money, and expertise. One of his students at the University of Montreal, Monique Bégin, recalls: 'We knew he had friends, spent evenings in bars, but his private life remained mysterious – mysterious because the little we heard about it from him referred to a life, a really private life, which was totally deviant compared to the official intellectual's life.'

John Jackson describes him as 'populist to the core; he has a love of humanity, and there is no pretence. The things he says, the people he hangs around with, and what he does with his own life don't fit any *known* academic mould. But it hasn't been easy for Hubert – to be in academia and not adopt a certain kind of life-style. It gives rise to certain anxieties, certain angers.' This helps explain why the politesse of the bourgeoisie and the social pretensions of the middle classes have no charm for Guindon. But it also explains why he has lived so uncomfortably within institutions, and why he rises so quickly to defend those whom he believes they are victimizing. Jeannine Guindon explains his stance towards authority this way: 'Authority had to be right or else come down. As he saw it, if you take responsibility you have to be nearly perfect, if not perfect ... he was not against all authority, but he was very critical of what they (those in authority) would do if he felt they were not doing the right things. And he had high standards and expectations.' As populist, self-taught lawyer, and astute sociologist he has provided formidable opposition to institutions and considerable assistance to those he has defended. And he has never forgotten that he once needed defending himself – in 1959 at the University of Montreal.

Guindon started teaching there in 1954, when Quebec's professional networks were small and informal. A letter from Father Mailloux informed him while he was still in Chicago that he had a job teaching in the university's new Department of Sociology. L'abbé Norbert Lacoste was chairman; Hubert Guindon, Paule Verdet, and Sally Cassidy, all from the University of Chicago, were the other professors. Fernand Cadieux, the motivating force behind the Social Research Group, who became one of Guindon's closest friends until his death in 1976, taught also, though he refused full-time appointments.[11] From the earliest days Guindon was a very popular teacher. Monique Bégin recalled that 'he taught us to doubt *with passion.* He was *our* professor in the old medieval definition – someone who is older than you in that field who has already explored more than you and whom you follow – literally follow – around, and you pick pieces and you organize them the best you can.'

That was also true in the large introductory lecture courses during the years at Sir George Williams University (now Concordia). His colleague John Jackson was unequivocal on this point: 'I suppose he was the best teacher in the world in the eyes of many, many, many students. Never have I heard a negative word.'

A student description from 1967 captures the flavour of Guindon's teaching 'methods':

Professor Guindon's lecturing style is very much peculiar to him, and he incorporates his personality into his subject matter ... He speaks with great ease, moving from one topic to another ... smoking like a defunct locomotive, spilling his 'cinders' over his suit. His comments interspersed with jokes allow for class intervention; that is, if anyone, as he puts it, 'can get a word in edgewise.' He is conscious of his eccentricities, and terms himself a 'smiling crocodile' ... Once one comes into contact with him, no matter what impression he makes, he cannot be forgotten.[12]

He was also a favourite guest lecturer. John Meisel accounts for his popularity in several ways: 'He was a man ahead of his time. He was a counter-cultural figure before the counter-culture – and then it was his *own* counter-culture. He was informal with students. He challenged them but they always felt free to speak openly with him. And, of course, he is an iconoclast – a man with a truly original mind.'

Relations with authorities were not always as congenial. John Jackson recalls Guindon's approving description of the administration of Sir George Williams University in 1966. 'The most impressive thing here,' noted Guindon, 'is that the administration is very humble.' At that time, Jackson continued, it was true. 'The administration *was* humble, that is, they did administer. It was principally a teaching institution.'

As it grew, Sir George Williams changed, taking its cues increasingly from research-based, formal institutions such as McGill rather than from its populist YMCA roots. Guindon's increasing disenchantment with a university he had once described to his sister as 'the university of the people' reflected that transformation. It also summoned up an earlier, more profoundly felt, disillusionment at the University of Montreal. There the transformation was wrought more dramatically and involved the clearing out of the old guard, and the introduction of new sociologists and a new sociology. From Guindon's perspective these developments resembled a coup, as they did to those of his students who returned in September 1960 to find the new order in place. What they had been taught previously, they discovered, had been 'bad' sociology; Guindon and his students had been christened 'les Hurons' by criminologist Denis Szabo (clearly a racial slur, which would presumably no longer be acceptable in the 'respectable' academy)[13] and the returning students had to be chastened, resocialized, and re-educated. Field-work was out – it amounted to little more than quaint ethnographic studies. L'abbé Norbert Lacoste captured this perception well: 'Hubert was less a class scholar, much more a field-worker. He was interested in marginal groups; he had some friends in the police force, and he went with them to see gangs. He was in the line of *Street Corner Society*, and was interested in students discovering the grass roots.' Those familiar with Guindon's sociological writings over the past thirty years can be excused if they have not picked up this aspect of his work. Yet l'abbé Lacoste's description is not his own invention. How can this discrepancy be explained?

Two interrelated factors seem to be at work. First Guindon's Chicago School inheritance – the commitment to studying the society first hand – together with his mistrust of preconceived systems of thought thoroughly informed his teaching of the discipline. In an era when sociology was trying to model itself upon the physical sciences, when general laws and abstract principles were the *sine qua non* of scholarly work, the messy, untidy task of apprehending and interpreting a historically specific society, and how it had come to be as it was, appeared as a less profound, even quixotic task.

Second, it would appear that Guindon's sociology was judged by the perception that was held of his personal life. To quote l'abbé Lacoste again, 'Hubert Guindon was a nonconformist, and the University of Montreal was building sociology on high academic standards.' Monique Bégin put it more bluntly: 'They used to take words from his physical appearance, from his private life – the word "disorganized" is the best that comes to mind – and say that that was not sociology.' In 1960 Hubert Guindon was given a two-year unsolicited sabbatical from the University of Montreal to complete his PH D. As he recalls, 'with a one-year sabbatical you know why they give it to you. But with two years, you wonder!' Or in l'abbé Lacoste's words, 'at a certain level you have to trim the tree – so Garigue trimmed the tree and so some branches fell off, and that's what happened with Hubert.'

There is somewhat more to the story. For when Garigue encouraged Guindon to leave he lost not just a 'disorganized' colleague from his faculty or the sociologist who was criticizing his interpretation of Quebec society, but also the man who clearly and publicly had opposed his nomination as dean. It was 1959 and Esdras Minville had resigned as dean of the Faculty of Social Sciences. Guindon and others had suggested that he be succeeded by Jacques Lavigne, a social philosopher, then teaching at the University of Montreal. Lavigne was a scholar of international reputation, and author of *L'Inquiétude Humaine*. When word got out that l'abbé Lacoste was trying to bring in Philippe Garigue, Guindon and Fernand Cadieux tried to prevent the appointment. They had been told that Garigue had not been renewed at McGill because he had been unpopular with the faculty and because had fomented animosity between sociologists and anthropologists within the joint department.

Despite the interventions of Guindon and others, Philippe Garigue was, to quote Guindon, 'named [dean] in the passive tense. *M. Garigue est nommé.*' For Guindon there had been two acts of institutional malfeasance: first in the treatment of Jacques Lavigne – 'Hubert considered it a treachery,' in the words of his sister – and second in its appointment of a person with an ambiguous and unpopular administrative record, which from the point of view of Guindon and others pointed to authoritarian tendencies.[14]

Guindon's worst fears about the new dean were soon realized. In the first year of his appointment Garigue let it be known that he would 'create a dossier' on an economics professor if he did not resign from faculty council. The stories of uncollegiality that had emanated from McGill University appeared confirmed. Sometime in 1959 Guindon was called to Lacoste's office and a series of 'charges' were levelled at him in the name of the dean and the rector. Guindon responded by returning to his office, drawing up the list of 'complaints,' photocopying them, and distributing them to his colleagues! Garigue called him to his office and dissociated himself from Lacoste's actions. Guindon explains these events: 'I think Lacoste knew what they wanted and tried to do it on his own; that is, he tried to provoke my resignation but, by spreading news of this attempt, I caught them before they were ready to act. So Lacoste was left holding the bag. By then I was a highly politicized young man – that is I was not naïve, not me, anymore. I became known as the leader of the opposition and I had some fun.'

But most of the time it was not funny. Whatever the reasons, by the time Hubert Guindon was 'offered' a two-year sabbatical in 1960, a seven-person department had been reduced to its founder – Norbert Lacoste. But he too did not go completely unscathed. Garigue asked Lacoste to step down as chair of the department by recruiting Guy Rocher, then at Laval University, for the post. Guindon remembers meeting the sociologist-priest on a sunny day in April. '"Monsieur l'abbé" I said to him, "do you know who your friends are?" And he replied, "I thought I did but I'm not sure anymore."'

Guindon went to Paris for the first year of his compulsory sabbatical in 1960 with mixed feelings. Like Jacques Lavigne, he was unwanted at the University of Montreal but all was not bleak. These were the days when the Learned Societies Meetings were small, and most of the sessions were plenary sessions. Social scientists from across the country had heard him deliver 'The Social Evolution of Quebec Reconsidered.' He accepted an invitation to teach in the 1961 summer school at the University of British Columbia, and although, in these days before the expansion of the universities, there were few jobs, there seemed little reason for career despair.

None the less, the year in Paris was one of great discontentment. In December he was back in Montreal, hospitalized for a suspected case of tuberculosis. Furthermore, even at a distance, relations with Lacoste's successor, Guy Rocher, had become uncomfortable. Upon hearing that Guindon had accepted the summer appointment at UBC Rocher had written a letter of reprimand: he had no business accepting such a job when he was 'supposed to be getting his PH D.' That very important person in Hubert's life Fernand Cadieux – the only person ever acknowledged in any of his articles[15] – intervened apparently through another professor at the University of Montreal, Pierre Elliott Trudeau – and Rocher visited him in hospital and apologized for what Guindon perceived to be an unwarranted intervention. Still, returning to the University of Montreal seemed more remote than ever.

In April he was back in Montreal again, this time because of the death of his mother. Josephine Guindon had suffered from great periods of sadness and depression while Hubert, her youngest child, was growing up. More than the other children he was the witness of those times, and he has lived depressions himself, the underside of his warm, jocular, ironic appreciation of life and of the 'human condition.'[16] Whatever the other consequences of her death, it seemed to confirm his decision not to return to Paris.

These were the early years of the Quiet Revolution; the stars of social scientists were rising in the state bureaucracy: in l'abbé Lacoste's words, the sociologists were 'the new high priests of society.' In the second year of his sabbatical Guindon worked in Quebec City for the Ministère de la Jeunesse with Arthur Tremblay, Roch Bolduc, Pierre Harvey, and Jean-Luc Migué, a former student. He describes his time there: 'They didn't know quite what to do with me. I used to send memos to everyone. I was not in the inner circle. As you know I have never been in any inner circle, and if so not for any length of time. It was Gérin-Lajoie, Bolduc, Tremblay, and Harvey, and I was on the margin of all that.'

It was a new regime, but he was still a critic. 'I remember writing about La Cité des Jeunes. The first was built in Vaudreuil in Paul Gérin-Lajoie's riding. It was a school of six thousand or seven thousand students. I thought it was a monstrosity of the first order to have that many people of the same age, all with very few adults, and I used to deal with this in these sarcastic memos.' Once again out of step. But his critique of the new bureaucratic order helps explain the defeat of Jean Lesage's Liberals in 1966 – a defeat incomprehensible, at the time, to most intellectuals inside and outside Quebec.

At the end of that year, a letter arrived from Dean Garigue asking for a decision: would he be returning to the University of Montreal? A chance encounter on St Catherine Street in Montreal with Harold Potter, whom he had known at Chicago, confirmed his decision not to return. Professor Potter was then the chair of the two-person sociology department at Sir

George Williams University. Somewhat defensively Potter asked him if he would consider a move to Sir George Williams. He would. Kurt Jonassohn – the other half of the department – remembers his reaction to Potter's enquiry about Guindon: 'I had heard his paper in Kingston, and had been tremendously impressed by this bright young man. I remember that my response to Harold was simple: grab him!'

In the early Sir George Williams years Guindon published two important articles. The first paper examined the social changes undermining the traditional culture of Quebec and the political legitimations of Canadian confederation. Published in 1964 as 'Social Unrest, Social Class, and Quebec's Bureaucratic Revolution,' it illustrated further Guindon's prophetic abilities. 'The emergence of a new middle class in French Canada,' he warned, 'is a structural change that cannot be wished away. Its status aspirations are challenging the historical pattern of the ethnic division of labour.'[17] The success of the emerging separatist movement would depend on the future character and direction of lower-class unrest and on the ability of political and economic élites to meet the status aspirations of this aroused middle class.

Guindon, then and now, was not sanguine about the imaginative abilities of the Canadian power élite. In 1964 he noted that 'it is doubtful that the current concept of "co-operative federalism" in its present confused and blurred state will tide us over.'[18] Fourteen years later in 'The Modernization of Quebec and the Legitimacy of the Canadian State' he made the same observation, but in blunter terms: 'Whether the Canadian people can respond to the challenge of the reshaping of the Canadian state is far from certain at present. Until now, in fact, very few, and least of all our current crop of political leaders have recognized its absolute necessity.'[19]

On the question of social unrest in the rural and lower classes, Guindon analysed the appeal of Social Credit as a manifestation of deep social discontent. It was a 'boomerang or latent resentment' against the middle-class–oriented Liberal political course in Quebec. The rural poor and the urban proletariat, bound by a fierce traditionalism, responded to the ousting of the Union Nationale from power with their own brand of class disenchantment. Cast off from the reservoirs of patronage by the bureaucratic political morality of the new middle class and net losers in the restructuring of public monies and 'goodies,' they found more merit in the Créditiste slogan 'you have nothing to lose' than in the Liberal vision 'maîtres chez nous.' But he was quick to point out that the Créditiste movement had a very uncertain political future. 'The traditionally conservative substructure of French Canadian society has expressed discontent of its own. Its course has not until now been in the same direction. But who can say with absolute confidence that it will never be.'[20]

The Parti Québécois would, of course, come – temporarily at least – to incorporate these cross-class discontents and aspirations, and Guindon would be its partisan and its critic.

It is for an analysis of the new middle class – its rise to prominence, its political victories and demise – that Guindon is best known. The fullest statement on neo-nationalism, the new middle class, and ethnic conflict is found in the 1967 article 'Two Cultures.' Here he argues that the initial claim to power of the new middle class in Quebec was modernization. The new middle class was critical of clerical rule for its incompetence and patronage. It promoted bureaucratic rationality and personal qualification as the basic prerequisites for office. But while this new middle class was ethnically homogeneous between 1945 and 1955 it was not ethnically conscious. And when they did resurrect nationalism it was as a decidedly modern ideology, freed of and even hostile to the traditional beliefs of agriculturalism, messianism, and antistatism. Their new concern was occupational mobility – vertical and horizontal. A two-pronged strategy to overcome the structural limitations to their growth – the small scale of their bureaucracies and the limited and specialized character of their organizational tasks – was adopted: 'a bureaucratic transformation of traditional institutions and a reaffirmation of linguistic identification.' The expansion of linguistic space and ethnic jurisdiction would also increase occupational opportunity. This would be accomplished by taking over the provincial state.

Reformist neo-nationalism also ushered in a new era in ethnic relations inside Quebec society. The historical patterns of segregated institutions where French and English lived apart and autonomously came under attack as the new middle class expanded its channels of mobility and took over and expanded the arenas of education, welfare, and health. The ethnic distribution of resources and income were now perceived as privileging the anglophone community. Guindon predicted that middle-class demands would broaden to include private industry, and ethnic conflict would, as a result, intensify, as areas of English monopolization were challenged.

These years at Sir George Williams, then, were intellectually productive. Indeed, Guindon's letter of resignation from Sir George Williams seven years after his arrival provides evidence of how deeply satisfying that period had been: 'My distress' at having to resign 'stems from the fact of having to sever close contact with a group of colleagues, second to none, whose scholastic promise, dedication to education and commitment to excellence were indeed, for me, a source of inspiration, personal pride and satisfaction. Over a period of seven years, in a climate of enthusiastic involvement, we shared a dream.'[21] That dream was to build a first-class sociology department that was at the same time student-centred, rooted in Quebec, but international in scope. A tall order.

How it was to be realized is best viewed through the Summer Institute. Guindon tells how it happened: 'The American Sociological Association was holding its annual meeting in Montreal at the end of the summer of 1964. We had the idea to get three or four big names to come early, teach a course, and stay for the meetings. You see, if McGill invites you the university is giving you status by inviting you. If Sir George invites you, you're giving it status by coming. That's what I call the external option of greatness.'

Starting that summer, and for several years after, the department brought well-known sociologists from the United States and Europe to teach undergraduate courses at the Summer Institute. Many scholars accepted the invitation – particularly when word spread that six weeks at Sir George meant being hosted by the Guindon-Jonassohn team who, in Jonassohn's words, 'made it as agreeable as it could be. We would get reading lists two or three months ahead, so the students were prepared. We made the visiting faculty feel we really wanted them – and the best part was getting to know them. The Summer Institute put Sir George on the map.'

Seven years later the Summer Institute was dropped by the department. However much it was appreciated by their colleagues, essentially it was a Guindon-Jonassohn project. Jackson described its demise as part of the general bureaucratization of the department, and the transition from a teaching to a research institution.

In turn, this change related to transformations in the university at large – changes that brought Sir George in line with the transition taking place at other universities. Jackson explains:

This change was not necessarily of the department's own volition because at the upper levels with respect to criteria for promotion and tenure, more and more publications and research grants were in the picture. And as we hired more, they were more straight academics and conditioned in graduate school that way: so there was a shift in the department. I think the Summer Institute partly suffered from that – it was a teaching function – to bring undergraduate students into contact with the best in the discipline.

Within this unmistakable shift in the nature of 'higher education' in Canada we can locate Guindon's progressive withdrawal from the department and his growing disillusionment with Sir George Williams University. 'What was now missing,' Jackson explains, 'was the commitment to students as human beings who were *part of the enterprise*, actors in the enterprise, not clients of it.' At one point, in 1969, Guindon resigned because the university withdrew institutional support for a program of graduate studies in the department of sociology. This was part of a larger problem of what Guindon terms the 'sad and somewhat shameful story' of the university's motivation and methods for introducing graduate studies. 'Graduate programmes were introduced as a result of "political panic" ... created by the Parent Report which spoke of limited charter universities ... A child of panic, rather than the product of concern for organic scholarly development, the Board of Graduate Studies proceeded to further disregard academic criteria by its methods of ... internal accreditation, rather than "external accreditation" by a panel of well-known and impartial scholars.'[22]

Having proceeded in this fashion, the university was then overtaken by a new panic, what Guindon described as the 'goodies' panic, so that 'resources will be allocated only to those programs already born in the noble way I have just described.' That sociology's claims were put on the back burner was, for him, a repudiation of his and his colleagues' best efforts 'to build along professional lines and establish live interaction and academic intercourse with the world of sociological scholarship in many leading centres of the world.'[23] Indeed, Guindon himself had served as president of the Canadian Sociology and Anthropology Association during that period and had been elected to the executive of the International Sociological Association.

His resignation prompted four immediate job offers, and he accepted a position at Carleton University in Ottawa: 'I especially liked the Institute of Canadian Studies. The students were so goddam good.' But ultimately Sir George had something going for it that was irreplaceable: it was in his beloved Montreal, and within weeks of 'moving' to Ottawa – that is, coming up on Tuesday and leaving as soon as he could on Thursday – he opened negotiations with McGill. That is when Kurt Jonassohn intervened and convinced his friend to return to Sir George. 'I thought he was bloody silly to have resigned because I didn't think he'd be happy anywhere else – not because of the universities, but because Montreal is home to him.' For its part the university agreed to institute an MA program in 1972, and the editors of this collection were in its first class.

For Guindon the new political realities governing the university proved galling at several levels, and he engaged in a number of all-consuming struggles, alone and with others, in efforts to contain or reverse what he perceived to be the worst abuses. For Guindon that usually involved an individual who was being victimized by the institution. There was, for example, in 1967, the famous case of Henry Worrell.

Worrell had worked for the university in the administration for thirty-three years when he was offered a demotion and a 50 percent cut in pay. 'That to me was degradation. The idea was that he was incompetent. Well, if he was incompetent, it was because he was here too long! So, if he's incompetent offer him his pension.' When Guindon was unable to rouse the administration internally he raised the issue on the pages of *Le Devoir*. In the end Worrell settled privately: 'He seemed satisfied and was grateful to me.'

But the incident left its impact on the administration's perception of Guindon. 'I'd been a marginal person at the university for some time. When there was talk of a new university of Quebec, Kurt and I wrote a memo saying it would be a good idea if Sir George became its English-speaking campus. It went over like a lead balloon! But now I was washing dirty linen in public; this was burning bridges with the administration.'

But was the administration's move against Worrell also a racist act? That's how Guindon read it. 'At the time I said, "you don't treat any white man that way." ' A decade later, the department turned down a colleague's tenure application. The man was black. Guindon successfully served as his advocate during a full three years of proceedings. Was the department's decision a racist act? 'If you believe in the unconscious it can be pretty easy to explain. The case against him was initiated by the chair and supported by the dean, both of whom mobilized a segment of the department. Such a mobilization was atypical of tenure hearings in the department – to say the least. The whole thing had a southern flavour. At one time the department even suggested to "my client" that he get another advocate!' Recently the administration turned down a tenure recommendation from the department. That candidate was a woman and, again, her case was argued successfully by Guindon.

Despite his 'withdrawal' from the department, then, he has been extremely active when he believed that an individual was not getting the benefit of 'due process.' As Jackson put it, 'If he perceives an injustice –

and it could be tomorrow – he's going to be in it, or if someone asks him to do something he will be there, because he says yes to anyone who needs help and is a victim of injustice.'

It would be wrong to leave the impression that Hubert Guindon is a bitter man. The advice he gives others about mistreatment is the same he took from a Dominican priest shortly after his departure from the University of Montreal: 'you should not forget, but you should always forgive. If you hang onto your resentments they will eat you up, not those who have done you harm.' Those who know him well, who have lived some of his turmoil with him, express amazement that he is spoken of so fondly everywhere. Quite a trick, if you can manage it!

Hubert Guindon's understanding of the politics of institutions, and the motivations of those who serve them, has informed his sociology, and his academic and personal politics – all of which, in his hands, are interrelated. We have often joked that his understanding of Quebec society is derived through osmosis – though our not infrequent charge that he doesn't read books is constantly belied – and is primarily derived from his own gently disparaging remarks about himself (and about us when we appear to put too great a reliance on the most recent sociological trend). Still, most of us would not dare trust our own perceptions and insights derived from everyday life, as he does. The Quebec demographer Jacques Henripin addressed this question in his welcoming address to Guindon when he was inducted into the Royal Society of Canada in 1978: 'Assez curieusement d'ailleurs, vos conclusions rejoignent les perspectives de certains démographes qui ont etudié l'évolution des groupes linguistiques au Canada. Etonnante convergence de vos intuitions, de votre sensibilité et de notre froide panoplie de méthodes de mesures.'[24]

The findings to which Henripin refers are those that underpin Guindon's trenchant critique of the federal bilingualism policy in 'The Modernization of Quebec and the Legitimacy of the Canadian State.' Here he argues the futility of coercive bilingualism policies both in Quebec and in the rest of Canada. Far from providing a *modus vivendi* for a shared fate between English and French, such policies feed a backlash among those outside the charmed circle of educated central Canadians. For unless minorities can work in their own language, their communities are destined to disappear – even if they have their own state-sponsored radio stations and other services, all sternly monitored by the commissioner of official languages. The English 'minority' in Quebec survived precisely because the language of capital remained English – hence Guindon's unconditional support for the language policies of Quebec governments (both Liberal and Parti Québécois) intended to make French the language of work.[25] This was the argument Guindon made to the Task Force on Canadian Unity while he was employed as researcher, and his impact is clear from its report.

Guindon's critique of the English Quebec response to the task force's recommendations was triggered by a pamphlet that he found in his mailbox – the kind of 'junk mail' most people give a cursory glance before depositing in the waste basket. The document in question was written by Donald Johnston, MP for Westmount, later president of the Treasury Board in Trudeau's cabinet. In a press conference Johnston had responded to the recommendations of the Task Force on Canadian Unity and, 'proud of his achievement' (in Guindon's words), had its contents translated and distributed (in both languages) door to door to his constituents.[26] Guindon subjected the contents of that pamphlet, including the 'giveaway' line that 'our French-speaking citizens ... will be condemned to live and work only in French,' to a scathing indictment in an article written in response to an invitation by Gordon Robertson, then chairman of the board of the Institute for Research on Public Policy for publication in its magazine, *Policy Options/Options politiques*. Although the invitation was never revoked, the article was not published – at least not in this journal, with its joint corporate and state funding. Indeed, the article might have been deep-sixed by Guindon who, as we pointed out, never sends articles anywhere. But copies of the paper circulated, and it was published in both *Canadian Forum* and *L'Action Nationale*.[27]

There are two points here. First, Guindon develops his interpretations through such mundane encounters with his culture as the literature stuffed unwittingly in his mailbox, conversations with his neighbours in the working-class area of Montreal's St Henri, where he now lives, and his friends on Boulevard St Laurent; observations of the behaviour of administrators, colleagues, and successive generations of students; and assorted literature including some scary tabloids like *Allo, Police, Midnight*, and *Time* magazine. Second, during these encounters he sees what others see, but more. The admonition of Herbert Blumer to look for the underlying meaning is taken up brilliantly and persuasively – though usually in ways that afflict the comfortable. And if he has been acknowledged for his original mind, he has also been silenced, and the *Policy Options / Options politiques* incident is far from the most important example.

In this connection we have wrestled with the question of why only one of Guindon's articles was published in French before 1977, and that one a full eleven years after it was published in English. Part of the answer to this question lies at the 'macro' level and is explained in Guindon's own interpretation of the Canadian confederation – an arrangement that produced the 'two solitudes of Hugh MacLennan.' Contrary to the understanding of well-educated and well-intentioned Canadian élites in the 1960s, these two solitudes were, in Guindon's words, 'intended not accidental, cherished not deplored.'[28] For this insight he credits the writings of Hannah Arendt, who has played as important a role in his thinking in the last ten years as C. Wright Mills did at an earlier time. Guindon has great respect for Hannah Arendt, finds her writing intellectually powerful and politically persuasive: in a word – his word – beautiful.

His first public discussion of Arendt's work was in his keynote lecture to the Canadian Sociology and Anthropology Association in June 1978. That lecture was written en route from Montreal to the meetings in London (probably not on the inside of a cigarette package – although that's what he said at the time). In that paper, 'Class, Nationalism, and the Nation State: The Case of Quebec in Canada,' he acknowledged his debt to Arendt in apprehending the larger historical context for his discussion. 'Her book *The Origins of Totalitarianism* constitutes, in my mind, the undiscussed classic in the whole area of imperialism and nationalism ... the definitive statement on the sociology of the nation-state.'[29]

Although she did not deal specifically with Quebec, Arendt's general analysis of British imperialism resonated with, and enriched, Guindon's earlier interpretations. The British Burkean tradition balked at extending the 'Rights of Englishmen' to others. In Canada the English had ensured, through shifting political arrangements – the Constitutional Act of 1791, the Union of the two Canadas, and ultimately, Confederation – that Quebec would be no different. Yet confining the French to Quebec, and making a division between federal and provincial powers, enabled the British, in Arendt's words, 'to escape the dangerous inconsistency inherent in the nation's attempt at empire building by leaving the conquered peoples to their own devices as far as culture, religion and law were concerned, by staying aloof and refraining from spreading British law and culture.'[30]

For Guindon, Arendt's writings provide an interpretation that explains and provides the intellectual and historical rationalization for Quebec nationalism. How can the French in Quebec agree to submerge themselves in a broader culture so heavily informed *not* by universalistic criteria embodied in the expression 'the Rights of Man' but rather by the particularistic rallying cry 'the Rights of Englishmen'?

In one sense, then, Hubert Guindon's marginalization from French-Canadian sociology reflects the carefully constructed two solitudes: he taught at an English-language institution; he wrote and published in English; and like the writings of many others, French and English, his remained on one side of the great divide. But the other part of the answer, we believe, lies in the particular circumstances of Guindon's life at the University of Montreal that we have discussed. For he was not simply another English academic whose work was not translated into French. He is French. He began his career, and indeed hoped to continue it, at the University of Montreal. We conclude, therefore, that the silences surrounding his work in Quebec during the 1960s and 1970s reflect his controversial scholarship and the nonconformity of his life-style. For, as Monique Bégin put it, his successors believed that what he did wasn't 'real sociology.' This denigration of his work found expression in his contested relationship with Philippe Garigue, and in the opinions of some of those who came to the Department of Sociology after he had 'been called' (to use l'abbé Lacoste's euphemism) to Sir George Williams University.

But it would seem that there was also a powerful gatekeeper at Laval University where Quebec's only sociology journal (until 1969), *Recherches Sociographiques* is published. One of the journal's editors from its founding until 1981 was Jean-Charles Falardeau, and that journal did not publish any of Guindon's work until 1977 when Falardeau's control was waning.[31] According to Guindon, Falardeau requested a copy of 'The Social Evolution of Quebec Reconsidered' when it was delivered at the meetings in Kingston, a request he followed up with a cable to Guindon in St Denis where he was doing field-work. Soon after receiving the paper, however, Falardeau informed him that *Recherches Sociographiques* would not publish it. This article finally appeared in French in 1971 when Marcel Rioux and Yves Martin's anthology, *French-Canadian Society*, was translated and published. The next two articles to appear in English, 'Social Unrest, Social Class, and Quebec's Bureaucratic Revolution' and 'Two Cultures: An Essay on Nationalism, Class, and Ethnic Tension,' have never been published in French.

His freeze-out from the University of Montreal at the end of the 1950s was succeeded by a more benign set of circumstances, yet one that perpetuated his marginalization within Quebec sociology. For the structural Marxist perspective, which swept Quebec academia with its close ties with the intellectual milieu of France, had little affinity with Guindon's style of historical sociology. Only with the fading of the 'Althusserian moment' – rather a long one in Quebec – was Guindon welcomed back intellectually to the University of Montreal.

In 1979 he was invited by Jean-Louis Martel, a *professionel de recherche* at the Ecole des Hautes Etudes Commerciales de Montréal, to participate in a research project on Quebec's co-operative movement. Guindon's contribution was pivotal, according to Martel. He suggested the oral-history approach. Through the life histories of activists, the life history of the movement could be reconstructed. With Martel he conducted the first twenty-five of what would be some one hundred interviews, and, in the process, discovered the Quebec of the 1920s, 1930s, and 1940s, especially the 'family compact' of the nationalist movement. Martel recalls the excitement of that project: 'Hubert and I met the important people ... some of whom were in the Ordre de Jacques Cartier ... a kind of secret society that was governing Quebec in those years. Two or three times we know that they had conferences about us: would they permit us to go further or not? Once they decided that we were to be trusted, we heard a lot. We gained a kind of real intimacy with those families.'

Interiewing was a rewarding and exhausting experience, with some of the interviews lasting seven or eight hours. From those interviews Guindon derived the set of powerful insights that underpins his interpretation of the demise of the Parti Québécois in the 1980s, and that led him to make the case for a more popularly based nationalist movement.

In 1981, while still working on this project, Guindon was invited by Louis Maheu and Robert Sévigny to give the introductory course in sociology at the University of Montreal, and his reintegration with Quebec sociology and sociologists proceeded apace.

But the pleasures of teaching once again in the sociology department at the University of Montreal were deeply mitigated by a growing physical and emotional malaise. The end of that calendar year of deteriorating health brought a diagnosis of cancer of the larynx and a serious operation that held the almost-certainty that he would lose his voice, and perhaps more. In the days leading up to that operation friends from all his social and academic milieux mingled for the first time with one another and with members of his family in his apartment and later in his hospital room. For the first time in most of our memories, Hubert did not wait until we called him, but gathered us all around for what he must have believed were his last conversations.

But the operation was a success. What Hubert gave up were his trade-mark Gitanes cigarettes, the dense smoke from which filled his hospital room even on the night before the operation! He also gave up his downtown St Marc Street apartment, which a journalist from *Saturday Night* described as reflecting his 'penchant for the Vegas lifestyle' in its décor: 'early 1950s Strip Hotel Lobby.'[32] He bought a lovely old French-Canadian–style cottage in the heart of St Henri and proceeded to surprise students, friends, and family with a newly cultivated domesticity. In Monique Bégin's words, 'the escape side of him is gone – and Hubert Guindon now cooks! And owns a home. That could not have existed before.' Until then breakfast with croissants and coffee had been Guindon's way to entertain; now, in St Henri, invitations are as likely to be for carefully prepared dinners.

The partial domestication of life-style did not herald a comparable transformation in his political and sociological insights, as the last two articles in this book indicate. On the contrary, the arguments are more forcefully made, his point of view more polemically delivered, the sense that he is writing about *his own* society more clearly apparent. We asked him about this in response to a comparison that he made between Everett Hughes and C. Wright Mills. 'Hughes is more suggestive than accusatory. Sometimes he is so suggestive that you don't know what he is suggesting. He never imputed motives – if he did it was in conversation or tangentially. Mills, on the other hand, was impudent. I remember him raising the question more than once – could one, should one, impute motives? And the answer was emphatically, Yes!'

'And you,' we asked, 'have you changed from being suggestive to being more accusatory?'

'No ... I can see why one could say that. I resolved some ambiguities. I became more involved and clear about my own politics. I am less naïve. Certainly there is a change from the referendum piece – it starts in the modernization piece – that's a turning-point. I'm less academic. Although I was quite controversial from the beginning. And accusatory? I'll be more accusatory if I'm given more time!' Having apparently contradicted himself, he proceeded to clarify: 'I think ultimately all social sciences are – what did Lasswell call them? – moral sciences. Let's say that society has concerned me more than sociology.' He meant something rather specific by this, which helps explain the direction his scholarly/political interventions have taken.

I think most people go into sociology running away from something – but once that's done, what's there left in sociology? Understanding your own times, society, and I suppose coming to terms with your own people and culture. In other words, coming to terms with yourself probably involves coming to terms with much more than yourself. I don't know how to say it, but I mean being yourself is much more of a culture thing than you suspect, and I think you become aware of that as you become older. When you're young you are more aware of the oppressive nature of that past that impinges on you, and as you grow older you're sensitive to the meaning of that culture.

Yet we have the sense that his work has been consistently sensitive to the meaning of the culture and that, in a way, Hubert Guindon was always 'older.' At school, when he was only nine or ten, he was with boys several years older. He was only twenty-four when he started teaching at the University of Montreal. But for Monique Bégin and her class-mates 'he was an adult. It is only looking back that I realize he was a very *young* adult.' Perhaps this is simply a way of trying to understand the tone that runs through his work: that at one and the same time he takes distance from – and cares passionately about – the events to which he bears such eloquent and perceptive witness. Bégin describes him at the University of Montreal in words that are still appropriate: 'Culturally speaking all of us were products of the pre-Quiet Revolution, and we were living the passage. Hubert Guindon had gone to the United States: he appeared completely *libre-penseur*, *dégagé*, and intellectually he surely was. And we had never seen that, really. Yet we still knew it was so close to his heart. He was still deeply committed.'

That commitment remains intense, as evidenced by his recent article on the rise and fall of the Parti Québécois. In this essay he delivers a stinging critique of the PQ's post-referendum polices and strategies, arguing that much of its demise was internally generated if not unpredictable when a social movement is pummelled into the strait-jacket of a successful political party. Guindon invites his readers to examine some of the errors of the Parti Québécois: the wage freeze and roll-back for public and parapublic employees, until then its most committed cadre; the betrayal of the nationalist movement through the bungling of the constitutional conference; the ritualistic dissociation of the party from a confrontational national politics that included the forced exit of the *indépendantiste* caucus and the election of Pierre-Marc Johnson; and the forging of an alliance with the Conservative party, the net political gain of which was a cheap revenge – the defeat of the federal Liberals in Quebec. In short, the process of institutionalization had overtaken activism. By the end of the second mandate, 'the goal of staying in office had superseded the goal of independence. By the time the last lacklustre leadership race took place, its membership was overwhelmingly composed of yuppies rather than radical nationalists.'[33]

Guindon's critiques are tough. Yet they come in an unusual guise, generally cloaked in irony and humour, and only those unable to defend themselves are spared. He was the first faculty member at Sir George Williams to be inducted into the Royal Society of Canada. Not insensitive to the honour, he none the less began his initiation address by asking, 'La Société Royale du Canada est-ce une chose sérieuse ou solennelle?' The rest of his short talk elaborated on this theme: 'La première reflexion qui m'est venue à l'esprit a été de penser aux élites d'une société. Sont-elles solennelles ou sérieuses? Il me semble que les élites d'une société ont un penchant et un gout marqués pour le solennel. Non seulement prennent-elles le solennel au sérieux mais elles insistent pour que le peuple fasse de meme. De cette façon, raisonnent-elles, elles seront prises au sérieux.'[34]

Perhaps, then, it is in this short talk, intended primarily for the amusement of his audience, that one may discern a certain clue to Hubert Guindon's 'passionate distance.' Critical of the pretensions of others, he has despite long years in the university, that most pretentious of institutions, avoided pretension. There is always an underside, always another layer of meaning, and it is often exposed through humour, which he says is 'not only the last fortress of sanity but very often the first condition of objectivity.'[35]

It would not behoove us, then, to end an introduction to his work on a 'solemn' note. With that in mind, it is perhaps worth pointing out that this is the first time his articles have appeared in one place. Even Hubert Guindon himself was unable to provide reprints of most of his articles, or copies of his unpublished texts! That is both the endearing and frustrating side of this man who has given sociology in Canada and Quebec such a good time in the last thirty years. His work, which spans and chronicles nearly three decades of dramatic transformations in Quebec society, can now speak for itself.

HUBERT GUINDON: ACADEMIC CHRONOLOGY

REGULAR APPOINTMENTS

1954–62 Assistant Professor of Sociology, Université de Montréal (1960–2: on sabbatical)

1962–66 Associate Professor of Sociology, Sir George Williams University

1966–69 Professor, Sir George Williams University

1969–70 Professor of Sociology and Visiting Professor, Institute of Canadian Studies, Carleton University

1970– Professor of Sociology, Sir George Williams University (merged with Loyola College in 1974 to become Concordia University)

VISITING APPOINTMENTS

1961 (Summer) Department of Sociology, University of British Columbia

1968 (Summer) Department of Sociology, University of Victoria

1969–71 Visiting Lecturer, Ecole des Hautes Etudes Commerciales

1969–70 Visiting Lecturer, Département de sociologie, University of Ottawa

1971 Visiting Lecturer, Department of Political Economy, University of Toronto

1980 (Fall) Visiting Lecturer, Département de sociologie, Université de Montréal

Invited lectures

Brock University, Carleton University, Duke University, Glendon College, McMaster University, Memorial University, Mount Allison University, National Defence College (Kingston), Queen's University, St Francis Xavier University (Cape Breton), St Mary's University, University of Alberta (Edmonton), University of Calgary, University of Guelph, University of Toronto, University of Waterloo, University of Windsor, University of Winnipeg, University of Wisconsin (Milwaukee)

ELECTED POSITIONS

1970–1 President, Canadian Sociology and Anthropology Association

1970–4 Canadian Delegate and Member of the Executive, International Sociological Association

1978– Fellow, Royal Society of Canada

TASK FORCES AND COMMISSIONS

1961–2 Senior Research Sociologist, Bureau de Recherches et Planification, Ministère de la Jeunesse, Quebec
1974–6 Member, Task Force on Urbanization (Castonguay Commission)
1979 Research Sociologist, Task Force on Canadian Unity (Pepin-Robarts Commission)

NOTES

1 Unless otherwise noted, all quotations attributed to John Jackson, Jeannine Guindon, Kurt Jonassohn, Monique Bégin, l'abbé Norbert Lacoste, Pierre Dandurand, and Jean-Marie Rainville were drawn from interviews with the editors held in Montreal in November 1986. Jean-Louis Martel was interviewed in Montreal by the editors in May 1987. John Meisel was interviewed in Kingston, in March 1987, by Roberta Hamilton.
2 For a bibliography of the writings of George Herbert Mead, see *Mind, Self and Society*, edited and with an introduction by Charles W. Morris (Chicago, 1934), 390–2. As Morris put it in the introduction to the book, 'Professor Mead never systematized his position and results in longer form ... [this] volume is in the main composed of two sets of excellent student notes on the course, together with excerpts from other such notes and selections from unpublished manuscripts left by Mr. Mead' (v–vi).
3 Guindon borrows what he calls this 'felicitous expression' from Stanley Ryerson's important book by the same name (Moscow, 1968).
4 Everett Hughes, *French Canada in Transition* (Chicago, 1943; reprinted with a new foreword, 1963), x
5 Philippe Garigue, 'Change and Continuity in Rural French Canada,' in *French-Canadian Society*, ed. Marcel Rioux and Yves Martin (Toronto, 1964), 137
6 'Social Evolution,' this volume, p. 24
7 Interview with Hubert Guindon, November 1986. Unless otherwise noted, all quotations from Hubert Guindon were drawn from a series of interviews held in November 1986.
8 'Social Evolution,' this volume, p. 26
9 'The Crown, the Catholic Church, and the French-Canadian People: The Historical Roots of Quebec Nationalism,' this volume, p. 104
10 Years later two Canadian sociologists – Wallace Clement and Dennis Olsen – took issue with this claim of Guindon's when he made it during the course of a public lecture. The title of one of his articles was, after all, '*Two* Cultures'! But Guindon had a quick retort – he had not titled the article; that was the work of the publisher.

11 L'abbé Norbert Lacoste told us he had offered Cadieux a full-time appointment. A book should be written about Fernand Cadieux, the man behind the scenes of the Quiet Revolution, behind the coming of the 'Three Wise Men' to Ottawa, described by Claude Ryan in the obituary he wrote as 'un des esprits les plus perçants de sa generation' (*Le Devoir*, 6 March 1976, 5).

12 Reprinted in *Forum: The Journal of the Students of the School of Community and Public Affairs* (Montreal, 1985)

13 This expression was recalled in interviews with Monique Bégin, Jean-Marie Rainville, and Pierre Dandurand.

14 This is not the place to provide an analysis of Garigue's character and politics, but we do draw attention to a published discussion commemorating the twenty-fifth anniversary of the Department of Sociology at the University of Montreal. On that occasion Professor Jacques Dofny recalled this interchange with Philippe Garigue: 'Je me souviens que lorsque j'ai proposé de donner un cours de sociologie comparée des mouvements ouvriers et que j'avais indiqué comme lecture importante Karl Marx, le doyen Garigue m'avait appelé dans son bureau en me disant: "On n'a jamais enseigné Marx ici, ca ne passera jamais." J'avais dit: "Essayez toujours on verra bien".' 'Table ronde: Le Département de sociologie de l'Université de Montréal,' *Sociologie et sociétés* XII (2): 190

15 A footnote to 'The Social Evolution of Quebec' acknowledges Fernand Cadieux 'for many years of intellectual companionship.'

16 Title of Arendt's book *The Human Condition* (Chicago, 1958).

17 This volume, p. 37

18 This volume, p. 37

19 This volume, p. 90

20 'Social Unrest... ,' this volume, p. 37

21 Letter of resignation, Hubert Guindon to Kurt Jonassohn, Chairman, Department of Sociology, 28 April 1969

22 Ibid.

23 Ibid.

24 Jacques Henripin, 'Présentation de Monsieur Hubert Guindon,' Montreal, 24 November 1978. Published in *Présentations* (Trois-Rivières, October 1979), 87–90

25 Guindon made this argument as researcher for the Task Force on Canadian Unity, the Pepin-Robarts Commission. He circulated his yet-unpublished article 'The Modernization' to the staff and commissioners. A reading of the task force's report will demonstrate Guindon's impact here. Of course the task force's recommendations were shelved by Prime Minister Trudeau even before they appeared.

26 'The Referendum: The Lessons of Defeat,' this volume, p. 119
27 This article appeared in French, under the title 'Le Référendum: Une autre décennie d'instabilité politique' in *L'Action Nationale* LXX (4) December 1980, 271–91, and in *Canadian Forum* under the title 'The Referendum: Another Decade of Apprehended Political Instability.'
28 'The Crown, the Catholic Church, and the French-Canadian People,' this volume, p. 100
29 That lecture has been revised and appears in this collection as 'The Crown, the Catholic Church, and the French-Canadian People: The Historical Roots of Quebec Nationalism,' p. 95
30 Hannah Arendt, *The Origins of Totalitarianism* Part Two: Imperialism (New York, 1951; reprinted, 1968), 10
31 'The Modernization of Quebec and the Legitimacy of the Canadian State' was published as the lead article in *Recherches Sociographiques* 18 (3) (septembre-décembre 1977), 338–66 under the title 'La Modernisation du Québec et La Légitimité de l'Etat Canadien.'
32 R. Collison, 'Academic Oracle,' *Saturday Night*, May 1978, 22
33 'The Rise and Fall of the Parti Québécois,' this volume, p. 162
34 'Le sérieux et le solennel' delivered in Montreal, 24 November 1978. Published in *Présentations* (Trois Rivières, October 1979), 91–6
35 'The Crown, the Catholic Church, and the French-Canadian People,' this volume, p. 94

QUEBEC SOCIETY:
TRADITION, MODERNITY, AND NATIONHOOD

The social evolution of
Quebec reconsidered

Any attempt to assess the direction of social change in a particular society is a risky business at best. Yet, inasmuch as sociology, in its official texts on method, rests its claim to scientific status on its predictive capacities, it must somehow, sometimes, take this risk and say something about what are the significant changes occurring in the social organization of a society. In order to achieve any such general assessment the social analyst needs, it seems to me, to consider the society as a whole, and through time.

Sociologists are generally reluctant to view the whole of a society as a proper subject of study and reluctant also to study social phenomena through time. Indeed, what is at present felt to be adequate methodology, or should we say prestigeful methodology, requires living respondents whose answers can be given statistical treatment, and therefore becomes largely irrelevant for studies with historical dimensions; and while it may be quite useful in measuring change it is quite helpless of itself to account for it. Furthermore its preference for piecemeal and detailed verifications makes it a rather awkward instrument to use when dealing with general analyses. Anthropologists, by tradition, have commonly achieved such analyses in the case of less complex cultures. Even they, however, when confronted with large societies, have tended either to adopt the sociological habit of narrow investigation or to postulate that an image of the larger whole can be gleaned through the minute study of a particular instance, a particular cell such as a village or a town. In choosing the first alternative, they abdicate what seems to have been a traditional objective of anthropology. In the second case, they stand in danger of missing the target through oversimplification.[1]

These considerations may or may not account for the fact that when sociologists speak of social change they usually become rather vague and elusive, and their commentaries, camouflaged in such all-embracing terms as the impact of industrialization, technological change, or cultural lag, create blurred images lacking both sharpness of perception and focus.

These same considerations will, however, help to state the aim and nature of this essay on the social evolution of Quebec. This paper is an attempt to give an over-all view of the changes that were wrought in the social organization of French Canada from its beginnings. This general view does not claim to be a completely verified construct; it only claims to be a coherent interpretative analysis of social structure up to and including contemporary French-Canadian society.

Historians sometimes feel that, for sociologists, French Canada started in the nineteenth century. It is quite true that sociologists have not attempted, until quite recently,[2] any systematic analysis of French-Canadian society prior to that time. That they have not done so is no cause for censure, despite the views of a latter-day student of French-Canadian society.[3] It makes little sense to accuse someone of not having done what he did not set out to do. Had the authors in question claimed to explain the emergence of rural society with no reference to the earlier context of social organization, the censure would stand. But neither Miner nor Hughes attempted to account for the emergence in the nineteenth century of a predominantly rural French-Canadian society;[4] nor for that matter has their critic. Or again, if French Canada had not been for a period of its history a predominantly rural society, or had Miner and Hughes claimed that it had always been a strictly rural society, the censure might be justifiable. But such was not the case.

The only merit of such criticism is that it does raise the question of how it was that French Canada became a predominantly rural society at the end of the eighteenth century, and remained so throughout the nineteenth century.

This paper will attempt, first, to account for the emergence of the rural society from the collapse of the feudal trading society; second, to describe what were the mechanics of social organization of the rural society; and finally to assess the impact of the recent massive industrialization on the preceding social structure.

I. NEW FRANCE: A FEUDAL TRADING SOCIETY

The settlement of New France was not, as to some extent it was in the United States, accomplished by dissident groups seeking refuge from an inhospitable homeland. It was initiated, financed, directed, and some-times stymied by the ruling administrators of the French Court. It involved the participation of five groups of people: colonial administrators, soldiers, business men interested in the fur trade, clergy, and an emigrant population. Of the four institutions involved in the colonial enterprise, the administrators and the clergy became the dominant groups in the colonial social structure. The influence of the military and the entrepreneurs in moulding social organization, while not inconsequential, was clearly of secondary importance even though administrators were quite often recruited from the ranks of the military. A common feature of the four institutional spheres was that the posts of command in each were generally held by people of aristocratic culture who were part of the lesser nobility orbiting around the Court of France. The manifest class distinctions between the leaders of these institutions and the bulk of their members involved more than differences in dress; the distinctions were apparent in basic styles of life, including types of social recreation, taste for literature and the arts, and in attitudes towards a 'glamorous social life.'

The conditions of a frontier society, however, are not ideal circumstances in which to reproduce a feudal system, and some aspects of such a social organization could simply not be naturalized in New France. An outstanding case, as Professor Frégault pointed out, was the hollow meaning of the feudal status of a seigneur in bush country.[5] Owing to frontier conditions, it was impossible for feudal society to have its metropolitan meaning, and this situation increased the avenues of social mobility for the eager and deserving young men of common ancestry who had succeeded in the military or commercial spheres of life. Thus the caste system was weaker in New France than in the metropolis, although the basic arrangement was feudal in nature.

This feudal organization of New France did make for a society with more strongly contrasting styles of life than the succeeding rural society. If the feudal game fell flat in the out-country, in the budding cities of Quebec and Montreal it could be, and was, played with more *vraisemblance*.

Political authority in this feudal system rested, in the final analysis, with the King's ministers. Conflicts within the local political structure were resolved by royal decree. The two principal groups of actors in the political game were the colonial administrators and the clergy. Both groups had formal and informal channels to the nerve centre of the political organism. Both had their lobbies at Court. Inasmuch as there was conflict within the colony, and there often was, it frequently pitted one against the other. The final authority in the colony was formally in the hands of the governor. The clergy was, however, a politically significant group and generally a cohesive group who seemed to have, on occasion, the power to influence the choice of governor, and, in times of extreme conflict, also the power of stalemating the governor, which amounted to the power of recall. Insight into the causes of these chronic conflicts can be gained by analysing the official and self-attributed roles of both groups.

The colonial administrators were expected to achieve simultaneously three objectives: (1) the exploration and claiming of new land for the Crown of France; (2) the protection and development of the fur-trading interests; and (3) the establishment of colonial settlements for French settlers. The clergy,[6] on the other hand, was expected: (1) to Christianize the Indians; (2) to cater to the religious needs of the immigrant population; and (3) to institute and staff various educational and welfare institutions such as hospitals and homes for the aged.

Conflicts arose because these official roles eventually led to competing, partially different, or sometimes opposed conceptions of the colony's social organization. In the early days of the colony the aims of the two groups did not conflict. Conflict began with the expansion of the fur-trading society. The development of this aspect of the colonial venture implied a basic social organization substantially different from that of the colonial settlement. The fur trade implied a semi-nomadic type of organization, the creation of ever-expanding outposts, and the elaboration of a commercial complex. Family life and ties were much weakened.

There was little concern for the establishment of permanent settlements; the ability to barter with friendly Indians, cunning, imagination, and occasional deception were all assets in trading assorted products of metropolitan culture, including whiskey and guns, for the valued furs. The *coureur de bois* has never been described as a family man, nor as a highly religious one; history rather depicts him as a smooth operator, not very reliable and with few moral scruples. In the colonial settlement, frugality, hard work, stability, and the creation of a domestic economy were crucial to survival and growth. So it came about that the very differences in the ways of the trading society and the ways of the agricultural society led to competing conceptions and to conflicts between clergy and stage officials.

The conquest of New France considerably altered the matrix of social organization. Some historians claim that it shifted French-Canadian society into a state of arrested development, which it can no longer overcome. The conquest certainly did hasten the transition from the feudal to the rural society. In a remarkably well-documented article, Professor Brunet has shown how it brought about not only the exodus of the political bourgeoisie, but also the replacement of the French commercial bourgeoisie by an English counterpart.[7] The latter was able to substitute the already established complexes of commercial communication between England and America for the French commercial system which had been disrupted by the war; the English thereby achieved decisive control of local commerce.

The conquest spelled the end of the trading society[8] and the feudal society. The political élites, who had more or less conceived of their residence in the colony as a temporary step in their occupational careers, left with the collapse of the French colonial venture and returned to the homeland. So did the military élites. The local clergy and the *habitants* stayed. The clergy became, by default, the undisputed leaders of the local colonists; thus was the triumph of the clerical conception of the proper social organization for French Canada achieved by the British military victory. The social organization of French Canada was simplified and proceeded along a single line of social development – rural development.

II. THE RURAL SOCIETY

Critical review of previous theories
With the cession a new social system emerges in French Canada. The type of livelihood and existence the *habitants* forged for themselves by their frugality and their domestic economy was one wherein they were dependent on very little direct assistance from outside the family. Thus the collapse of the whole administrative and political apparatus had little impact upon them. While they were somewhat marginal to the previous social organization, they were to become central to the emerging rural society. The rural society was built upon the remnants of the feudal and trading society.

What, then, was the nature of French-Canadian rural society? The social organization of rural Quebec has been described by Gérin, Miner, Hughes, Falardeau, and Rioux. In recent years Professor Garigue has challenged the validity of their analysis, which he has labelled the Chicago School's view of French Canada. As a result of Professor Garigue's challenge, the whole subject stands in need of a critical assessment, especially in view of the sharpness[9] of Professor Garigue's attack and the wide publicity that has accompanied his 'challenging new concept' of French-Canadian society.[10] Much of the earlier analysis, he claims, is outright myth.[11] The authors under attack were misled by Gérin whose central hypothesis in regard to French-Canadian rural society was not substantiated, and mainly because they were ignorant of the history of French Canada. This ignorance led them to presuppose, by sheer imagination, the concrete realities their basic hypothesis required, and to forget completely the factual data that would have contradicted it.[12] The myths are also due to partly unconscious bias. Professor Garigue forthrightly states that were the tools of the sociology of knowledge applied to their theories, the naked *ad hoc* structure of their theories could be exposed.[13]

Professor Garigue summarizes his own work in the following passage: 'Not only have we deepened the already existing studies, but we have also challenged their basic conceptions on the nature of French-Canadian culture. Not only must the mythical or ideological character of certain commonly held concepts on French Canada be shown but also the mythical and ideological character of certain statements made by many social scientists, notably the Americans Redfield, Miner and Hughes.'[14] Fortunately, Professor Garigue believes, as we all do, in the scientific tradition of alert criticism for his own views as well as others. This enables us to evaluate the relevance of his critique.

What exactly is the case set forth by Professor Garigue against the so-called Chicago School's analysis of French Canada? His argument is built along three lines of reasoning that can be summed up this way.

1. The Chicago School used the folk-society concept to analyse French Canada because of its ignorance of previous French-Canadian society, which was not a peasant and folk society but essentially an urban and commercial one. Furthermore, sound epistemology and methodology have discredited the use of such 'ideal type' concepts in social research. They should be replaced by specific historical hypotheses.[15]

2. Secondly, the Chicago School was misled by uncritically appropriating Léon Gérin's basic hypothesis on the nature of rural Quebec. This hypothesis was both unsubstantiated by Gérin and was the result of his becoming the intellectual victim of his own training in Paris under disciples of Le Play.[16]

3. Finally, the Chicago School's analysis leads to the conclusion explicitly stated by Falardeau that 'the traditional French-Canadian culture is sociologically inadequate and it is destined to disappear for the very good reason that it cannot prepare the French Canadians to face up to the exigencies of an urban industrial way of life.'[17] This conclusion stems from the conception of French-Canadian culture as an 'archaic and

simple one' which is thought to be in conflict with, and disintegrating under the impact of, the secular rationalism of urban culture, the dynamic of which is English in origin.[18] The facts are quite different, Professor Garigue claims. He has found that the patterns of social institutions prevented the rise of a specifically rural culture and that French-Canadian culture already had incorporated within itself all the elements necessary for large-scale urbanization.[19]

This, in summary, is what has been called Professor Garigue's challenging new concept of French Canada. What are the merits of his criticisms? The complete irrelevance of his charge of historical ignorance can be demonstrated. If Miner and Hughes fell unwittingly into the booby-trap set by Gérin, it was because they were ignorant of French-Canadian history.[20] A fortiori, Gérin formulated his basic hypothesis because he was ignorant of French-Canadian history. But Léon Gérin was not only aware of previous French-Canadian society, since he wrote a book on it,[21] but his conception of French-Canadian social organization was not that it was a predominantly peasant society, but a predominantly trading society. Indeed, his thesis is that the weakness and vulnerability of the social system of New France lay precisely in the fact it was not a predominantly agricultural society.[22] With the conquest, the trading society collapsed, and the *habitant* was to become 'la clef de voute du Canada moderne.'[23] Professor Garigue has never referred to this work of Gérin; and the countercharge can be made that had he known of Gérin's historically oriented work on the social structure of New France, he would not have made the charge that the allegedly erroneous conception of the Chicago School stemmed from its ignorance of French-Canadian history. Professor Garigue, who is wont to underline what he considers other writers' 'unguarded moments'[24] seems to have had a major lapse himself.

Despite the somewhat irresponsible character of the first criticism, one must assess on its merits the criticism of Gérin's central hypothesis about the nature of rural society in French Canada during the nineteenth century. Gérin described the rural society of Quebec as 'a juxtaposition of families which were very nearly all equal; nearly all engaged in farming; nearly all self-sufficient; but none of which puts any ambition before that of transmitting intact the family property to one of its children, although favoring, within the limits of its resources, the settlement of the other children outside the family home.' The land was tilled as a family enterprise and the goals were, first, the creation and maintenance of a unit of property sufficiently large to supply the family's daily needs and to provide subsistence for the aged, and, second, to provide as best might be for the settlement of the non-inheriting children. As Hughes commented:

The rural society turns, then, about a relation of family to land. The farm must be fertile enough and large enough to feed and clothe the family – ideally, enough so to provide money for education or a start elsewhere for the children who do not inherit land. The family, in turn, must be large enough and possessed of enough skill and solidarity to run the farm and keep it free of burdensome debt. But such a family, by its very size, endangers the farm in every generation. It becomes a function of the family to scatter its members, leaving but one son behind to inherit and to sire the next generation of farmers.[25]

Hughes, in Gérin's footsteps, saw in this demographic contradiction the vulnerable spot of the social system.[26] Miner, in describing the social equilibrium, says it was a culture with a high degree of internal social integration based on a short-term adjustment to the environment.[27] This is the structural basis upon which the 'traditional culture' of nineteenth-century French-Canadian society was built. This, for Professor Garigue, is the myth of French Canada, a myth he claims to have slain.[28]

Let us see. Miner's and Hughes's error was traceable, in Garigue's view, to their ignorance of history and to prejudice.[29] In the case of Gérin, error springs from misleading devotion to his intellectual masters, and unsubstantiated *a priori* conceptions.[30] To check the accuracy of Gérin's central theory, Professor Garigue undertook in the middle fifties a revisit to St Justin. His main conclusions[31] put him at odds with Gérin. The family is not related to the land in the manner suggested by Gérin. The maintenance of family continuity is not paralleled by continuity in landownership. The passing of land through a single heir is only part of a wider cultural system in which it is an item of secondary importance. The society is not dominated by the family as the main determinant of social experience. There is a decided readiness to accept technical changes. Leadership is widely distributed and not limited to the parish priest. The loose segmentation of the community gives a great deal of scope for both social mobility and for autonomous action in certain fields. Although the parish is a religious unit, its religious organization has little to do with economic development.

What, then, should be said about Professor Garigue's critique of Gérin? The gist of his argument is that the relation between land and family that Gérin described as pivotal to the rural society is unsubstantiated. To invalidate this description Garigue has attempted to show that family continuity was not paralleled by continuity in landownership. Out of a total of 137 farms still existing in St Justin seventy years after Gérin's study, Garigue has found that only thirty-one, or 22.6 per cent, still remained in the same family line.

Is this datum very convincing? Let us assume that there are 100 farms, and that over a period of seventy-five years they will have been inherited roughly three times. Let us also assume that if in seven cases out of ten the described relation of land inheritance holds, it is the dominant trait. In the other three instances, the family land may pass to other family lines for various reasons, such as the lack of a male heir, the premature death of the father, economic mismanagement, or innumerable other contingencies. In the first handing down of the 100 farms, in this context, only 70 per cent of the original 100 would remain in the same family line. After fifty years, only 49 per cent would remain, and after seventy-five years only 34.4 per cent. Because Professor Garigue finds that only 22.6 per cent of farms have remained in the same families, he has not demonstrated, to my satisfaction at least, that the relation described by Gérin was spurious. Professor Garigue has not investigated why farms passed into other hands. One may even wonder if his data do not defeat his interpretation.

From my own revisit of St Denis, we get a substantially different picture on this particular point. Of seventy-seven farms still intact since 1882, thirty (or 38.9 per cent) are still in the hands of direct descendants. Seven more are within the extended family group (including in-law inheritance), for a total of thirty-seven (or 48.1 per cent) of the original seventy-seven farms. This indicates that, in St Denis in 1882, the norm was operative in more than seven cases out of ten. Should we proceed to a more refined analysis of the causes for the sale of the farms to others, we find that fourteen out of forty, or approximately one out of three, were *initially* sold because of the lack of a suitable heir (see table). I shall not further stress this aspect of land inheritance other than to say that Professor Garigue will need both to get more refined data and to use stricter rules of inference before claiming to have disproved Gérin's central hypothesis on the structural basis of French-Canadian rural society in the nineteenth century.

Gérin's account of the basic structure of French-Canadian rural society of the last century can be used to interpret both continuity and change in the social organization. The stability of the system arose from maintaining intact the unit of land through the generations. Change in social structure became imperative when arable land became scarce and migration difficult. This imperative I have previously called the demographic

Pattern of land inheritance in St Denis, 1882–1959

Within family		Outside family		
Immediate	Extended*	No suitable heir†	Debts and dislike of farming	Outright‡
30	7	14	3	23

* This includes cases of the passing of the land to nephews and cousins and three cases of women inheriting farms.
† Cases of widowhood, bachelors with no heirs, sickness of appropriate heir.
‡ In about half these cases, once the sale was made in the early stages of the time sequence, the basic type of land inheritance is resumed. For the other half, the selling pattern continues.

contradiction within the rural system. French Canada's responsiveness to changes in social structure can be traced to this structural fact. The solution to the demographic contradiction will, indeed, be the growth of industrialization.

This leads us to the third and final criticism of the 'Chicago School' by Professor Garigue – his disbelief in the cultural conflict or disintegration caused by the impact of industrialization on the traditional French-Canadian social system. After closely studying the texts on this issue I am left with the definite impression, to risk an interpretation of my own, that Professor Garigue is, to quite an extent, a victim of his own vocabulary. Cultural conflict and disintegration are not basic to the vocabularies of either Miner or Hughes.

Miner, on this question, states the problem in these terms: 'Social systems change to meet their structural problems. When the traditional ways cease to solve the problems of life, social behaviour varies from the old ways until a solution is found. If the new ways are successful, they in turn will become traditional.'[32] His interpretation of how this was done in French Canada can be gleaned from this passage:

Land pressure alone created the structural problem in the society and accounts for the necessity for change and some of the actual cultural changes, but an even greater amount of change is only indirectly related to the basic structural problem. The growing lack of land forced parents to seek other outlets for their children. The society was experiencing trial-and-error behaviour in an attempt to find a solution to its problem. The conflict between the old patterns of establishment and the lack of land was a gradually growing one. There was no sudden disruption of the traditional ways, only an increasing attempt to find other ways. All the new ways involved dependence upon the industrial civilization surrounding the old culture.[3]

The fears that Hughes, writing in the late thirties, entertained about the future of French-Canadian society are far from being fears of the disintegrative effect of large-scale industrialization, but quite the contrary; they are based on the uncertain prospects of what would happen to French Canada's surplus population should industrial expansion stop:

The really great runoff [of surplus population] has been to towns and cities. New England which took unlimited quantities of labor in the late 19th century and on until the war of 1914–18, is crowded. Its industries are moving out to areas where labor is unspoiled by high standards of living and correspondingly high demands. Quebec, with its growing industries, has been insatiable until lately. But an end may come to the rapid growth of Quebec's own towns and industries ... for the city population itself is prolific enough to provide the next generation of city labor if no great expansion of industry occurs.[34]

Hughes does state that the new economic institutions were not products of French-Canadian culture, but were largely the products of an alien culture. He raised the question of what could happen with the shift, or transition, as he so aptly put it, of French-Canadian social structure from a rural to an industrial society. In other words, French Canada was entering a new phase. What would the new society be like? To me this is a valid statement of a problem. It is a valid question, not a prejudiced one; it is not a myth and it deserves an answer. The rest of this essay will attempt to outline what I conceive to be the shape of French Canada in the new epoch.

Although I have just voiced strong, and, I admit, at times passionate, dissent with Professor Garigue's criticism of the pioneers of our subject, I should not like to part company with him on such a sour note. The use of the folk-society concept for the study of nineteenth-century rural social organization does have its drawbacks. There were no problems in its usage when the total society was composed of the observed group, as was often the case in primitive societies. But what was macroscopic in primitive society becomes microscopic in a more complex and articulated one. So it is, as Steward has pointed out, that anthropology in its earlier applications to more complex societies was somewhat a victim of its own traditional methodology.[35] Thus Miner, by focusing exclusively on the parish, might have missed some of the significant aspects of French Canada's rural social organization. French-Canadian society was more than the parish. On this point I agree with Professor Garigue. But then the rural parish was pivotal to the essentially rural French-Canadian society of the last century. And here I disagree with Professor Garigue, who does not conceive of that society as an essentially rural one. Miner was not guilty of a personal sin; if sin there was, it was a collective one, traceable to the state of anthropology.[36]

The advantages of the use of the folk concept, at least in its methodological consequences, lie in the fact that it enabled Miner to give us a very minute, detailed study of the everyday life of people in the parish context, at every stage of the life-cycle; of how this culture coped with nature, death, and the struggle of daily living; and most of all of how it was changing, and groping for new solutions to meet its own internal contradictions. For these reasons, any student of French-Canadian society will ever remain very much indebted to him.

Social organization prior to massive industrialization
The defeat of France in Canada brought about the collapse of the feudally operated trading society. The rural establishments, marginal to the previous context of social organization, became central to the emerging rural one. The emerging society, in its early phases, rested on an economy of subsistence farming by landholding families grouped in local communities called parishes. The parish was the pivot of the rural organization. Only such institutions existed as could be financed by such an economy. The development of the new society meant the development of such communities. Quebec was a complex of these expanding local communities. Supra-parochial institutions were initially very weak. The history of the rural society, in a sense, is also the history of the development and strengthening of these supra-parochial institutions.

The local character of the basic structure is underlined by the fact that the economic and social relations of the majority of its population existed completely within its limits. The administrative structure of these communities centred around the parish and the *mairie*. The parish grouped the local *habitants*; the landholding families, tilling the soil, were settled in the *'rangs* of the parish.' In villages, the *rentiers* or retired farmers settled near the church together with the local *commerçants*, a few professionals, and the parish priest. The latter three groups were the local bourgeoisie anchored in the rural society. This bourgeoisie travelled more than the rest of the population. By trade, vocation, or occupation they linked the local community with others like it and with the gradually strengthening supra-parochial institutions of business, politics, and religion. For the *habitants*, to travel farther than one could go by horse was a major event, a break in the routine of everyday experience. Typically, a village in its completed form had its priest and church, a school operated by nuns, its notary and doctor, and its small business men who rested their trade on supplying what the subsistence economy could not produce. Many villages could not, at first, afford all the features of this internal institutional structure. Some, such as St Denis, have never been able to afford them all.

The first supra-local set of institutions was to be found in the *chef-lieu* of a group of such local communities. There, another set of institutions, wider in scope and supra-local in character, appeared. In these small towns one might see the bishopric, the bishop's seminary, an orphanage, a hospital, regional staff-houses of religious orders, a court, a prison, a newspaper, some small recently created industry, and more important commercial concerns. It was these sites that the roving eyes of American and English capitalists were to choose in their search for unspoiled labour, as Hughes put it. There, more often than not, lived the *député*. This set of institutions linked the local communities with the supra-local spheres of politics, religion, and business. Yet, as Gérin intimated, the institutions to be found in the *chef-lieu* rested on the yields of the rural hinterlands.

This rural society produced its own bourgeoisie, created from the ranks of the *habitants*. It thus cut across the ranks of kinship structures. The main channel of social promotion was rather neat and simple. It consisted in attending the bishop's *petit séminaire*, very often with the benevolent help of the clergy, and becoming an officer of the religious institution. For those who failed to become priests the liberal professions were open. In either case one became part of the bourgeoisie. The bourgeoisie was clerically created and the avenues of social promotion were clerically controlled; the clergy taught not only religion and profane science, but also manners – bourgeois manners, a style of life very different from that of one's family; in brief an image of bourgeois life that had been carried over by the clergy from the feudal aristocracy of New France. After a sojourn in the houses of clergy, one could come back and claim one's local prestige in the parish in one's new occupation. The more ambitious and the more successful competed for the higher offices in the emerging and strengthening supra-parochial spheres of politics and religion.

The game of politics was centred on the parish life. The gradual introduction of the British game, with its territorial basis of representative government, strengthened the importance of parishes. The buoyant participation of the local population in politics is traceable to this fact. The local population, by the British rules of the game, decided who among the competing cliques of local bourgeoisie would be given the rewards and the spoils of victory. Political parties, like all other supra-parochial institutions, were strong on the parish level, but became weaker the farther away from the parish one moved. The issues were defined by the urban bourgeoisie and its internationally minded small élite, disseminated by the local bourgeoisie through the help of their partisan regional newspapers, and settled by the quite illiterate population who were sometimes told what to do straight from the pulpit, in the name of God and salvation, by the parish priest at the goading of an aggressive bishop. Otherwise, one could easily get an illusion of intense democratic life and tradition from the politics of the period. The mainstay of political parties consisted in the continuous efforts of the competing bourgeois cliques to create and keep the support of the local population. Some families did achieve quite unchallengeable local support. Most of the time their positions were not so secure.

Among the supra-local institutions, religion was the strongest one. Even though the clergy itself, in the beginnings of the new society, was relatively weak both in numbers and in institutional equipment, it was strong in moral leadership. Leading deeply Catholic and sometimes superstitious populations, it organized the parish around the church. The local resources were tapped to make the church the most impressive structure of the parish. Sometimes the *habitants* squealed and did not co-operate with very much enthusiasm. Sometimes some even rebelled; but then the wrath of God and the fear of hell and the bishop's decrees of excommunication led them back to obedience. Yet, most of the time, they took pride and joy and comfort from the very majesty of their church, and its meaning for the after-life.

The clergy interpreted both the supernatural and the natural world. It defined the ethics of everyday life, and when politics strayed from its proper path, it scathed the erring politicians and warned the population. Sometimes the sway of erring bourgeois intellectuals was strong enough over their local followers to withstand the clerical storm, but not for any great length of time. Anti-clericalism made enough headway among a minority of bourgeois intellectuals, at one time, for them to proclaim their status publicly, to initiate institutions of their own, and to participate as anti-clericals in political parties. Two bishops declared open warfare on them. The dissenters countered by using the existing juridical institutions of British tradition to defend themselves. They won most of their battles but lost the war. Anti-clericalism became a political liability and has ever remained so. Its public existence was squashed, never to reappear. It resumed its proper place in the context of hushed conversations of disgruntled intellectuals, cynical politicians, and bitter business men. It may have grown with industrial society, but it is still a silent minority, officially and publicly non-existent, politically insignificant. The anti-clericals of the period participated in a more international culture. But, then as now, the clergy interpreted not only the supernatural and local worlds, but the international one as well.

As an administrative framework, the religious had a definite advantage over both the political and the commercial. It had a centralized bureaucratic structure organized on a regional basis into dioceses with the best communication system of all institutions, and a discipline and staff approximating the effectiveness of the military. It controlled the avenues of social promotion by its control of the educational structure. It socialized, in tender youth, all the budding professionals and politicians and even the future anti-clericals.

So it was that if the actors of politics were lay, and if they enacted the political roles of the game, most of the script was clerically censored, when not clerically written; and the actors were clerically rehearsed and directed. One should not project in this picture an image of tyranny. For the social script, such as it was, enjoyed social consensus. It still does. Nor was there cupidity and lust for power on the part of the clergy. In their conception of the world their control was the natural and proper order of things, of the good society, of the healthy society, uncorrupted by the evils of nineteenth-century modernism with its erroneous doctrine of separation of church and state. The sometimes brutal and systematic eradication of the enemies of such a conception stemmed from the very deep conviction of the truth of their own view. They did not however abdicate their role as leaders, and when conflicting conceptions seemed to take some hold and footing in the social structure they did not hesitate to take measures ranging from moral persuasion to economic boycott in order to eradicate the budding dissenters.

There existed a division of labour between politics, business, and religion. But the religious was the commanding institution; its ascendancy assured the spread of its ideology, its vocabularies of motives, and its languages, within the realms of the other two.

By and large the system of social institutions traditional to French Canada was built upon rural society, financed by its economics, controlled by its own ethnic élite with a cultural flavour of its own.

III. THE IMPACT OF INDUSTRIALIZATION ON THE RURAL SOCIETY

The rural society of French Canada contained its own weaknesses, its own structural contradictions. Gérin was the first to spot it. Arable land was scarce. The balance between land and people was precarious. Emigration helped to keep equilibrium, but limited growth. Gérin, who had seen that the weakness of New France stemmed from its lack of an agricultural basis, could now see the weakness of his contemporary society in its predominantly agricultural structure. The solution rested on progressive industrialization. When Hughes's study was undertaken, the process of industrialization was still in its earlier stages; its growth was slow, and temporarily halted by the depression of the thirties. The conclusion of Hughes's study was, in fact, a question. How would industrialization mix and mould with the institutions of French Canada's essentially rural social organization?

The conclusion of this essay is a largely tentative statement of how French-Canadian society has responded to the new situation.

Questions
Did massive industrialization change the composition of the previously existing structure of power? Did the strategic importance of the clergy in the new society decrease? Did new men of power rise on the scene, claim and get membership in the inner circles of power, on the basis of structural shifts? What impact did industrialization have on the institutional spheres themselves: on politics, business, and religion? These are the questions that I shall shortly attempt to answer.

My answers to these questions presuppose the general accuracy of the existing studies on French Canada, from Gérin to Miner and Hughes. Although my analysis both postulates the general validity of these studies, and claims a logical fit with them, it is not merely a logical explication of views already implicit in their works. Be kind enough not to see in this statement a devious way of staking a claim for originality. My only purpose is to plead that Miner and Hughes and the other members of the 'Chicago School' be spared whatever burden of guilt and errors my analysis may deserve. They will then be free to agree or dissent, strongly or mildly. Thus will I be assured of the honour, dubious as it may be but which I claim as rightfully mine, of standing convicted alone of my own sins.

Traditional élites, industrialization, and the developing society
The basic idea of this paper about the emerging shape of the new society is

that the traditional élites are still the commanding ones in French-Canadian society. While the changes wrought by massive industrialization could have considerably altered the composition of the power structure at the top levels, they have not done so. The decisive importance of the clergy and its ascendancy over the French-Canadian political and commercial spheres have not decreased in the transition from the rural to the industrial society. Quite the contrary: the clergy's importance has been strengthened. The structural pivot of power was gradually shifted from a rural landholding population towards the urban population. The structurally significant group of the recently urbanized population is not the urban workers, but the new middle class, a rapidly increasing group of salaried white-collar workers with no definite political ideology. This new middle class staffs the ever-developing bureaucracies of government, business, and the church. The collective role of this new middle class is to be the improvised agent of an 'administrative revolution,' and this 'administrative revolution' constitutes a new basis for the accrued power of the traditional élites. Their claim is being honoured without any major dissent.

I should now like to show how this new society is emerging. The rejuvenation of the traditional élites can only be accounted for by as neat a set of converging interests of clergy, political parties, and foreign capitalists as can be imagined.

The capitalists by their very presence and their money produced drastic changes. They were the ones who, in the final analysis, transformed the French Canadians into urban dwellers. The population needed no persuasion since it needed work. The capitalists gave the surplus population something to do and a place to go. In exchange, the local power élites let the capitalists dictate the industrial rules of the game. And in their game, unions were quite unwelcome players. Furthermore, their interest in local society was specific. They sought maximum yields with minimum involvement in the local game of politics, religion, and urban development, a requirement that dovetailed nicely with what the local power élites required, and still do, of invading aliens.

This tacit informal pact can also account for the local power élites' basic coolness and distrust, if not outright hostility, towards unionism and its supporting socialistic ideology. For while the capitalists with their money and industries brought structural relief, the unionists carried only words and caused social unrest. The structural relief became the basis of continued, though renewed, control by the traditional élites. Social unrest could only lead to the challenge of their continued exercise of power.

This spontaneous agreement can also account for the élite-created, predominantly political theme of nationalistic ideology up to the early fifties. The demand for economic nationalism, brought about by the flirtation of some currents of nationalist doctrine with socialism, may not be much more than an indirect demand, by the local élites, for a greater part of the yield of the new economic system.

This tacit understanding also accounts for the absence of unions in the contemporary composition of top-level power. The significant demographic basis for the new bureaucratic exercise of power is not the urban workers, but the new middle classes, salaried all, and busily engaged in operating the administrative revolution for the benefit of traditional élites.

The process of rejuvenation of traditional élites
How could the commanding élites of a rural society react so swiftly and channel so successfully, to their own advantage, such drastic changes as were brought about by the secular forces of industrial capitalism? How could the clergy, for instance, traditionally viewed as a convervative group, succeed in altering its attitudes and self-defined roles quickly enough to turn the structural shifts to its continued advantage? Its psychological preparation for setting out vigorously on the new course needed in the new circumstances can be traced far back into the last century. It was a psychology of fear learned as witnesses of European history. The crumbling of bourgeois Catholic institutions and of European monarchies, and the dechristianization of the masses that eventually resulted, provided the context in which the fear grew. And when disgruntled intellectuals in French Canada openly praised what was happening elsewhere, the clergy concluded that the danger was also at its own doorstep.

The clergy was thus psychologically prepared well in advance to act, and act swiftly, when the perils of industrialization were perceived to be of essentially the same nature. A mixed socio-religious theory of social reconstruction justified the new course of action. The clergy, out of fear, aggressively embarked on the administrative revolution. In the previous rural society, it had already taken hold on all the major institutional spheres; besides religion itself, the fields of education and social welfare were its unchallenged domain. With the advent of industrial society, and the pressure of numbers, it had to modify its techniques of control.

The basic mechanism it adopted was that of rapidly building and investing in large-scale institutions of assorted sizes and qualities. While it continued its old roles, it undertook to create completely new ones. The clergy became bureaucratic overlords and the rate of growth of clerical bureaucracies is simply amazing. The clergy's credit has long been established within the world of business. It also possesses a very effective privately operated taxation system whose yield reflects the health of the expanding economy; the faithful practice of weekly contributions has never diminished. With the growing size of its para-religious institutional holdings, it has adopted, with no qualms whatsoever, the system of community drives. Its accumulation of wealth for the financing of its expanding bureaucratic empires was not hampered by its privileged status in terms of public taxation.

It had choice lots in the cities whose values skyrocketed with the speculation for city land. Its investments are handled by its own specialists who are by no means the laughing stock of the trade. Lay stockbrokers compete for their patronage. With the increasing size of its bureaucracies, it has centralized both its administration and its finances. The parishes have become administrative units accountable to the *corporation épiscopale*. The symbolism of the name is self-evident. The *curé* whose income used to be a function of the wealth of his parishioners has been stripped of his old status to become a salaried functionary, a status more in line with new structural facts.

In the industrial society, the clergy kept all the institutional roles it had historically acquired, but it had to specialize for the successful maintenance of these roles. The very scope of the administrative revolution required the help of new groups. Its institutional pyramid needed a very wide assortment of professionals. The Church thus opened its own channels of social promotion. The agents of this administrative revolution are the salaried ranks of middle-class white-collar people.

There has been increasing pressure from the Church's white-collar ranks and from its assorted professionals for more income, which is necessary if they are to play their own status games in their drive towards professionalization. These professional groups are the agents of the administrative revolution; they do the actual cultural borrowing and the actual implementation of the clerically initiated or at least the clerically censored new policies. The clergy is now not only the distributor of the treasures of heaven but very much also, for a sizeable part of the population, the distributor both of status, in terms of institutional rewards, and of the very earthly rewards of weekly or monthly pay cheques. The pressure of demands from the new middle-class staff members of its own bureaucracies gave the Church an added claim to exert further pressure on the provincial treasury to augment its subsidies. All the while, its institutions, known as semi-public, enjoy the advantages of private bookkeeping, autonomous administration, and governmental subsidies.

The latest emerging phase of the logic of the developing clerical bureaucratic power has now taken definite form. It has been in the making for the last five years, and was publicly revealed last year. The pressure from the clergy for increasingly higher subsidies to finance its bureaucratic empire had met with stiffer resistance from the late Premier Duplessis. Signs of conflict were everywhere. Duplessis's mastery of politics dated back to a period when the political game still had a dominantly rural aspect. A persistent theme of his political oratory was his opposition to 'bureaucracy.' Even if ideologically neutral, the theme was becoming increasingly impertinent structurally. His great knowledge of the rural basis of politics enabled him to withstand the coming onslaught of the bureaucracy. The clerical powers were insistently claiming a new deal. For, willy-nilly, politics in Quebec structurally require a deal between clergy and politicians; this is the significant fact of democracy in Quebec. The old rural deal, based as it was on personal acquaintance, informal grants to priests and bishops for their assorted lot of cherished projects, no longer satisfied the claims of the increasingly competent leaders of the clerical bureaucratic empire. In the rural society, quasi-ritualistic exceptional grants sufficed to win clerical co-operation. The other aspect of the game consisted in spending public funds as our government dictates, spreading the money around a system of geographically dispersed private enterprises competing for the favours of government contracts of all sorts. Thus the gradual enrichment of these local commercial élites of easily identifiable men was the direct result of political action. The script was simple and obvious. It did not offend the sensibilities of the rural people; the rewarded business men knew clearly what their role was, and the parish priest accepted the same rule of the game. The priest was not asked to participate actively but only to be on the receiving end of the outstretched political hand; he had only to agree to accept the gift at timely moments.

What was really offensive to the sensibilities of the politically aggressive clerical members of the bureaucratic empires was the rather indecent openness of the whole deal. Their offended sensibility was shared by the salaried professionals of the clerical bureaucracies. Though completely unaware of the structural reasons that linked them to the new deal they responded in unison. From sheer structural location, and bureaucratic socialization, they felt that the proper ways were the ways of bureaucracy. They felt uneasy with the old rural game of politics. They felt it brought shame to the province. The leader of the government was depicted as a dictator, a tyrant having a corrupting influence on political *mores*. Young progressive clerics, in a daring move, celebrated all over the country, publicly fustigated the corrupt practices of the old game of rural politics. The public castigation in moral categories of the old game of politics can only be interpreted in terms of symbolic rituals. The young priests, very deserving, sincere, and well educated in the social sciences, valid examples of the young progressive clerical executive who will implement the new bureaucratic deal for the benefit of clergy and the new middle class, solemnly proclaimed the death of the old rural game of politics. The onlooking population, whose interests were aroused by the salaried middle class of the surrounding society, were keenly interested, and seemed to be rejoicing in the imminent coming of age of French-Canadian politics, that is, its coming of bureaucratic age. One bishop, from a rural diocese appropriately enough, raised a feeble voice of protest. Significantly, the voice of a bishop, which traditionally would have silenced that of any priest, had little effect.

The script of the new bureaucratic deal was quickly revealed and suddenly concealed by the untimely death of Premier Duplessis's successor, Premier Sauvé. Although he took the leadership of the very party whose political power had been anchored in rural politics, it was sufficient for him to proclaim the new deal to see all the previous bitter denunciations of the very same party vanish into thin air. All the middle-class salaried professionals in the extremely short period of one month unanimously – I was unable to find one dissenting voice – chanted his personal merits, and the rosy character of the future. The new deal was simple: the aggressive demands of clerically controlled bureaucracies would be met; universities, hospitals, and the staff of the government's own salaried middle class would be the beneficiaries. The ending of the old game was acclaimed by all. The solution had been found. The clerical bureaucracies required and demanded a regular flow and a substantially increased subsidy from the provincial coffers to forestall the unrest among their staff. By acquiescing to clerical demands, Premier Sauvé achieved imperishable fame in three short months of tenure. Never, in so short a time, did any politician, by a single declaration of policy, receive such spontaneous acclamation and such emotional endorsement. His premature death was felt by all as a tragic national loss. Some, who had never met him personally, were moved to tears. That this late Premier was more of a symbol than an actual ordinary human being is to me anthropologically obvious. He symbolized the new deal; its vocabulary is couched in the bureaucratic concepts of competence, planning, and so on.

The recently imported language of the salaried middle class will from now on shape the language of politics. The decisive political significance of the new middle class is now clearly assured. Its first act when it reaches actual power, I predict, will be to organize a truly competent civil service, a task which had been impossible under the old game of rural politics. Naturally, a truly competent civil service means a smoothly operated bureaucracy accompanied by enhanced status for the new middle class. Administrative social science, which, in the final analysis, is the only kind of social science wanted by these dominant bureaucracies, will have its heyday. Administrative efficiency will be rewarded and administrative laxness punished. And rural society will resume its proper place in the now almost completed new society.

The true sociological meaning, in terms of power, however, will be the establishment of a wider and more efficient communication system between the strictly political and the clerically controlled bureaucracies, because in the new system a bigger traffic between the two spheres is anticipated as the flow of money to clerically administered coffers increases. As overlords of bureaucracies the clergy is learning and accomplishing its role quite well. What the clergy is collectively incapable of seeing, however, is that the problem is not one of efficiency. The problem is a much more basic one, with deep meanings. With the systematic maintenance of the clergy's increasingly diversified number of roles, the image of what a priest is, why he exists, becomes blurred. After having achieved complete control over the social organization, the clergy may discover, perhaps too late, that its population no longer knows what religion and its cherished symbols mean. The symbols may become hollow and meaningless for the population, and even for parts of the clergy. And not because of alien and foreign culture, but as a direct result of the clergy's own successful control of the whole society.

NOTES

This paper, originally published in *The Canadian Journal of Economics and Political Science*, November 1960, was presented at the annual meeting of the Canadian Political Science Association in Kingston, 10 June 1960. The author is particularly indebted to Mr Fernand Cadieux of the Social Research Group. The basic ideas of this paper are the outcome of some years of intellectual companionship with him.

1 J.H. Steward, *Area Research: Theory and Practice* (Ottawa: Social Science Research Council, 1950), Bulletin 63, 21–2
2 One notable exception is Léon Gérin, whose book *Aux sources de notre histoire* (Montreal, 1946) is an analysis that gives great insight into the social system of New France.
3 Philippe Garigue, *Etudes sur le Canada français* (Montreal, 1958), 8, 14, 15
4 Horace Miner, *St. Denis: A French-Canadian Parish* (Chicago, 1939); Everett C. Hughes, *French Canada in Transition* (Chicago, 1943)
5 Guy Frégault, *La Civilisation de la Nouvelle France* (Montreal, 1944)
6 The clergy, in this context, obviously includes nuns.
7 Michel Brunet, 'La Conquête anglaise et la déchéance de la bourgeoisie canadienne, 1760–1793,' *Amérique française*, xii, no. 2, juin 1955
8 Gérin, *Aux sources de notre histoire*, 228ff., 253, 254
9 Garigue, *Etudes sur le Canada français*, 15
10 Robert Olsen, 'A Challenging New Concept of French Canada,' *Maclean's*, 14 February 1959
11 *Etudes sur le Canada français*, 6
12 Ibid., 15
13 Ibid., 9
14 Ibid., 6
15 When Professor Garigue says that the previous French-Canadian society was an urban and commercial one, are these characterizations not themselves 'ideal types'?
16 Professor Garigue blurs the historical record when he says ('Mythes et réalités' in *L'Etude des sciences de l'homme*, iii, 1956, 129) that Gérin was Le Play's disciple. Gérin studied under Edmond Demonlins, one of Le Play's disciples.
17 Quoted by Garigue, freely translated by me. See Garigue, *Etudes sur le Canada français*, 8
18 Ibid.
19 Ibid.
20 'Seule leur ignorance de l'histoire du Canada français permet de comprendre que les sociologues aient pu accorder à une telle hypothèse une importance de premier plan' (ibid., 14).
21 *Aux sources de notre histoire*
22 Ibid., esp. chaps. xiv, xv
23 Ibid., 254
24 *Etudes sur le Canada français*, 49
25 *French Canada in Transition*, 8
26 Ibid., 7

27 *St. Denis,* 237

28 Here are a few stanzas: 'Grâce aux nouvelles méthodes de recherche et à
l'élaboration de nouveaux instruments d'analyse, nous pouvons affirmer
que nous avons dépassé les pionniers' (*Etudes sur le Canada français,* 6). Or
again (ibid., 15): 'Je pense avoir démontré que beaucoup des idées qui ont
été émises par les sociologues de l'école de Chicago sur le Canada français ne
sont pas valides. Il reste maintenant à montrer ce qu'est le Canada
français ... Malheureusement, mes recherches personnelles ne me permettent
pas encore de répondre à cette question. Et ceci pour l'excellente raison que
les critères scientifiques que j'utilise demandent la mise en action de
recherches très larges, faites avec des équipes de plusieurs personnes, et
demandant des ressources financières importantes.' On the basis of this last
sentence, Professor Garigue does not conceive of himself as a soldier in
the army of science but rather as a field general. There is nothing particularly
wrong in the ambition, for most social scientists cherish the same one
secretly; but the common practice is not to voice it quite so openly and
aggressively.

29 Ibid., 5: 'L'argument que nous esquissons dans ces études est que de
nombreux préjugés one existé et existent, dans les milieux dits scientifiques,
sur la nature du Canada français ...'

30 Ibid., 14

31 Ibid., 46–9

32 *St. Denis,* 235

33 Ibid., 237

34 *French Canada in Transition,* 20

35 *Area Research,* 22

36 Ibid., 51

Social unrest, social class, and Quebec's bureaucratic revolution

Political structures in a mass society are fragile things. Since the Second World War, we have witnessed the collapse of age-old political regimes. The break-up of formal political empires, with the intellectual backing and sympathetic understanding of the majority of liberal intellectuals of the Western World, is now nearly complete. Seldom was the use of force necessary to achieve this. Massive ideological agitation with wide popular support achieved what armed might would not have attained. In most cases, the two structural conditions prerequisite to national liberation were: (1) a newly created native elite, highly educated, politically conscious and through nationalist identification effectively engineering the revolt of expectations within (2) an awakened, restless native population whose aspirations are to be fulfilled by political independence. National independence has often been achieved though the heightened expectations usually have yet to be met.

Political structures need legitimations. Formal political empires collapsed because of a bankruptcy in legitimations. Legitimations are created by intellectuals and become sacred values for the other social groups.

Withdrawal of support from political structures by wide segments of the intelligentsia therefore becomes a crucial clue of imminent political instability. When this disenchantment of intellectuals is widely publicized and finds massive support in the lower social strata, the political regime, short of tyranny, is doomed. For a political structure is, in the final analysis, a moral order requiring for its existence consensus.

Confederation is a political structure. For growing numbers of French-Canadian intellectuals its legitimations are unconvincing. The Massey-

Lévesque brand of national feeling, the mutual-enrichment theory of ethnic co-habitation, seems, in 1964, so quaint, archaic and folklorish, that for many young French-Canadian university students it is hard to believe it was formulated as late as 1950.

In the early sixties we have therefore witnessed the collapse of the latest legitimation of Confederation produced for the post-war period of peace. The Dunton-Laurendeau Commission, in my opinion, is searching for just that. Whether it will be successful is still very problematical. For the first time in the history of royal commissions concerned with national identity, dissent from many English-speaking Canadians is loud, clear, and emotional. Traditionally, such dissent came from a marginal, vocal group of French-Canadian nationalists. Their voice today is still vocal, but marginal it no longer is, for it stems from official circles with the blessing of academia. Lionel Groulx in the thirties, Michel Brunet in the early fifties could be dismissed as narrow-minded chauvinistic nationalists both within and without French-Canadian society. René Lévesque in the sixties cannot be so easily dismissed and he, in fact, is not so dismissed.

In terms of my opening remarks where does Confederation as a political structure stand within French Canada? Intellectual disenchantment with Confederation is widespread within the French-Canadian intelligentsia, including the social scientists. This disenchantment of intellectuals, artists, writers, newspapermen, film directors, etc., has been widely publicized in all forms of mass media. Furthermore, wide segments of French Canada's new middle class are either openly committed to, or sympathetic with, this heightened nationalist feeling if not with separatism itself. This disenchantment, measured by belief in separatism, has not yet found massive support in the rural and lower urban social strata, but has met rather with indifference, apathy, and scepticism, seldom however with outright hostility. Had massive support from these social strata been forthcoming, the separatist idea would have been acted upon. Paradoxical as it may seem, it is the uneducated, unskilled and semi-skilled French Canadian farmer and worker, the 'ignorant,' 'joual'-speaking French Canadian, oft-maligned and spoofed at by his ethnic middle class and the perfect fit of the anti–French-Canadian stereotype, it is he at present who quite unconsciously is holding Confederation, unsettled as it is, on its shaky legs.

This leads me to raise specifically, the questions I shall attempt to answer in this essay. Why has the lower-class French Canadian been relatively immune to separatist agitation? Why has the new French-Canadian middle class become virulently nationalist and, to an important extent, separatist? Why has the emergence of this new middle class heightened ethnic tensions in Confederation? What is the nature of social unrest in the lower social strata?

II. SOCIAL UNREST AND THE NEW MIDDLE CLASS

The emergence of what is commonly called the new middle class is not something specific to French Canada; quite on the contrary, the growth of such a class was rather belated, in fact, essentially as post-war phenomenon. With the growth and the increased size of large-scale formal organizations of business and government, the middle class was overwhelmingly transformed into a bureaucratically employed white-collar group with professional and semi-professional status, displacing the dominant 'entrepreneurial' self-employed character of the middle class in the last century. The new middle class is a product of the bureaucratic expansion of organizations.

1. The growth and characteristics of the new middle class in French Canada
Structurally, the French-Canadian new middle class is the same as its counterparts in industrially developed societies. But the circumstances of its emergence and some of its characteristics are somewhat at variance with most.

The bureaucratic revolution is, demographically speaking, the result of mass exodus from country to city. The demographic pressure created a need for expansion of the urban institutions serving this influx. In the process of expansion the urban institutions changed character, becoming large-scale organizations, marked by increased specialization. This bureaucratic revolution opened new channels of upward mobility. It required diversified staffs, trained in new skills. The growth of bureaucratic urban institutions became the structural basis of a new social class called the new middle class.

The French-Canadian new middle class, I have said, is somewhat different in some of its social psychological characteristics from other new middle classes. First of all, its emergence was more dramatic and sudden than in many cases. Secondly, the ethnic cultural traditions from which it came provided no models for the broad spectrum of the new occupational roles. Thirdly, French-Canadian bureaucracies are to be found overwhelmingly in the public and semi-public sectors as against the area of private enterprise. Finally, the bureaucratic revolution, in French Canada, has not changed the power elite of French-Canadian society; it has not displaced, but rather rejuvenated traditional elites. Much of the unrest, in my opinion, in the French-Canadian new middle class can be related to these special characteristics.

2. *The Duplessis era and the new middle class*
New–middle-class unrest dates back to the mid and late fifties. The post-war period saw a massive migration of French Canadians to the cities, mostly the major ones. This massive urbanization altered the existing nature of urban institutions. Urban institutions of welfare, health, and education had rapidly to increase their size, their staffs, and their budgets to meet the new demographic needs. This bureaucratic growth was being stifled by Duplessis's discretionary habit in spreading out public funds. In the process, the economic and status interests of this new middle class were not being met. Salaries could not be increased. Why? Because of Duplessis. Staff could not be hired. Why? Because of Duplessis.

Duplessis became a symbol of oppression, of reactionary government. He was depicted as a tyrant corrupting political mores. A persistent theme of Duplessis's political oratory was his opposition to 'bureaucracy.' Even though ideologically neutral, the theme was becoming increasingly impertinent structurally. The celebrated attack on the political mores of the Union Nationale party by Fathers Dion and O'Neill paved the way for a new bureaucratic type of political morality. The growth of semi-public bureaucratic institutions required greatly increased and predictable amounts of money from the provincial treasury. Because he refused to meet these class demands, Duplessis was emotionally and unanimously resented by the new middle class. Where Duplessis failed, Sauvé succeeded. By a single declaration of policy, namely, increased grants to universities, hospital insurance, and increased salaries to civil servants, he immediately got the emotional endorsement of the new middle class for the very same party. His untimely death was perceived by members of this social class as a tragic personal loss. Duplessis stifled the class interests and the status aspirations of the new middle class. He was resented. Sauvé decided to meet them; he was acclaimed.

3. *The new middle class and the Lesage regime*
With the death of Duplessis, the critical importance of the new middle class on politics became unchallenged. Following in Sauvé's footsteps, the Liberal party under Jean Lesage proceeded to base its political strength on the enthusiastic support of the new middle class, recently become politically aroused and vocal.

The link between the Liberal party and the new middle class can easily be established. Its existence can be shown in terms of (a) the 'nucleus' of its political support, (b) the choice of 'competent' administrative personnel in the civil service, and (c) the nature of its legislative reforms. The 'volunteer' workers of the Liberal party in the past elections were urban, more highly educated, younger, new–middle-class people. The concern for qualified personnel in the expanding provincial civil service spells the end of the 'self-made' man or politically appointed party supporter. The party man must also be professionally qualified.

The Liberal legislative reform is a bureaucratic reform. It has sought to expand and strengthen the bureaucratic services of education, health, and welfare. The Quebec renaissance or silent revolution, or whatever it is called, is a bureaucratic revolution. The tremendous expenditures in education and health are coupled with a constant concern with increasing the salaries of white-collar occupations in these institutions. Current concern for portable pensions equally reflects the interests of the new middle class.

4. From anti-Duplessisism to separatism
It is not, in my opinion, by sheer coincidence that separatism became a social force only after the death of Duplessis. By stifling the status aspirations of the new middle class, Duplessis became a scapegoat upon which its frustrations could be vented. Middle-class unrest did not die with Duplessis. The middle classes, however, did lose a scapegoat.

The Liberal party, champion of bureaucratic reform, endeavouring to meet the aspirations of this social class, could not easily be indicted. Unrest in new–middle-class circles took on the form of separatist agitation. The class origins of separatism can be ascertained both in terms of the social location of its supporters and the class nature of its grievances.

Separatist leaders as well as their rank and file are to be found among the better-educated, younger, professional and semi-professional, salaried, white-collar ranks. This class constitutes the core of its support. The nature of separatist grievances also underlines its class bias. Separatist discontent, in the final analysis, boils down to protest against real or imagined restricted occupational mobility. The objects of separatist indictment are the promotion practices of the federally operated bureaucracies, of crown and private corporations. This class bias is also the reason why the separatist appeal has gone by largely unheeded by the rural classes and the lower social strata of the cities.

5. Nationalist unrest, the Liberal regime, and confederation
Sheer coincidence cannot alone account for the fact that separatism and disenchantment with Confederation appeared on the political scene, in its massive form, after the Liberal regime came into power and not during the Duplessis era.

Meeting the status aspirations of the new middle class in French Canada, as the Liberals surely know by now, is an expensive proposition. It is more costly than most service since, as I have mentioned, French-Canadian bureaucracies tend to be in the public or semipublic sectors that typically rely on public funds for a sizeable proportion of their budgets. The income squeeze that resulted from trying to meet new–middle-class demands created a political crisis in dominion-provincial relations.

Ethnic tensions, unheard of during the Duplessis era, were brought back once again to the forefront of public discussion. *Maîtres chez nous*, the Liberal party's slogan in the last election, is actually the official endorsement of a forty-year-old slogan first put forward by Lionel Groulx. 'Le seul choix qui nous reste est celui-ci: ou redevenir maîtres chez nous, ou nous résigner a jamais aux destinées d'un peuple de serfs.'[1] Lionel Groulx's was a voice in the desert until the new middle class made it theirs. His historical, economic, and social views were academically marginal and politically ineffective until the emergence of the new middle class and its access to political power. His views have become the unifying ideology giving political cohesiveness to this new social class.

Many of the current themes of political concern are to be explicitly found in his writings. Ambivalence towards foreign capitalists and foreign labour unions, indignation at the handing over of natural resources to foreign investors, the lack of an entrepreneurial bourgeoisie, the positive role of the state in economic affairs, the lack of proper academic institutions and training for the world of business, the 'bi-national' theory of Confederation, all of these themes are clearly and eloquently pleaded in his writings.

The financial strain of the French-Canadian bureaucratic revolution and the nationalist ideology of the French-Canadian new middle class, have brought about a reinterpretation of Confederation specifically and of ethnic co-habitation generally. The reinterpretation is not new; its widespread acceptance in the new middle class is.

Confederation is on probation. The French-Canadian new middle class does not view it as something valuable in itself. It is to be judged on its merits as a means to achieving national aspirations. It has, for a long time, been viewed as an instrument of British-Canadian nationalism.[2] With the rise of ethnic tensions this view is becoming widespread in many circles and a postulate of the political analysis of separatist groups of every tendency.

What, in effect, needs clarification is the history of ethnic co-habitation in Canada. Ethnic accommodation, it seems to me, has been historically constructed, successfully in Quebec, on a basis of mutually desired self-segregated institutions. In the fields of education, religion, welfare, leisure, and residence, institutional self-segregation has been total. The only two areas of societal living where inter-ethnic contact has been institutionalized are those of work and politics.

The pattern of ethnic contact in the area of work was established with the introduction of industrialization. Anglo-Saxon industry moved into a society faced with an acute population surplus, a distinctive political and religious elite, a developing set of institutions anchored in the rural parish. This society, politically stable, economically conservative, and technically unskilled, provided ideal conditions for investing Anglo-Saxon capitalists; they could invest their capital, open industries, and be supplied with an abundant source of unskilled labour seeking employment. The managerial and technical levels were filled, with no protest, by the incoming group, who also brought along their own set of institutions, servicing their own nationals.

This social setting provided an easy introduction to industry. The French-Canadian elite was ideologically co-operative, sensitive only about its continued control over its demographic substructures. This fitted in quite well with the aims of the incoming groups, who could develop their economic pursuits and enterprises with minimum involvement in the local society. There was a minimum of involvement in local politics. The local elite of politicians and the clergy welcomed the transaction of business and the development of business institutions. All this took place with no unrest whatsoever. Industry was relieving the economic burden of the demographic surplus of French-Canadian rural society. The local elites' leadership was not being challenged.

This pattern of mutually satisfying, self-segregated institutions worked with no dissent up to and including the Second World War. This historical pattern is now being challenged. It is being challenged by the recently emerged French-Canadian new middle class. Making room for this new social class in the managerial levels of industry and government is the crucial test of Canadian unity. This cannot be achieved without the shedding of old habits that surrounded the traditional ethnic division of labour.

III. SOCIAL UNREST IN THE RURAL AND
LOWER URBAN SOCI'AL CLASSES

1. The Créditiste episode
'Nous sommes simples, nous autres habitants, et vu notre ignorance, nous sommes contraints de mettre à la tête de nos municipalités et de nos administrations des citoyens instruits mais qui, au fond, nous exploitent ... ' – Isidore Gauthier, a farmer, 1862.[3]

New–middle-class unrest, vocal and well publicized, overshadowed another social unrest, that of the lower social class of country and city, until the unforeseen sweep of rural Quebec by Réal Caoutte's Créditiste movement.

Indeed, for the first time in Quebec's political history, the rural lower classes transgressed the political script described by Isidore Gauthier. Instead of sending to the federal parliament traditional middle-class professionals, they elected class peers to represent them.

Unforeseen, this political development brought about a reaction of bewilderment, astonishment, and nervous laughter in middle-class circles. The Créditiste surge was viewed with alarm, ridicule, and embarrassment. The French-Canadian new middle class had the identical reaction as its English-Canadian counterpart towards the Créditiste sweep. It focused immediately and exclusively on its unorthodox economics not on the social discontent that gave rise to it.

The Créditiste appeal successfully tapped the unrest of farmer and unskilled worker where the middle-class separatist protest failed. The Créditiste criticism of the traditional parties found fertile soil in the economically deprived regions of rural Quebec. 'You have nothing to lose' went the slogan. Another major theme was the right to economic security. Economic security to middle-class people means decent pension plans. To a sizeable part of the French-Canadian population it means something quite different. It means stable employment, a year-round job, the right not to live in the constant fear of unemployment. Caouette, who is no new–middle-class symbol by any means, but a small entrepreneur, the product of the barren Abitibi region, spoke their language. His charge that the old parties really do not care or cannot change their socio-economic plight, comes dangerously close to regional historic truth, for this state of economic insecurity has been a pattern that dates back close to a century.

The dramatic emergence of the Social Credit party in rural Quebec can be viewed as a boomerang or latent resentment of the class-oriented

Liberal course in Quebec. Duplessis, whatever his shortcomings, based his political machine on the rural and lower-urban social strata. After the ousting of the Union Nationale from power, these classes felt unrepresented, uncared for, with no significant voice in the political arena. Duplessis had never been viewed as a dictator or tyrant in these strata. The Lesage resolve to dissolve patronage increased the Créditiste supporters because of disenchanted rural Liberals who had expected the continued exercise of patronage by their own group.

The possibly unanticipated effect of the crackdown on patronage, in actual fact, was to halt or substantially reduce the flow of provincial funds to the lower social strata. Holding up the new 'bureaucratic' political morality was a hidden net reorienting public expenditures to other social classes. In the light of this interpretation, the Créditiste slogan 'you have nothing to lose' takes on added meaning. Whatever the dubious ethics of the political organizers of Duplessis may have been, and whatever the size of the cake they kept as their part, they managed, in their own devious ways, to let the rest funnel down in numerous bits into kinship systems. With the Liberal regime, the cake is properly and ceremoniously cut up, but the slices are fewer and the number of guests greatly reduced.

Whether the Créditiste movement will manage to hold its own politically is uncertain; whether it does or not, is of little interest; the social unrest that gave rise to it is, however, of considerable importance. To make intelligible the social forces behind its success, whether temporary or not, is the legitimate and necessary concern of the social scientist.

2. Messianic social movements and deprived social classes

Messianic social movements tend to take roots in the economically deprived social classes. The utopian dream they hold up may seem unattainable and irrational to middle-class logic, but its purpose and function are different. Its function is to present an alternative to the state of things for those who benefit the least from the status quo. In the process, the present state of society is shown to be man-made and therefore amenable to change. The 'funny money' policies of the Créditiste movement can be understood in the light of such classical social-movement theory. The Créditiste attack on the financial 'sharks' and its insistence on monetary reform served this purpose. To set off the printing presses is an alarming idea for those who have money because of its inflationary effect, for those who do not have money, it becomes a pleasant dream; a dream about magical access to middle-class status. And when believed in, it becomes a political force.

Eric Kierans's brave foray from the Board of Trade's executive suite to Créditiste territory with an orthodox economic gospel, quite unprecedented as it was, only underlined the establishment's sombre assessment of the situation.

The Liberal solution to the economic plight of these deprived regions goes little beyond the faint hope of recruitment over the generations to middle-class status through education. This is equally utopian; it has yet to be achieved anywhere in Western capitalist society. The fact of the matter is that no operational solution to these pockets of poverty has actually been found.

3. The Conservative urban proletariat and the uprooted new middle class
The French-Canadian urban lower classes behave improperly in terms of classical theory. They remain Catholic, faithfully go to church, never vote socialist, and in times of family crisis will spontaneously turn for help to their extended kinship group, their priests, and their landlords, and only as a last resort, and with a loss of self-respect, to social agencies, social workers, and union leaders.

The traditionalism of the urban lower class has been the scourge of socialist efforts. It has also stubbornly resisted appeals from the nationalist circles to become an ethnically conscious consumer. They do not share the anti-Americanism of both French-Canadian and English-Canadian nationalism.

The rural-urban transition, eased by the kinship group, has not been, as textbooks usually describe it, as personally unsettling and culturally shocking as earlier massive urbanization may have been in other societies.

Uprootedness is more characteristic of French Canada's new middle class than of its urban proletariat. The traditional pattern of land inheritance, of keeping the farm intact and handing it over to only one heir, coupled with the high rural birth rate, has meant that moving, looking for work, settling elsewhere, is not a dramatic event in the life-cycle of the rural surplus population and it has been provided for in the cultural script.

What have not been provided for by the cultural traditions are the role models for the new–middle-class occupations. For this reason, the traditional culture is something far from sacred and useful, very often the object of contempt and ridicule within new–middle-class circles. Part of the anxiety and anguish of the new–middle-class psyche may be traced to this lack of cultural continuity.

IV. SUMMARY

The emergence of a new middle class in French Canada is a structural change that cannot be wished away. Its status aspirations are challenging the historical pattern of the ethnic division of labour. Whether its heightened national mood will lead to the separatist experiment is dependent upon two things: (a) on how successful the present political and economic structure of the Canadian society will be in coping with its bureaucratic aspirations, and (b) on the future direction of lower-class unrest.

The bureaucratic revolution of the last few years in Quebec has brought to the surface latent resentment in French-Canadian society. The traditionally conservative substructure of French-Canadian society has expressed discontent of its own. Its course has not, until now, been in the same direction. But who can say with absolute confidence that it will never be?

Bold, imaginative, and responsible decisions are in order from the power elites of this country, whoever they may be. It is doubtful that the current concept of 'co-operative federalism' in its present confused and blurred state will tide us over.

NOTES

Originally published in *Queen's Quarterly*, Summer 1964

1 Lionel Groulx, *Directives* (Montreal, 1937), 20

2 See Michel Brunet, *Canadians et Canadiens* (Montreal, 1952), 47–9. 'Une autre manifestation du nationalisme Canadian, le Rapport Massey.'

3 Quoted in Léon Gérin, *Le Type économique et social des Canadiens* (Montreal, 1938), 54

Two cultures: an essay on nationalism, class, and ethnic tension

In highly industrialized societies, the increasing scale of economic organizations goes hand in hand with a corresponding degree of concentration of political power in the central governments. Canada, however, in the last decade has in a climate of political tension experimented in another direction; namely, an increase in the political and economic relevance of the provincial governments at the expense of the federal government. One of the factors bringing this unexpected turn of events has been in no small measure, as most observers will agree, cultural dualism, within which the French-Canadian culture has been more aggressive and forceful. The question therefore becomes: What are the changes, the social forces, within French-Canadian society that brought about this development?

In this essay the social and cultural factors that seem to have been of paramount importance in producing change in French Canada – a new middle class and a resurgence of nationalism – are singled out and analyzed. There are three parts to this study. The first deals with neo-nationalism and traditional societies. In this section, an attempt is made to trace the emergence of modern nationalism in Europe and in traditional societies. Furthermore, elements of a conceptual model that could be useful in interpreting nationalist movements in a comparative fashion are described in some detail. The second section of the essay is an attempt to utilize the model in analyzing social and cultural changes in French-Canadian society. In a final section, the impact of the aforementioned cultural and social changes on ethnic accommodation is raised.

NEO-NATIONALISM AND TRADITIONAL SOCIETIES

In his essay on nationality, Lord Acton gives a brilliant account of its emergence.[1] Until the French Revolution the exercise of state power was legitimized by dynastic rule. The rights of nationalities were neither recognized by governments nor asserted by the people. Wars between countries were not wars between nations and did not capitalize on national feeling, but were wars involving dynastic rivalries and conflicting claims between monarchs. Dynastic rule became despotic, claims Acton, with the brutal suppression of Poland because of the nature of its monarchy. A monarch without royal blood, a crown bestowed by the nation, was an anomaly and an outrage in that age of dynastic absolutism. 'This measure awakened the theory of nationality in Europe, converting a dormant right into an aspiration, and a sentiment into a political claim'[146].

The legitimacy of dynastic rule was destroyed by the French Revolution. With the overthrow of dynastic rule and feudal social structure, a new legitimation of the power of the state had to be created. Since tradition meant feudalism, it had to be discarded, and 'descent was put in the place of tradition and the French people were regarded as a physical product: an ethnological, not an historical unit' [148]. In this way the idea of the sovereignty of the people, uncontrolled by the past, gave birth to the idea of nationality independent of the political influence of history. Nationality sprang from the rejection of the two authorities – of the state and of the past. 'Every effaceable trace and relic of national history was carefully wiped away – the system of administration, the physical divisions of the country, the claims of society, the corporations, the weights and measures – even the calendar' [149].

Nationality had been ignored by the Old Regime; the revolutionary wars and the Napoleonic Empire proceeded to outrage it. Napoleon attacked nationality in Russia, delivered it in Italy, and governed in defiance of it in Germany and Spain. Men were made conscious of the national element of the French Revolution not by its rise but by the conquests. With the demise of Napoleon and the Restoration, the governments of the Holy Alliance devoted themselves to suppressing with equal care the revolutionary spirit by which they had been threatened and the national spirit by which they had been restored. The antinational character of the Restoration, most distinct in Austria under Metternich, had the opposite effect of transforming the theory of nationality – that is, the right of national groups to statehood – into a political doctrine. 'Beginning by a protest against the domination of race over race, its mildest and least-developed form, it grew into a condemnation of every state that included different races and finally became the complete and consistent theory that the state and the nation be coterminous' [156].

Lord Acton's account of the emergence of the principle of nationalities as a political doctrine can be supplemented by a consideration of De Tocqueville's brilliant analysis of the continuity between the Old Regime and the Revolution.[2] Revolutions seldom start outright with an attack on the legitimacy of the political structure as such but rather as a plea for redress of injustices within the structure itself. His analysis of the *cahiers de doléances* that preceded the Revolution abounds with the practical characteristics of such complaints, covering a wide area of social arrangements. What stunned De Tocqueville was the fact that the centralized bureaucratic structure that had largely been set up under the Ancien Regime was left untouched by the Revolution. Indeed, the kings had progressively substituted their own politically appointed administrators, the feudal lords, to handle bureaucratic requirements of daily life, thereby extending territorially the political dominance of the Crown over the feudal lords. While the former did the work, however, the latter pocketed the proceeds, a factor that De Tocqueville considers of great importance in focusing unrest and resentment of the people upon feudalism. In fact, in those areas of France where the feudal lords still performed their administrative duties as well as reaping the rights and privileges of their office, the Revolution was resisted. This would suggest that revolutions build up gradually from discontent over the unequal distribution of facilities to meet the prosaic requirements of daily living, to the gradual focusing upon agents responsible for this state of affairs, to demands for a change of structure, and finally, to a challenge of the legitimacy of the overall political structure.[3]

The centralization of bureaucratic power under the monarchy was retained, however, because of its functional utility as a structure to maintain the political power and cohesion of the state under the new symbols of legitimacy. Had this bureaucratic centralization not occurred and had it not been maintained, the chances of France remaining a unified political state would have been greatly reduced. In summary, the theory of nationality in Continental Europe provided the symbols whereby the nation-state was made legitimate after the liquidation of the feudal political order.

THE EMERGENCE OF NATIONALISM IN TRADITIONAL SOCIETIES

From a consideration of the development of nationalism, it is important next to consider some of the structural features of contemporary or 'current' nationalism. Paradoxical as it may seem, at the very time that the principle of nationality was reorganizing the political shape and foundations of Europe, the European powers were expanding, developing, and consolidating their imperial holdings over other parts of the globe. National groups of the imperial powers controlled the political apparatus of the colonies. These endeavors were carried on with the help of the army and the churches.[4] In order to deal with local cultures, the imperial elite within the colonies would work with indigenous political structures of a tribal or feudal character or create such native political leadership. Administrative and political boundaries were carved with little or no regard for the ethnological homogeneity or heterogeneity of the indigenous populations.

The symbol of 'legitimation' for the empire-builders was the 'spread of civilization.' In providing this legitimation, the Christian churches were of paramount importance. The religious legitimation took the form of converting the indigenous populations to Christianity, thereby heeding the prescription of the Gospel. The 'spread of civilization' involved the armies, to assure political stability; the capitalists, to spread the benefits of industrialization; and the clergy, to bring them the Kingdom of God.

Colonial rule swiftly and deeply affected the local traditional cultures as well as the traditional social structure of the various indigenous groups. Not frequently, the nature of traditional indigenous culture before the Western presence is clouded in mystery and is the object of historical speculation and of archeological investigation. The very success of the imperial ventures gave rise to an indigenous middle class recruited from the various indigenous groups, a middle class whose status, power, and prestige were derived from its formal though subordinate participation in the expanding institutions of the imperial regimes. While the newly acquired status of the middle class was honored by its co-nationals, it was bestowed upon them by the ruling aliens. The social mobility of the middle class was accompanied by a high degree of acculturation. The local clerically staffed schools gave its children their basic education and not infrequently the more promising would have some years in the metropolitan centres overseas.

Irrespective of the occupational dissimilarities, whether they were minor civil servants, teachers, industrial white-collar workers, or non-commissioned officers in the army, the members of this newly arisen middle class had many common characteristics: they were bureaucratically employed, they were culturally marginal to the traditional local cultures, they had been shaped by the same school system, they had alien ethnic superiors, and social distance kept them from intimate social contact and integration with the Western elite. These common characteristics made them a status group with a distinctively characteristic style of life, with common class interests that led to class awareness, if not to the growth of political class consciousness.

Thus the growth and extension of colonial governments and administrations gave birth to a new indigenous middle class. It is within the ranks of this new indigenous middle class that nationalist movements were born.

THE STRUCTURAL DILEMMA OF NATIONALIST MOVEMENTS

Next, an analysis may be made of what may be called the structural dilemma of nationalist movements in traditional societies.[5]

Nationalist movements in traditional societies seldom, if ever, begin as revolutionary movements launching a full-fledged attack on the legitimations of the political structure of the state. The first phase is more aptly labeled a quest for social and political reform. This quest, which more often than not takes the form of a request from legitimate authorities, is voiced by the new indigenous middle class and very frequently in terms of its class interest. The symbolic basis for the requested changes invariably reflects the ideological acculturation of the native elite. For instance, in the British Empire it was based on the extension to the colonies of increased 'home' rule, i.e., increased and extended political participation of the citizenry. This, however, only reflected the colonists' acceptance of the political ideology that brought about such changes in Britain itself.

The second phase of nationalist movements begins when there is an effort to extend the social base of national claims and of the nationalist movement itself. The initial social base of nationalist movements, as has been noted, is the native bureaucratic or liberal bourgeoisie. It is a social class of recent emergence and of relatively small size. As a class it possesses very little political leverage to bring about political reforms because of its restricted social base. In its search to extend its social base it faces what might be called a structural dilemma.

Two sets of structural constraints must be overcome by the nationalist movement to expand its social base. The first set of constraints stems from the nature of colonial rule and the local groups which have a vested interest in the persistence of the status quo. The constraint is that these groups, politically established or supported by the state, control the means of violence in the country. The other set of constraints stems from the preindustrial character of the local culture and its traditional commanding institutions. While they accommodate with the status quo, they are marginal to, if not resentful of, the ongoing social changes.

In order to overcome these structural constraints, the national movements must successfully launch a twofold symbolic attack: on the alien presence and control of the state on the one hand, and on the traditional culture and the social control of traditional institutions and traditional political leaders on the other.

This leads the nationalist movements to the third phase wherein they are transformed from reform to revolutionary social movements. They are revolutionary because they attack the very legitimacy of the exercise of power of the state as presently constituted; they are equally revolutionary because they attack the legitimacy of basic values legitimizing indigenous traditional social structures. As a class, the newly emerged native elites have an economic and political stake, not in arresting but in pursuing the socioeconomic changes initiated by the colonial regimes. Thus not only their marginality and acculturation but their class interests compel them to pursue and accelerate socioeconomic changes. The attack upon the legitimation of colonial rule as well as of the traditional social structure is centered in the positive acceptance of industrialization. It then focuses on the fact that the purpose of the colonial regime's political apparatus is to protect and assist the economic interests of the investing capitalist from the imperial center, not to accelerate the economic development of the local people.[6]

The same core values of modernization and industrial development are used to challenge the traditional culture, its social institutions, and its traditional leadership. Neo-nationalist movements based on the values of modernization therefore are necessarily ambivalent toward the traditional culture, which was not based on such values. However, the need for ethnological continuity in the new nation-state requires not that all the elements of traditional cultures be rejected but that some be retained, glorified, and used as a basis to form a new consensus.

The fourth and final phase of successful nationalist movements is to force a new consensus in support of the new nation-state. This requires, to varying degrees, wrestling the masses from the symbols of tradition, creating and celebrating a new kind of man, a product of the changing society, by initiating and controlling the formal and informal means of socialization – the schools, the public mass media, etc. – and finally, establishing a considerable degree of bureaucratic control and centralization over the whole territory to avoid the fractionalism of tribal or local cultures once the political dominance of the aliens has been removed.

NEO-NATIONALISM, THE QUIET REVOLUTION, AND THE NEW MIDDLE CLASS

From an assessment of the emergence of modern nationalism in the Continental Europe of the nineteenth century and a consideration of the social basis of neo-nationalism in the traditional societies of the present, elements of a conceptual model that might prove useful in analyzing social changes in contemporary French-Canadian society have been developed. This model will now be used in assessing, in global terms, the direction of change in the ideologies and the social structures of French Canada.

The French Revolution was a social revolution designed to overthrow the feudal social order. The major social changes brought about in a violent fashion as a result of the French Revolution were an end to the dynastic exercise of power and to the political, fiscal, and economic privileges formerly held by the feudal lords and landed aristocracy, the accession to political ascendency of the liberal bourgeoisie, the abolition of the prvileges of the estates, and changes in feudal ownership of land.

That no similiar situation existed in French Canada is quite obvious. The feudal system of land tenure never had serious content within New France. Bush country was no major attraction for whatever feudal nobility emigrated to New France. In fact, agricultural settlement was marginal to the social organization of New France and did not keep pace with the agricultural settlements of the British colony to the south.[7] What feudal trappings there were in New France were an urban phenomenon and revolved closely around the political control of the administrative structure of the colony. The main economic drive was the development and exploitation of the fur trade industry, carried out by a metropolitan bourgeoisie, supported by the military, and viewed with suspicion by the clergy. With the British conquest the traditional society collapsed. The military were recalled and what liberal bourgeoisie of any significance were left were supplanted quickly by their British counterpart from the south.[8]

The pattern of land ownership, formally feudal in the political form of its distribution and allocation, was not so in social fact. It was neither politically oppressive, socially resented, nor economically burdensome. Upon pressure to develop agricultural settlements in order to maintain ownership, the feudal landowners could manage to meet this requirement only by parceling out ownership as an incentive or inducement to settlers to carve out arable land in bush country. This process had one major effect: it avoided the development of a class of indentured agricultural workers. The colonist was never an indentured servant, although some of the *corvées* of the feudal agricultural system were implemented. Léon Gérin was therefore correct in stating that the French-Canadian rural society, which was left untouched by the conquest, consisted in a 'juxtaposition of [landholding] families which are very nearly all equal; nearly all engaged in farming; nearly all sufficient unto themselves.'[9]

With the collapse of the political ties with France, the exodus of the entrepreneurial bourgeoisie, the absence of feudal landownership as an oppressive social structure, the withdrawal of the military and political elites, all this some thirty years before the revolution in France, it should not be a subject of amazement that the French Revolution, its ideology, its break with the past, and its new set of legitimations of the present, did not receive a sympathetic ear within the ruling elite of French-Canadian society – the clergy, the intelligentsia, or the *habitants*. The differences between metropolitan French and French-Canadian social structures were so great as to render meaningless in French Canada the revolutionary upheavals in France.

Nationalism did not feed therefore on a rejection of the past, of tradition, or of feudal social structure, which did not exist, as it had in Continental Europe. Since Canadians were unattracted to French republicanism, because of the difference in social structure, the Crown, whether British or French, was not an object of resentment, and loyalty to the monarchy was not considered national treason. As a result, when the American Revolution or Rebellion, quite bourgeois in character and interest, occurred, the loyalty of the new British subjects of French descent, while crucial for the British Crown, could be easily pledged by the French-Canadian peasants and its clerical elite in exchange for political concessions assuring its cultural survival, namely, the right to stay French and Catholic. The tradition of political guarantees for cultural survival of the French Canadians as a community was thereby begun.

If French-Canadian national feelings were unaffected by the Continental context, the same is equally true of the British who moved into the newly acquired country. The British Canadians were not deprived of their military forces and their political elites. Rather than spurring a rejection of the British connection, the immigration of the United Empire Loyalists from the American colonies strengthened the emotional ties to the Crown and motherland. The effect of the American severance from Britain gave impetus to British-Canadian nationalism and its determination to forge a British North America. Furthermore, the political upheavals of Continental Europe had not had the same repercussions in England, where the accession of the liberal bourgeoisie to political dominance had been achieved without revolutionary upheavals.

The theory of the nation-state, of the right to statehood on the basis of national homogeneity, was a product of Continental Europe where despotic rule and feudalism were violently overthrown and where it served the political unification of feudal territories into nation-states. Neither French Canada nor English Canada, although for different reasons, was greatly affected by these ideologies. The granting of some political guarantees to French Canadians' survival as a culturally distinct community assured French-Canadian acquiescence to a common state. The absence of political repercussions to these doctrines in England, together with the multi-national character of the British Empire, also inclined the British-Canadians to consent to a multi-national state in Canada.

French-Canadian society in the nineteenth century was a rural society. It consisted in a loosely integrated collection of rural parishes geographically expanding. As a social system it required an equilibrium between land and people.[10] Since the pattern of landholding was one of diffuse ownership among small farmers with large families, the stability of the system could only be maintained by handing down the family farm to one inheriting son. The equation between land and people could thus be kept intact. But this also meant that the system required an ever-expanding geographical base in order to absorb the surplus population. As long as arable land remained plentiful there was no major problem. When it became scarce this social system became acutely vulnerable. It is within this context of geographically expanding parishes that a developing set of supraparochial institutions gave birth to an ethnic elite. Faced with a surplus population with no land to till, the traditional elite was in need of structural relief for its continued survival.[11]

Structural relief could only consist in industrialization, which is the one thing the traditional elite could not deliver since it was not and had not been primarily an entrepreneurial bourgeoisie and therefore lacked capital. The vulnerability of the traditional elite set the stage for an easy introduction of industrialization even if it meant dependence on foreign capitalists. The capitalists transformed the French Canadians into urban dwellers. To service the needs of the recently urbanized masses, the traditional power elite had to transform its institutions into large-scale bureaucracies, giving birth in the process to the new middle classes of French-Canadian society. Industrialization helped finance the development of urban bureaucracies, but the new middle class was formed within the context of traditional institutions headed by the traditional power elite, but undergoing fundamental changes to meet the demographic need of the urban masses.

The institutional segregation of the new middle class sets it off in one respect from the new middle class of traditional societies under colonial regimes. There, its emergence was the direct result and outgrowth of the colonial political and economic structure. The bureaucratic overlords were cultural aliens, of more or less recent arrival, and in direct political control of the bureaucratic structures. In French Canada, the new middle class was an outgrowth of traditional institutions, ethnically homogeneous in composition, in the process of urban transformation.

MODERNIZATION: ITS INITIAL CLAIM TO POWER

The new middle class equated its social role with progress and the growth of its institutions with modernization. Its cohesion was thus first achieved under the banner of modernization, not nationalism. This value of modernization was a product of the training and education of the new middle class. In the process of developing urban social bureaucracies, the need for functional specialization and training brought the new generation in contact with the various specialized social, human, biological, and economic sciences of industrialized societies. This new training was the basis of the internal status of that class within the developing hierarchies. This new competence had been achieved through cultural borrowing, and the new theories of organization welcomed within the developing bureaucracies were foreign to the traditional culture. Not only was this new knowledge the basis of status; it also became the yardstick by which traditional institutions were evaluated.

Marginal to traditional culture by training, the new middle class became politically restive by class interest. Because it settled mainly in bureaucracies that did not produce profits, it required outside financial resources, namely state funds, to expand its scope, develop its services, and perform its social role. Functionally indispensable in bringing about the institutional changes required in the urban setting, it became politically aroused and aggressive.

Its demands were directed toward the provincial government headed by the Union Nationale. By refusing to acquiesce quickly to its demands, the Union Nationale incurred its wrath and Duplessis, its leader, became its favorite scapegoat, and Premier Barrette, an ex-railroad employee of working-class origin with no formal training who represented a rural riding with strong rural traditions, could not become a symbol of the new social order. He was defeated, his incompetence being adequately celebrated in political cartooning by emphasizing his 'boîte à lunch.' In such a context, the slogan of the Union Nationale, 'vers les Sommets,' seemed ludicrous and no match for the structurally appropriate slogan of the Liberals: 'Y faut que ça change.' The Liberal party thus became the political expression of the new middle class, the champion of its interests and aspirations. It heralded a bureaucratic revolution under the banner of modernization and was spontaneously acclaimed internally and externally. Its election in 1960 publicly consecrated the political dominance of the new middle classes in French Canada.[12]

THE NEW MIDDLE CLASS: SHIFTING IDEOLOGIES AND THE SHAPING OF SOCIETY

The positive acceptance of modernization has been and still is the unifying ideology of the new middle class. The violent controversies manifest in the various segments of its intelligentsia do not center on the desirability of this assumption, but rather on conflicting views of the methods of accelerating its historical implementation.

Social change seldom begins with attacks on the legitimacy of a social structure. The new middle class in French Canada conformed to this expectation. Rather than the legitimacy of a party, an agency, a government, the first attempts consisted in trying to secure a bigger share of facilities, financial and administrative, to develop modern competent bureaucracies. Failing to secure these facilities, the new middle class identified a responsible agent – the Union Nationale and its leader. Their challenge was reformist, not revolutionary; the political structure was not attacked, but the incumbents of political offices were, as incompetent. Incompetence was defined in terms of ruling arbitrarily, of retarding progress, of allocating funds to cronies rather than to qualified people.

In the bureaucratic institutions of health, education, welfare, and public service, the challenge to priestly rule or political appointees was not an attack on religion or on the older people, but on incompetence. It no longer was sufficient to be a priest to run an agency or a university department, a nun to run a hospital board or the nursing department, or a public official with a long record of service to head a ministry. What was necessary was that one should be professionally qualified. If he were not, he must forfeit the right to bureaucratic power. That scientific or technical competence should be the overriding concern in the selection, hiring, and promotion of bureaucratic personnel marked the claim to supremacy of bureaucratic leadership over traditional leadership.

A second characteristic of the attack on traditional leadership was that competence and training were the only prerequisites to claim office. A university teacher competent in his discipline and in his role as a teacher need not be Catholic even in an officially Catholic institution. In this way the Weberian idea of bureaucracy was the yardstick by which to measure institutions. The allocation of institutional position should be rational and open to achievement rather than ascription.

Modernization, bureaucratic rationality, and personal qualification became the tools for the new middle class to assess the worth of not only the institutions but also the ideologies of the past. Ethnically homogenous, the new middle class was not initially ethnically conscious. In fact, nationalism was suspect during the first decade after World War II. Faced with the depression, the mainstream of French-Canadian nationalism withdrew its support from capitalism. It could not endorse socialism, however, because of its atheistic materialism and its cultural matrix, which was Anglo-Saxon and Protestant and therefore foreign to the traditions and philosophical world view of a Latin and Catholic people. It endorsed instead corporatism as the ideal sociopolitical structure of the state.[13] The new middle class, at least those members of it who were trained outside the ethnic universities, did not take corporatism seriously. It had no sympathy for its political elitism and was fully aware of its economic sterility.

Not only did the new middle class of the period reject the political philosophy of the nationalism of the thirties and early forties but it remained skeptical about its indictment of American culture. Rather than fearing the assimilative effect of American culture, it admired the technological and scientific basis of that culture and found in American society the model for modernization it sought to establish in French Canada. The attempts by nationalist groups in the thirties and forties to make the French Canadian an ethnically conscious consumer had failed and were looked upon by this postwar-trained middle class as an indication of naive ignorance about the economics of the market place.

What is somewhat more surprising is that in the early postwar period the new middle class did not deeply share but rather remained skeptical of the nationalist suspicions toward the government and its encroaching jurisdiction within the network of French-Canadian institutions. While the Massey Report, one of whose authors was Father Lévesque, founder of the Laval Faculté des Sciences Sociales, tended to legitimate centralization, and while it was castigated publicly and violently by the French-Canadian nationalist intelligentsia, it left the new middle class rather indifferent. Maurice Lamontagne's book on Canadian federalism[14] was an attempt to show how the modernization of French Canada could best be achieved within the context of a strong central government. It was strongly criticized by the same intelligentsia but was warmly received in academic and political circles, labor unions, and by the majority of the new middle class. Maurice Duplessis, in turning down federal aid to education, was not initially acclaimed by the new middle class for doing so but incurred its censure instead. Indeed, his action was applauded only by the Action Nationale and the nationalist wing of its intelligentsia. He made the decision politically and eventually his attitude toward federal aid to education became the cornerstone of the strategy of political parties in Quebec in their public platforms.

Finally, to illustrate the little inclination toward nationalism of the new middle class from 1945 to 1955, one may refer to the celebrated asbestos strike,[15] which rallied the sympathy of the new intelligentsia for the workers and directed its attack on the provincial government for interfering in collective bargaining and supporting management and for its callous disregard for the workers' health. The strike was viewed as a class conflict, not an ethnic conflict; the government was attacked not for ethnic treason but for political interference with the rights of the workers. The new–middle-class ideology in the immediate postwar period claimed change in the name of modernization and democracy. The values of the middle class were those of modern liberalism with emphasis on progress and social change articulated partly in class interests but not in terms of ethnic conflict.

If modernization was the initial claim to power of the new middle class, if at the beginning the middle class was rather hostile and suspicious of traditional nationalism, this is so obviously not the case in the sixties as to require some explanation for the change and shifts in the ideological positions of the middle class.

THE RESURGENCE OF NEO-NATIONALISM

In the mid-fifties neo-nationalism as a force dissenting from traditional nationalism made its appearance. The main exponents of neo-nationalism were French-Canadian historians, Michel Brunet being the main spokesman of the new wave. Brunet made a celebrated attack on three tenets of traditional nationalism that were described as myths impeding modern development that should be cast aside. These myths were called: *l'agriculturisme*, or the glorification of the rural life; *le messianisme*, or the concept that French Canadians had a spiritual mission in the North American context; and *l'anti-étatisme*, or the conservative suspicion of the propriety of state-initiated social and economic activity. This declaration for modernization under the aegis of nationalism and the attack on traditional nationalist tenets heralded the emergence of the social power of nationalism within the new middle class. Traditional nationalism was offensive not because it opposed modernism and industrialization, which it did not, but because it subordinated them to what was felt to be a more basic, more important value, namely, religion.[16] Brunet did not disagree with the tenets of the thirties; he shared their suspicions of the central government.[17] Brunet's pessimism was based on what he perceived to be an inevitable fact – the incapacity of total social development for French Canada because it lacked statehood. He viewed the federal government as a political structure ethnically appropriated by English Canadians and as a tool of English-Canadian national interests and aspirations. This he stated as a sad yet inescapable fact which French Canadians must recognize and accept and which worked necessarily in the direction of depriving French Canada of a necessary tool to achieve modern development. Co-operation necessarily meant being short-changed, and in such a set-up French Canada could only be perceived as a burden by the rest of Canada. French Canada, because of ethnic appropriation of the central state, was doomed to a condition of arrested development. The only solution lay in relying exclusively on the government of Quebec to transform its province into a national state and to use the full powers of its limited scope to achieve partial development.

For a decade the new middle class remained aloof from, if not hostile to, the tenets of nationalism since its emphasis subordinated modernization to traditional religious values. Nationalism became ideologically compatible when it became decisively modern, slaying as myths the traditional beliefs of agriculturism, messianism, and antistatism. It became, in the last decade, increasingly nationalist in its effort to overcome the structural constraints of its growth. The constraints to the growth of the new middle class are a function of the specialized character and the smaller scale and size of the bureaucracies it staffs. The specialized character restricts the channels of mobility and the smaller scale and size restrict the level of mobility. A direct outgrowth of urbanization rather than industrialization, fathered by a clerico-political elite rather than an entrepreneurial bourgeoisie, the channels of mobility of the new middle class were not located in the bureaucracies of private enterprise, secondary manufacturing, finance, and trade. Thus its channels of mobility were both restricted and specialized.

If the channels of mobility were restricted by the specialized nature of the bureaucratic tasks to be performed, the levels of mobility were equally restricted by the smaller scale of bureaucracies themselves. The French-Canadian bureaucratic pyramids have a narrow base – geographically, socially, and organizationally – because of their small scale. This means that upward mobility is more restricted, less diversified, and less extended.

Given these two constraints, one can view the new middle class as seeking and needing space for expansion, occupationally and organizationally. This, indeed, is the most important structural clue to understanding the restive or restless character of the new middle class in French Canada and the various competing ideologies, the political attitudes, and the ideological agitation so rampant within its ranks in the last five years. To overcome the restricted social mobility of its small bureaucratic pyramids, it has adopted a twofold strategy: (1) a bureaucratic transformation of traditional institutions, and (2) a reaffirmation of linguistic identification, so that by expanding linguistic space and ethnic jurisdiction it can also increase job outlets.

THE NEW MIDDLE CLASS, NATIONALISM, AND ETHNIC ACCOMMODATION

Even since 1760 the French and the English in Canada, for better or for worse, have had interlocking destinies and a shared fate. The pattern of ethnic interaction in the two centuries that have since elapsed can be roughly divided into three periods: (1) from conquest to Confederation, (2) from Confederation to 1950, and (3) from 1950 to present.

From conquest to confederation
The conquest, as it has been said, involved the takeover by the British of the political and economic institutions of New France. This was greatly facilitated by the massive exodus of the middle-class entrepreneurs and political administrators of New France. It was thus achieved swiftly, completely, and without conflict, for the French Canadians who remained were either farmers or priests. French Canada became a rural society with a clerical elite. Since French Canadians were concerned with ethnic and

religious survival and were living in quasi–self-sufficient rural parishes, their interaction with the English political rulers and the economic elite was mediated by a clerically led ethnic elite. The habitants in the rural parishes could and did live out their lives in a French environment, with no direct contact with the ruling aliens. The parochial institutions that did exist were staffed by co-nationals. Until 1867, the history of French Canada is a history of rural expansion and consolidation. Inter-ethnic contact was thus held to a minimum, mediated by an ethnic elite.

While the French Canadians were rural dwellers, the English were urban, and the social and economic and ethnic division of labor was also to a large extent geographical. Nor did the rural French Canadian meet the English farmer, who was geographically concentrated in the Eastern Townships, so that even rural settlements were neatly divided along ethnic lines. The rural French, for the better part of a century busily involved in reproduction and parochial settlement, were not to meet the English. Contact with the English came about with industrialization, but even then its impact was cushioned by social distance – since the English were status superiors – and by informal interaction, since the linguistic environment of work, while formally English, was and still is informally French for the working class.

From confederation to 1950: patterns of mutually satisfying institutional self-segregation
The second era in ethnic accommodation extends from Confederation to the postwar period. During this time two major sets of events affected the pattern of ethnic interaction. The first of these concerns the extension of Canadian sovereignty to the Pacific with the settling and development of the West. The second concerns the progressive industrialization of Quebec. Both of these affected the course of ethnic interaction between French and English in Canada: the first set of events affected the patterns of accommodation of the French minorities outside Quebec; the second set the stage for ethnic interaction within Quebec.

Minorities outside Quebec
It is doubtful whether Canadian nationalism existed in any meaningful way within English Canada before Confederation. While the French Canadians were concerned with ethnic and cultural survival, the English Canadians were concerned with political supremacy and political sovereignty. Political supremacy was threatened internally by the demography of ethnicity. A potential external threat to political sovereignty was

always present in the successfully secessionist neighbor to the south. Political sovereignty could only be upheld by depending on the military strength of Britain. Political supremacy could only be achieved by demographic growth and development of the political structures of the country.

In these conditions Canadian nationalism could not and did not exist. The birth of Canadian nationalism coincides with Confederation, the political structure that facilitated the geographical extension of sovereignty from the Atlantic to the Pacific. Nationalism is often closely related to geographic expansion and conquest. The conquest and settling of land co-ordinates group activity, channels energies, provides a common vision and dreams, nurtures and develops nationalist sentiments. In a process of circular reinforcement, nationalism in turn legitimates the spatial enterprise. Former Prime Minister Diefenbaker intuitively knew this when, in his attempt to revitalize Canadian nationalism, to stir the national soul, and to activate the national purposes, he proposed his vision of opening up the North. Not only was Diefenbaker's vision of the North good sociology, but it was also good history. For the birth of Canadian nationalism indeed coincided with the settling of the West. Initiated in the East, English-Canadian nationalism was realized in the West. Its dream enacted in the Prairies, Canadian nationalism has ever since found its most coherent and sharply defined expression in the Prairies.

Notwithstanding what might or might not have been the intentions of the founding fathers of Confederation, notwithstanding whether Confederation was or was not a pact between two races, in empirical fact the settling of the West set the stage for the pattern of ethnic conflicts in Canada. The national dilemma of the 1960s reflects the same basic strains in national consensus that arose in the 1870s. George Grant,[18] who laments the defeat of Canadian nationalism, none the less recognizes in Diefenbaker a true Canadian nationalist defeated by the concerted and co-ordinated efforts of the antinational ruling classes whose economic interests are tied to the continental economy and who, by the way, did not respond to Diefenbaker's vision of the North. Grant explains Diefenbaker's unpopularity in French Canada and the traditional ill fate of the Tory party with French-Canadian voters quite accurately.

A product of Prairie nationalism, Diefenbaker could not appeal to French Canadians because of his basically American conception of federalism. His emphasis on unhyphenated Canadianism, quite an acceptable doctrine as far as the rights of individuals were concerned, became a threat to the rights of French Canadians as a community. While

Grant's diagnosis is correct, his contention that Prairie nationalism is a deviation from traditional nationalism is much more open to question.

The West was settled by the action of the central government, which financed, directly or indirectly, the system of transportation and facilitated immigrant settlement in the western enterprise. When ethnic conflict arose on the school question, Ottawa upheld legislation that curbed the possibility of the existence of French Canadians as communities. That this occurred not only in the West but also in New Brunswick and later in Ontario would indicate that unhypenated Canadianism enjoyed a central rather than a marginal status in traditional Canadian nationalism. The 'nuisance value' of French Canadians, to quote P.E. Trudeau's expression, is still celebrated today, as the Dunton-Laurendeau Commission discovered, and this celebration increases as one moves farther away from Quebec, east as well as west. The consequence of the assimilationist impulse of traditional Canadian nationalism has been greater in Quebec than among the French minorities in other provinces. The latter, reduced to immigrant status as they moved out of the boundaries of Quebec, developed ethnic institutions as demographic density permitted, centered around the national parish. The greater impact, however, of these historical events took place in Quebec.

The French Canadian in Quebec

In Quebec the consequences of the assimilationist impulse was to restructure loyalty to and identification with land and institutions. Loyalties of individuals and groups tend to take root and must find expression in space and time. They therefore are affected by proximity and daily interaction. This is why emotional ties to farm, town, and neighborhood need little conceptual elaboration and remain constant in times of stress, national fervor, or national indifference. These kinds of ties, basic to patriotism, are constant, irrespective of the direction of nationalist sentiment and feeling associated with larger social structures. A German Jew can still remember fondly his city of birth and childhood despite the nightmare of National Socialism. Localized, these loyalties are not parochial and are very often more deeply embedded, more deeply internalized, than loyalties toward larger and more abstract structures, such as national governments. The French-Canadian loyalties in Quebec, as a consequence of the assimilationist impulse outside Quebec, became restricted in space and selective in institutions. The army, the central government, the federal bureaucracies, while legitimate sources of employment and appropriate institutional set-ups within which to eke out a living, or even a career, were thus, from their very beginning, not objects of emotional commitment and of devotion.

For the French minorities outside Quebec, the assimilationist pull from the civil and industrial society was counteracted by the norms of kinship and religion. The solution to the dilemma created by the contradictory pull of these opposing norms was and is perfect bilingualism. That way, full membership and participation in all of the institutional life of a community could be achieved. Thus could one be spared the sanctions of both imperfect citizenship and loss of ethnic membership. Without it, one's loyalties had to be two-fold and camouflaged. The French-Canadian could stay French in public as well as in private, in official as well as in unofficial life only in Quebec. His linguistic environment within the confines of his province encompassed his school, his place of work and worship, his hospital, his town hall, and the public streets, and his loyalties could be more sharply differentiated.

Quebec: industrialization and the pattern of self-segregated institutions

From Confederation to the postwar period the pattern of ethnic accommodation between French and English in Quebec developed within the context of rapid industrialization, especially after the turn of the century. Historically ethnic accommodation has been constructed successfully in Quebec on the basis of mutually desired self-segregated institutions.[19] In the fields of education, religion, welfare, leisure, and residence, institutional self-segregation has been total. The only two areas of societal living where inter-ethnic contact has been institutionalized are those of work and politics. The pattern of ethnic contact at work was established with the introduction of industrialization. Anglo-Saxon industry moved into a society faced with an acute population surplus, a distinctive political and religious elite, and a developing set of institutions anchored in the rural parish. This society, politically stable, economically conservative, and technically unskilled, provided ideal conditions for investing Anglo-Saxon capitalists. They could invest their capital, open industries, and be supplied with an abundant source of unskilled labor seeking employment. The managerial and technical levels were filled, with no protest, by the incoming group, who also brought along their own set of institutions servicing their own nationals. This social setting provided an easy introduction to industry. The French-Canadian elite was ideologically co-operative, protective only about its continued control over its demographic substructures. This fitted in quite well with the aims of the incoming groups who could develop their economic pursuits with a minimum involvement in the local ethnic society. Industry was relieving the economic burden of the demographic surplus of French-Canadian rural society. The local elite's leadership was not being challenged. This led to a mutually satisfying pattern of self-segregated institutions. The English could live in Quebec as autonomous and separate communities, with their own churches, hospitals, schools, and ethnic neighborhoods. Very often, especially in the provincial cities, they could and did incorporate as separate towns, where the limits of the town often coincided with the limits of class and ethnicity. The pattern of self-segregation conditioned the social setting of inter-ethnic contact, which was held to a minimum. The lower classes, the working class, met the English in the formal structure of the job, while the middle classes met the English much less frequently, and when they did it was almost always on ritual occasions and in a ritualized manner. This pattern of mutually self-satisfying, self-segregated institutions worked with no dissent up to and including World War II. This historical pattern is now being challenged by the recently emerged French-Canadian new middle class. The traditional ethnic division of labor is now under attack and the present climate of uncertainty has arisen as a result.

From 1950 to the present: ethnic tensions and social mobility
With the postwar emergence of the new middle class, a new era in ethnic interaction has set in, and a search for a new deal in ethnic accommodation is being sought by the French-Canadian new middle class under the impetus of reformist nationalism. As noted above, neo-nationalism in traditional societies is linked with social change in the direction of modernization. Reformist in outlook, the new middle class seeks to extend its scope, size, and mobility. It becomes revolutionary when it successfully enrols the support of the peasants and working classes in taking over control of the state by successfully indicting colonialist rule. This situation is not paralleled in French Canada. Despite the inroads of separatism, separatist ideology has not succeeded in enlisting the support of the working classes or the rural people, and the colonialist indictment has been rejected. Historically, the exploitative view of the English presence is inaccurate and does not reflect the way it was initiated. Rather than rally to separatist unrest, the lower classes joined the Créditiste ranks in proclaiming the possibility of the middle-class dream for all.

The new middle class in French Canada, like its counterparts in traditional societies, however, has a stake in modernization. Having achieved political dominance, the provincial state to a large extent is seeking to meet its demands. In seeking to overcome the constraints to its growth and continued mobility, it is seeking a new social convention in ethnic accommodation. The old pattern of ethnic accommodation and its institutional arrangements met the needs of incipient industrialization. At that time, the ethnic division of labor reflected the complementary needs of both ethnic groups, and ethnic competition did not take the form of occupational competition.

The new middle class, however, by training, outlook, and culture increasingly similar to its ethnically alien counterpart, is also increasingly in competition with it. In its search to expand its channels of mobility and widen its areas of development it is examining the assumptions of institutional self-segregation. Now that it is politically in control, its views may be acted upon. Thus the traditional patterns of financing education, welfare, and health – wherein the pattern of institutional segregation has often meant better services, better facilities, and better salaries for the English involved in these areas within the confines of the province – are being questioned. The differentials in resources and income are not new, but the fact that these differentials are viewed as special privileges is recent and new. That in its search for resources to expand its bases the new middle class will seek to change traditional institutional arrangements in these areas is a foregone conclusion. That such changes are upsetting to the English Quebecers is already apparent. Bred by the church, having achieved control of the provincial state, the French-Canadian new middle class is now anxious to move from social to industrial bureaucracy. Bureaucratic state capitalism as well as linguistic expansion in the management of private industry are only assorted tools in its ongoing attempt to increase its social and occupational space.

NOTES

Originally published in R.H. Leach, ed., *Contemporary Canada* (Durham, NC, 1967)

1 John E.E.D. Acton, *Essays on Freedom and Power* (London, 1956), 141ff.
2 Alexis de Tocqueville, *The Old Regime and the Revolution*, trans. Stuart Gilbert (Garden City, NY, 1955)
3 This model is to be found in explicit form in Neil Smelser, *A Theory of Collective Behavior* (New York, 1962), chap. iii.
4 Hans H. Gerth and C. Wright Mills, *Character and Social Structure: The Psychology of Social Institutions* (New York, 1964), 192ff.

5 This whole development is to a great extent dependent on Smelser's model on collective behavior.
6 These themes are to be found abundantly in the writings of C. Wright Mills, notable in his *Causes of World War III* (New York, 1958).
7 See Léon Gérin, *Aux sources de notre histoire* (Montreal, 1946), and also Hubert Guindon, 'The Social Evolution of Quebec Reconsidered,' *Canadian Journal of Economics and Political Science*, xxvi (November 1960), 533–51 [this volume, 3–26]
8 Michel Brunet, *Canadians and Canadiens* (Montreal, 1954)
9 Léon Gérin, *Le Type économique et social des Canadiens* (Montreal, 1938), as quoted in Everett C. Hughes, *French Canada in Transition* (Chicago, 1963), 4
10 See Horace Miner, *St. Denis: A French-Canadian Parish* (Chicago, 1939), chap. xi.
11 Guindon, 'The Social Evolution of Quebec Reconsidered,' 545–6 [this volume, 9–10, 18]
12 Hubert Guindon, 'Social Unrest, Social Class, and Quebec's Bureaucratic Revolution,' *Queen's Quarterly*, LXXI (Summer 1964), 155 [this volume, 30–1]
13 Consult the works of Esdras Minville and especially those of François Albert Angers during the thirties and forties. See also the review *Action Nationale* during this period.
14 *Le Fédéralisme Canadien* (Quebec, 1954)
15 P.E. Trudeau, *La grève de l'amiante* (Montreal, 1956)
16 This is the striking difference between nationalist intellectuals like Minville, on the one hand, and Michel Brunet, on the other.
17 *Canadians and Canadiens*
18 *Lament for a Nation* (Princeton, 1965)
19 Guindon, 'Social Unrest, Social Class,' 157 [this volume, 33]

CAMROSE LUTHERAN COLLEGE
LIBRARY

The modernization of Quebec and the legitimacy of the Canadian state

The process of modernization is more often than not politically unsettling. For all practical purposes, formal political empires have been universally dissolved. Their legitimations were no longer convincing. Bringing civilization to the uncivilized, Christianity to the heathen, while historically powerful rationales in the past, have long since become hollow justifications not only for the intelligentsia but for churchmen in secularized states.

States which, by political disenfranchisement, exclude social and cultural majorities from the proceeds of modernization are increasingly under pressure. Rhodesia is in the process of accepting the inevitable and hoping for the best. South Africa's conception of independent statehood for its black population is so unconvincing that it is universally defined as a sham.

While Western industrialized states seem to have clear vision abroad, they tend to suffer from blurred vision at home. The rise of Scottish nationalism, fed by the promise of black gold off the shores of Scotland, has led the British Parliament recently to institute some form of home rule for Scotland in an attempt to ward off graver consequences. The tragic armed struggle in Northern Ireland with its weekly toll in human lives is dutifully and dramatically reported in the press and universally deplored but has led to very little political analysis of what brought this tragic situation about.

The access to power of the Parti Québécois was a world event probably because it was the first time that the political integrity of a Western liberal democratic industrialized state was being challenged internally through the democratic process.

Disbelief is the first reaction of the media of the Western world. How could it happen? Was it for real? The integrity of the Western liberal democratic industrialized states is so much taken for granted. Sacred rather than secular attitudes toward the state are so prevalent that social scientists have failed to study the state and its behaviour with the clinical detachment they generally so greatly cherish. This does affect the questions they ask and their construction of reality.

It is customary to regard political discontent within the Western nation-states as existing merely in pockets of unrest which, when peaceful, have been depicted as rather quaint, anachronistic resistances to modernization. This may, in some cases, be fair. But in the Quebec instance, and possibly many others, more insight is to be gained from viewing the political challenge to the integrity of the state as the consequence of modernization, of the aggressive espousal rather than the refusal of its values and rewards.

Is there any validity in the political challenge to the legitimacy of the Canadian state? If so, what is it? Until these questions are faced and answered, there is little hope for policies that could generate a new consensus. The remainder of this essay will address itself to these questions.

THE QUIET REVOLUTION AND THE MODERNIZATION OF QUEBEC SOCIETY

The ushering in of a new social order
The urban shift of Quebec's population, the need to develop large-scale institutions in health, welfare, and education, and the emerging new middle class of professionals and social scientists set the stage, during the fifties, for a growing opposition to the regime of Premier Duplessis. For the first time, during the prolonged strike of asbestos workers of 1949,[1] a vocal part of Quebec's intelligentsia and two dissident bishops openly sided with the workers against the provincial government. The strike was lost, but a formal, public split between the intelligentsia and the state, between some members of the Church and the State had taken place. This split was to widen and deepen. The opposition's mouthpiece was *Cité Libre*, a review founded by Pierre E. Trudeau and Gérard Pelletier. It was committed to modernization of Quebec society and strongly attacked the 'clerico-nationalist' ideology, vehicled by the Jesuit Relations, legitimating the relations between Church and State that underlay the Church's leadership and control of education, health, and welfare. The new

professionals were chafing under this traditional leadership. La Jeunesse Etudiante Catholique was challenging the secular role of the Church and was restless under the paternalistic authoritarianism of the hierarchy. By 1959, after the celebrated attack by Fathers Dion and O'Neill[2] on the political morality of the Union Nationale, and after the Association des Professeurs de l'Université de Montréal's successful campaign against the granting of a university charter to the Jesuits,[3] the end of an era was in sight.

The Quiet Revolution was launched by Premier Paul Sauvé with his celebrated *désormais* (from now on). Statutory grants to universities would be implemented. A royal commission to study the feasibility of free hospitalization was to be created, and the pay scale of civil servants was to be revised.[4] In other words, the aspirations of the new middle class and the growth and development of the institutions they staffed were to become the political priorities of the provincial state.[5]

Reform was the order of the day. Education, financed by the state, was to expand rapidly, welfare was to be professionalized, health services were to be secularized, the Church was to retreat from its secular roles into matters of private rather than public concern.

This coming out of the 'Dark Ages,' as the ancient dispensation used to be labelled by many, was widely acclaimed. Quebec had entered the modern era.

Modernization, elite-building, and the eclipse of community
Under the aegis of a 'catching up'[6] ideology Quebec was putting its house in order, in a new order more in line with the structural features of developed industrial societies.

This new order was a bureaucratic one. It involved a high degree of state-initiated political integration and bureaucratic centralization. If the modernized health, education, and welfare services were to be made universally accessible, if these services were to be upgraded to modern norms, the only level of government that could implement such reforms – given the constitutional division of labour in the Canadian state structure – was the provincial state. Local government had neither the resources nor the territorial base to ensure the universality of the reforms.[7] In the previous dispensation, these services were territorially based, locally financed, and organizationally overseen by local community elites. State modernization spelled the end of this territorial local integration of social life and its institutional underpinnings.

Elite-building became a state function, and the role of elites, to a large degree, was to shape, formulate, implement, and enforce state policy. In the process, loyalties and commitment were no longer to be expressed in a territorial manner. 'The countervailing power to the State would become the professional association and the professional corporation for the elites, and the trade-unions for the organized workers. Therein lies the structural basis for the eclipse of community in modern society. For the elites, its eclipse was not distressing since its life-style does not require it; for the poor and the unorganized, impoverished community structures would become a rather inefficient coping mechanism.'[8]

The political subordination of institutional elites
With increased state funding, bureaucratic imperatives required the formalization of tasks and rewards. Bureaucratic planning required budget forecasting of total expenditures – of capital expenditures as well as labour costs. In the process, the state had to set the parameters for collective bargaining as well as the rate of institutional growth. This severely restricted the traditional management prerogatives of the authorities of such institutions as local school boards, hospital administrations, etc. This also set the stage for the development of the common-front strategy of the labour unions and the eventual confrontation politics between the state and labour of the 1970s. This politically centralized bureaucratic model of social modernization had an impact on the traditional pattern – typical of the previous political dispensation – of ethnically self-segregated institutions.[9] This new political dependency of institutional managers on the state had the added effect, in the case of the Anglophone institutional managerial elite, of transforming them into a minority dependent on majority decisions, or, what is more to the point, on the majority's definition of the rules of the game. This had been a secular experience for French-Canadian institutional leaders elsewhere in Canada[10] but it was a new experience for Anglophones in Quebec.

The asymmetrical character of Quebec's new middle class and its two-fold consequences
One of the rather strange features of Quebec's Francophone new middle class is its overwhelming concentration in the public and parapublic sectors.[11] Its conspicuous absence in the large corporate private sector can quite easily be accounted for. At first, in the early sixties, the public and parapublic sector was able to absorb all of its members, since this was the period of intensive institution-building. The public service, the reformed and expanded educational system, the municipal civil service, and the

health institutions were in need not only of social scientists and professionals but also of MBAS and engineers. State-initiated crown corporations were another major outlet.[12] In the second place, to integrate in the public and parapublic sector did not require *acquisition* of the bilingual fluency that a successful integration in the corporate private sector would require. Given the fact that the reward structure in the state-dependent system was competitive at most levels, it naturally follows that the majority of the Francophone new middle class would follow the path of least resistance.

Language became a political issue when the cadres of public institutional development were to a large extent filled. It is within this structural context that sociological sense can be made of the language issue within Quebec. It can explain both the language movement within the Francophone sector and the mobilization of the Anglophone sector and its dependent immigrant component.

Another consequence of the asymmetrical nature of the social location of the new middle classes in the socio-economic structure accounts for the 'radical' nature of labour conflict in Quebec.[13] That the trade unions became the only countervailing power to the state as employer has already been explained in terms of the dissolution of territorial loyalty and commitment of the new middle classes. Another consequence was the increased unionization of professional cadres in the state-dependent bureaucratic apparatus. Within this structural context, strikes became total societal events, global events, shaking the polity to its very roots.

There is nothing cultural in this. Latin temperament has nothing to do with it. It can all be explained in terms of the nature of Quebec's political economy. Quebec is the only province in Canada that has a double economy, in labour-force terms, neatly segregated along language lines. The credibility of the Canadian federal state will ultimately stand or fall on this issue. Until now, it has not even perceived it.

THE MODERNIZATION OF QUEBEC AND THE FEDERAL STATE

We have defined, briefly, some of the major political problems generated within Quebec society by the state-initiated social modernization of its institutions. This provides a framework within which to analyse the policies – or lack of them – of the federal state in response to these structural changes. We will turn our attention to the Official Languages Policy on the one hand and the nature of economic development in Quebec on the other.

The official languages policy

A massive thrust in the wrong direction
The preliminary report of the Royal Commission on Bilingualism and Biculturalism (RCBB)[14] began by proclaiming a state of crisis in Canada.[15] Deep cleavages were said to exist between the Francophone and Anglophone components of the country. This alarmist manifesto concluded with the urgency of defining a federal language policy for the Canadian state, its state agencies, and Crown corporations, that could become the basis for a new consensus for the two 'societies' sharing a common state.

Some ten years later, in the summer of 1976, the defeat of the federal state's policy was publicly consummated with the Canadian Air-Traffic Controllers' (CATCA) and the Canadian Air Line Pilots' (CALPA) associations' successful resistance to the implementation of the Official Languages Policy.[16] For the first time (to my knowledge) in Canadian history a special interest group was able to dictate to the Crown a 'free vote' in Parliament on matters that were not related to issues of personal conscience.[17] That this clause was not perceived as a direct threat to the very essence of British parliamentary democracy is quite revealing. It is even more so when one realizes that this policy had been endorsed by all political parties. Obstacles to democracy do not always come from Quebec.

Such a spectacular 'crash' of federal state policy needs to be accounted for. CATCA and CALPA could not have succeeded were it not for the mobilized emotional support of English-speaking Canadians. The Prime Minister, in his usual sombre manner, proclaimed that this was a threat to national unity.[18] More mundanely, other ministers of the Crown stated that they had failed to do a good 'selling job' of the Official Languages Policy to English-speaking Canadians.[19] Now is perhaps the time to address ourselves to the content of the policy itself, and to question whether that may have something to do with the problems the policy has generated for the state. Maybe it was doomed to fail.

A critique of the Official Languages Policy might profitably start with a recall of the political and social context within which the Royal Commission on Bilingualism and Biculturalism (RCBB) was instituted. It was established by Prime Minister Pearson after a series of editorials by André Laurendeau in *Le Devoir*.[20] His lead editorial quoted from a memorandum written by a French-Canadian federal civil servant for the attention of his

French-Canadian subordinates. This memorandum was leaked to the press and in part read as follows: 'Since everyone in the Department is bilingual, all reports must be written in English.'[21] In this civil servant's mind, this was not a political act, but a suggestion to increase internal administrative efficiency. In the larger political context, such a memo meant, if not 'speak white,' at least 'write white.' In the broader political scene it underlined two things: the unilingualism of the public service, the fact that Anglophones could enter the civil service and be unilingual, while French Canadians could only enter government service if they were fluently bilingual. Proceeding from this barrier to entry, it followed that French Canadians were highly underrepresented in the civil service, increasingly so as one moved up the bureaucratic hierarchies of the public service and Crown corporations.[22] The alienating effect of these features for the French-speaking population of Canada toward the federal state was underlined. One of the RCBB's major objectives was to resolve this contradiction. It therefore sought to define a policy that would increase the use of French in the federal civil service and increase the proportion of French Canadians within its ranks at all levels of its bureaucratic hierarchy.[23]

Another major objective of the RCBB was in response to a *leit-motiv* of French-Canadian nationalism of the fifties. This *leit-motiv* concerned the treatment of minorities. Quebec was seen as a model of majority-minority relations – a model that contrasted sharply with the way French Canadians were treated in every other province in Canada. The provinces, from the time of the Manitoba schools question and Ontario's 'Rule XVII,' had severely curtailed the legal status of French within their public-school system. In the previous dispensation, when most institutions were territorially integrated within communities, locally financed, and locally administered, the English-speaking population of Quebec did have local autonomy and full legal status within the public-school system of the state. As a consequence, Quebec was seen as the model for French-English relations, and the RCBB set out to exhort provincial legislatures to effect changes that would bring the status of French Canadians outside Quebec more in line with the status of Anglophones in Quebec, especially as regards the legal status of French in provincial public-school systems.

These two concerns – increasing the participation and the upward mobility of French Canadians within the federal state's bureaucracies, and increasing the institutional support of French Canadians outside Quebec – became the major objectives of the commission's bilingual policy.

Given these objectives, the royal commission could not seriously consider a territorially based language policy.[24] And without such a policy, language was doomed to become a case of political irritation in English Canada, and of political irrelevance in a modernizing French Quebec. Unfortunately, social scientists should not underestimate the state's capacity to commit itself to both.

Noble illusions and political disaster
The commissioners appointed to the Royal Commission on Bilingualism and Biculturalism were all fundamentally bilingual. While this may have ensured its basic commitment to bilingualism, and facilitated the efficiency of internal communication for its members, it certainly constituted a 'rare event,' untypical of what happens nationally at the level of professional associations, voluntary associations, corporations, and even federal-provincial summit conferences.

A sense of *noblesse oblige* can easily permeate a body of distinguished bilingual citizens gathering together to forge a national language policy after a proclaimed crisis in national unity. Having personally achieved the 'noble' thing, such distinguished gentlemen are quite as aptly liable to forget that *noblesse oblige la noblesse*, not the ordinary common mortal. One can only speculate as to what sort of policy might have been hammered out had the commissioners been people like Judge Thorson[25] of B.C., Mayor Jones[26] of Moncton, and Raymond Lémieux[27] of the Ligue pour l'Intégration Scolaire of St Léonard. The outcome would certainly have been quite different, definitely less noble, certainly less illusory.

While factually incorrect in terms of its report, as a psychological fact it is quite correct to state that the commission generated the impression in the public view that a good Canadian ought to be bilingual. This impression was further strengthened by the commission's recommendations seeking to facilitate bilingualism for federal civil servants. This cast the unilingual Canadian in a defensive moral posture he duly and rightfully resented.

No matter how lofty its ideals, the legacy of the Official Languages Policy was politically disastrous.

1. It did not appreciably increase the Francophone share of the federal state's bureaucracies[28] (public service and Crown corporations), and yet it did give rise to the shibboleth of French power that has become the battle cry of social groups that feel threatened by its implementation.

2. It is not successful in arresting the accelerated assimilation of French

Canadians outside Quebec, nor will it increase the viability of French communities outside the Sault Ste Marie–Moncton perimeter.

3. It hinders rather than facilitates the changes needed as a consequence of the social modernization of the Québécois.

4. It contributes to a climate of ambiguity for immigrants in Quebec and uncertainty for the large private corporate sector in Quebec.

A short list but a major indictment that needs some elaboration.

THE LANGUAGE POLICY AND THE PROMOTION OF FRENCH CANADIANS IN THE CIVIL SERVICE AND CROWN CORPORATIONS

While the promotion of French Canadians to higher executive positions was one of the major aims of the royal commission, its policies, after a decade, failed to bring about any substantial changes. The number of Francophones in such posts increased from 13 per cent in 1966 to 14.4 per cent in 1971.[29] Furthermore, within that increase, it is known that Québécois are highly underrepresented. At that rate, it would take fifty years for the number of French Canadians in executive positions to match the statistical proportion of French-speaking Canadians in the total population.[30] Furthermore, since most of that increase is recruited from French Canadians outside Quebec who are, therefore, already bilingual, its political irrelevance for Quebec becomes even clearer.

The failure of the immersion programs to increase the French competence of Anglophone civil servants was admitted by the past Commissioner of Official Languages in one of his annual reports.[31]

In short, the number of French Canadians in executive positions is not increasing significantly and the English-speaking civil servants are not becoming significantly more bilingual. Instead of questioning the validity and the nature of the whole language policy, Keith Spicer insisted on remaining within a dream world and recommended that the resources be directed toward teaching French to school children. Myths die hard, especially when they are noble ones.[32]

Given the negligible increase in the Francophone representation at the various levels of the federal bureaucracy and its Crown corporations, one can only wonder what could have given rise to the shibboleth of French power that underlies the anti-French backlash which the Official Languages Policy generated across English-speaking Canada – the backlash that peaked with the CATCA and CALPA strikes.

The backlash, in my opinion, is traceable to one of the basic principles emanating from the RCBB and incorporated in the Official Languages Act. That principle, which can be labelled the 10 per cent principle, specifies that when a French or English minority is sufficiently great (roughly 10 per cent), government services, in such cases, should be made available in that minority's language, whether English or French.[33] When implemented, this principle has systematically brought about ethnic tensions. Let us briefly refer to a few examples.

The first incident refers to decisions of the Canadian Radio and Television Corporation (CRTC). The decision to change into a French radio station the CBC's Toronto radio station, which happened to be a popular one with a loyal audience, a rare thing for the CBC, created intense dissatisfaction and widespread local opposition.

Metropolitan Toronto, an area comprising nearly three million people, has fewer than 100,000 French Canadians, who, moreover, are nearly all perfectly bilingual. In such circumstances, it is clear that there is no market for a French radio station in the private sector. That the state should force an English station to become French, in such circumstances, can only give credibility at the local level, to the shibboleth of French power. The French are so 'powerful' that they can take away a popular English station and make it a French one where no one in the metropolitan area ever met a French Canadian, for the simple reason that if he met one, he would have been unaware of it since the French Canadian spoke English well enough to pass. The CRTC met with similar dissatisfaction when it moved to implement the policy in British Columbia as regards its institutional services.

Under the same principle, the CRTC moved to grant an English radio and cable-TV station in the heart of the Saguenay–Lac St Jean area. The local population saw the situation in the same manner. While English power is not nearly so new a slogan and much more of a social and economic fact, it was perceived as an illustration of that power and as an attempt by the state to further the assimilation of the Québécois.

In all these cases, state policy has the real effect of undermining the national consensus it wants to build.

Finally, when the Commissioner of Official Languages, again under the same principle, decided to proclaim all of Quebec a bilingual district,[34] the proposal generated such widespread spontaneous opposition that it was quietly shelved.

It would seem that the federal state's language policy brings out the worst in the people of Canada. It clearly makes no sense at the level of social reality as perceived by local communities. Conceived at the level of lofty ideals, its local implementation at the community level smacks of the bureaucratic arrogance of the state against which the local population feels powerless. Should one therefore be surprised that the local communities complain bitterly that French is being 'shoved down their throats' and that they consequently strongly believe that 'French power' is solidly entrenched at the cortex of the federal state.

Local resentment would be a reasonable price to pay were the state's objective to be realized. Should the resentment be temporary and the long-term objectives ensuring national unity be achieved, historians would certainly describe such persistence as an example of statesmanship. Unfortunately, it is increasingly evident that its main objective – creating a bilingual and bicultural Canada, A mari usque ad mare, by ensuring the viability of French communities outside Quebec – is an illusion. In such a case, persistence obviously becomes political irresponsibility.

THE VIABILITY OF FRENCH COMMUNITIES OUTSIDE QUEBEC

The grievances of Québécois nationalism in the fifties rested, in part, on the contrast between the treatment of French minorities outside Quebec and the status of the English minority in Quebec. In response, the RCBB first documented this unequal treatment, and then set out as its objectives both to redress these historical inequalities and to ensure that Canada be a bilingual country in its geographical totality. Given this aim, it could not and did not conceive a territorially based bilingual policy for the country. It therefore discarded, with strikingly unconvincing reasons,[35] previous consideration of any territorially based language policy. It opted instead to try through exhortation to the appropriate jurisdictions (mainly the provincial governments) to initiate what is called 'institutional bilingualism' whose main principle has already been outlined. The story and social consequences of the federal government's own attempts to follow through its institutional policy have just been described.

If it can now be shown that 'institutional bilingualism' from sea to sea cannot possibly ensure the viability of French communities outside Quebec, the whole thrust of the Official Languages Policy becomes highly questionable.

Institutional bilingualism: administrative idealism and the sociology of language
Even with ten years of hindsight, it is startling to remember that the RCBB

managed to develop a whole series of urgent language policies without any studies on the sociology of language. Simply defined, the sociology of language involves a study of language interaction in different kinds of social setting, at the community level, at the level of public space, at the level of voluntary organizations, at the level of institutions, etc. It raises such questions as: Who becomes bilingual, when, and why? How do bilinguals remain bilingual? When does language become an issue of community conflict? How do language conflicts get solved in minority/ majority contexts? When and why do language conflicts become larger societal events and give rise to language movements and counter-movements? When and how do language frontiers shift? What are the consequences of such shifts on local institutions?

Since the RCBB managed to avoid any and all such questions in its deliberations and commissioned research, and since it did make specific recommendations, one must therefore raise the issue of what its assumptions about the sociology of language were. It is this set of assumptions that I have labelled 'administrative idealism.'

Bureaucracies are notoriously prescriptive and normative. According to Weber – and we ignore him at our peril – one major effect of modern bureaucratic rationality is that the scope for an official (whether petty or high) to exercise his personal discretion in the application of a body of codified rules is minimized and that thus the pitfalls of particularism and ascription in the life and practice of institutional behaviour are avoided.

While the extent to which bureaucracies conform to this ideal type is still a matter for empirical investigation, the belief in the ability of bureaucratic institutions to achieve goals and translate them into social practice is itself very seldom questioned. This faith in bureaucratic efficacy is obviously reinforced by the fact that the overwhelming majority of middle-class professionals enact their careers in the bureaucratic settings of the state and large corporations. As such they witness daily the efficacy of bureaucracy, its capacity to mobilize human and financial resources, to overcome obstacles, and to make alliances and linkages to sister bureaucracies in all institutional fields. The feelings of expendability, powerlessness, and alienation they may personally experience within them, far from shaking this overwhelming belief, reinforces it. Only in times of crisis, when bureaucracies crumble, can one glimpse the limits of their power. Yet, even then, what is perceived is not so much the fall of a bureaucracy, but the apprehension that the 'world' is falling apart.

In fact, the 'world,' in the bureaucratic view, is an 'unknown.' It becomes something 'known' and therefore amenable to rational action only when it intersects with the world of the bureaucracy, through the instruments that the bureaucracy develops to sample it.

The perfect instrument with which to 'puncture' the unknown world and make it amenable for bureaucratic ministration is 'survey research.' A rather blunt instrument, it can force a respondent to define the world in its terms not his. Inept at measuring the nuances of meaning and life, it nevertheless efficiently supplies the gross data for bureaucratic planning. Life and society are more subtle, thank God, than this. And one field where the yields of survey research are negligible is the sociology of language.

It is clear that survey research was the RCBB's major means of apprehending social reality. Its 'administrative idealism' as regards its language policy is evidenced by its belief in 'institutional bilingualism.' Committed as it was to reinforcing the bilingual character of Canada, the first thrust of its policy was toward increasing Francophone presence at all levels of the state bureaucracies and agenices. In this it failed, as we have already seen. Acutely aware of the historical institutional depriva- tion of French Canadians outside Quebec, it assumed that by increasing the institutional supports for Francophone life outside Quebec, it would not only right a historical wrong but ensure the 'bilingual' character of the country. Is this assumption warranted? This paper argues that it isn't.

French communities have indeed managed to survive remarkably well until the recent past. Not surprisingly, the very processes that made this survival possible are becoming increasingly visible now that they are in a state of collapse. What were these processes and why are they collapsing?

The conditions that enabled the survival, indeed the growth, of French communities outside Quebec preceded the massive urbanization and industrialization that has restructured the political economy of Canada.[36] They could and did develop in a rural world of small-scale family farms, which sometimes bordered on self-sufficient economies. The Church was the pivotal institution of social life around which small voluntary associations as well as elementary schools could be developed. The bilinguals in such a setting were those who dealt with the 'outside' world. Those who lived most of their lives within the community lived it in French. These were still the days of the high birth rate, and Quebec had a surplus population that needed outlets.

The industrial setting under which very similar conditions could obtain is to be found at the level of the primary sector of the economy. Labour-intensive industries involved in the extraction process, whether it be mining, lumberjacking, or fishing, provided a similar basis for

Number of persons of French mother tongue vs number of
French origin, in the four western provinces, by age groups,
1961 Census

Age group	Ethnic French	M.T. French	Apparent loss (%)
45–54	25,639	19,125	25
35–44	35,227	24,533	30
25–34	40,767	26,617	35
15–24	45,159	24,579	46
5–14	68,993	27,656	60
0– 4	43,060	14,412	67

SOURCE: Richard J. Joy, *Languages in Conflict* (Toronto, 1972), 39

community survival. This Quebec demographic overflow gave rise to
what Joy has called the Sault Ste Marie–Moncton belt.[37]

The days of marginal or self-subsistence farming, the days of labour-
intensive extractive industries are over. As their relative importance in the
political economy shrinks, so does the economic base of the communities
they supported. The increasing productivity in farming has meant an
increased need for capital, not farm hands. Technological improvements
in extractive industries also diminish the need for labour. In other words,
economic development dooms these communities to stagnation. What
made them viable, paradoxically enough, was economic underdevelopment. While one could live out one's whole life in French in St Isidore de
Prescott, as many did, no one can live out his whole life in French in
Cornwall.

The consequences of the inevitable urbanization of the younger
generation of French Canadians from French communities outside Quebec were already clearly visible at the time of the RCBB's deliberations.
They have been well outlined by Richard Joy in his book, *Languages in
Conflict*. He demonstrated that outside the Sault Ste Marie–Moncton line,
assimilation was the order of the day. Such data were readily available in
the census.

These data served to confirm conclusions already eloquently spelled
out by Joy himself:

With the exception of a few small pockets, such as that around St. Boniface, where
the French-Canadian population has been large enough to permit a continuation
of French-language instruction in the schools and, even more important, to

minimize social intermingling and the incidence of linguistically mixed marriages, the younger generation outside the Soo-Moncton limits has been largely lost to the French language. Increasing urbanization and the greater mobility of adolescents may well destroy even the present few pockets of resistance within another generation.

There are, of course, persons of both language groups who claim, in all sincerity, that the provision of French-language schools and television from coast to coast would permit survival of the present French-speaking minorities. This seems to disregard the social and economic factors leading to assimilation ...

If the children are not educated in French, then the minorities will dwindle away through assimilation; if French schools are provided, then the probability exists that their graduates will migrate to Quebec when the time comes to leave home and seek employment. In either case, the end result is the same: no younger generation will remain to replace the ageing group who now speak French outside the Soo–Moncton limits.[38]

This illustrates in a nutshell what is meant by the deeply rooted administrative idealism of the RCBB.

Within the urban context, French Canadians outside Quebec had to deal with an English world: the world of the market, the world of state institutions from the courts to city council, the world of higher education, as well as the world of public space. This required fluency in English. The only acknowledgment the RCBB made to the sociology of language was a casual reference to the fact that they realized that people became bilingual because of necessity.[39] This said, they dropped the topic, to pursue their normative bureaucratic analysis.

Bilingualism: a note on the sociology of language
Bilingualism for an individual is a way out of a dilemma. It is a way of coping successfully with counter pressures: pressures to learn a language and pressures to retain a language. These pressures are best thought of as 'frontiers,' rather than boundaries, because in a real sense they do represent different worlds. They are, naturally, group pressures, group frontiers which delimit intergroup relations. In this perspective, bilingualism is a social passport around language frontiers. Perfect bilingualism is the smoothest way to handle the dilemma of counter pressures. In such a case, the individual can participate in both worlds, in both groups, in most institutions of either language, without his identity being highly visible. His identity can be conveniently ignored or forgotten in the process of interaction. With strangers, and in public places,

such a perfectly bilingual person can successfully claim either identity at will.

If bilingualism is a social passport across language frontiers, this means that these frontiers are not crumbling but are maintained, upheld. Furthermore for them to be clearly delimited requires that language norms governing social interaction be enforced.

This is not always the case. Behind the progressive loss of their ethnic language by immigrants is a history of a collapsing frontier. For instance, while grandmothers may still be essentially fluent only in the ethnic language, their grandchildren may be fluent only in the second language. Bilingualism in such a case may mean that the grandmother may still expect her grandchildren to understand the ethnic language, although they may be unable to speak it. Conversely, however, the grandchildren may expect their grandmother to be able to understand English although she may still be unable to speak it with any degree of fluency. The death of the grandmother may mean the death of the only person who in fact enforced a language norm in kinship interaction, and, therefore, may signal the final collapse of a language frontier.

In the case of French Canadians outside Quebec, under the earlier conditions of rural isolation the strength of the group structures and local community institutions along with kinship networks and the Catholic parish was usually sufficient to counterbalance the pressures of the state and economy. The only persons to become fluently bilingual were those who by occupation or profession were brought into sustained contact with these institutional areas.

In the urban settings in which, inevitably, French Canadians outside Quebec find themselves, every individual has to transact with the English economy, the state school system, etc. Everyone must become perfectly bilingual to cope adequately with their social setting.

The crucial question thus becomes: under these conditions can the frontiers maintaining fluency in French be upheld? The answer is no. The waning influence of kinship, the attenuation of the social relevance and moral power of the Church, the professionalization of welfare, health care, and education, the substitution of state bureaucracies for community elites in the same fields – all these factors spell the collapse of the traditional institutions that upheld fluency in French. Television and radio stations and bilingual schools will not stop these social forces in a minority context.

Once French Canadians outside Quebec are fluently bilingual, they face a whole new set of decisions. Do they speak to each other in French?

When and to whom? The fact of the matter is that when everyone is fluent in English manning a frontier in order to maintain a level of fluency in French is no longer socially grounded. While the language folkways defining interaction with the English-speaking world of the job market, public spaces, and state institutions are socially grounded and maintained, upholding a French language frontier becomes an artifice not grounded in the needs of social interaction; and those who try to do so are more apt than not to be viewed as narrow-minded if they are young, old-fashioned if they are not. As a consequence, fluency in French steadily decreases with infrequent use. All this because the enforcers of language frontiers are not policemen or bureaucrats, but unilinguals. Under normal circumstances, unilinguals are not politically motivated in their enforcement function. These language norms are territorial and social folkways, and they are conformed to, as in the case of all folkways, because they are the 'proper' ways to behave – accepted uncritically, handed down from generation to generation – and because conformity is socially expected. The person who does not conform is either a newcomer to be socialized or a trouble-maker to be ostracized.

If this small note on the sociology of language, a field as yet undeveloped, has any degree of validity, it becomes apparent that the 'institutional bilingualism' of the Official Languages Policy is indeed an illusion, a product of what I have called 'administrative idealism.'

THE POLITICAL IRRELEVANCE OF CANADA'S BILINGUAL POLICY IN A MODERN QUEBEC

Ineffective in increasing the French-Canadian participation in the federal bureaucracy and its subsidiaries, unable to ensure the viability of French-speaking communities outside Quebec – two of the major objectives it sought to achieve – the Official Languages Policy proved to be a political irritant in the rest of Canada and, as I shall presently argue, politically irrelevant and retrograde in a modernized Quebec.

The modernization of social institutions in Quebec was initiated by the provincial state. The new middle classes, as new elites, are a direct outgrowth of this state-initiated modernization. For the better part of a decade, its members could be, and were, absorbed in the public and parapublic institutions. These institutions are now fully developed and fully staffed. If these new elites are not to become blocked elites, new outlets must be found. The normal outlets for such elites, in all provinces except Quebec, in all nation states of the liberal democratic tradition, are the white-collar ranks of the large corporations in the private sector. The new elites have not found their place in these ranks. And it is precisely because this did not take place that language became a political issue when it did.

The traditional ethnic division of labour in Quebec is too well known to need describing again in detail. Suffice it to say that, historically, the native Québécois provided the unskilled and semi-skilled labour in the industrial sector. Clerical, middle- and upper-managerial levels in the private sector, especially in the large corporations, were, and still are, an English workplace.

The absence of French Canadians in the private corporate world has been noted often and variously explained. In the fifties, the conventional wisdom of the period accounted for the relatively low participation rate roughly along the following lines. Quebec's educational system was not geared to an industrial society.[40] Controlled by the Church, it was suited to develop an elite bound for the liberal professions, the only kind of elite that a pre-industrial society generally develops, composed of notaries, lawyers, doctors, and priests. Furthermore, among French-Canadian entrepreneurs economic rationality was not aggressively pursued but was interfered with by extraneous values such as kinship, with the consequence that their firms were less competitive and stayed small.[41] Finally, in the case of national corporations, it was pointed out that the patterns of upward mobility generally required geographical mobility and that the 'cultural attachments' of French Canadians interfered with their career interests. By refusing openings in other parts of Canada, they eventually were overlooked for promotions. To top off these various explanations, reference was usually made to the Weberian thesis of the different value systems between Catholics and Protestants as an ultimate ethereally enduring explanation of variations in socio-economic status.[42]

Thus it is that, in the fifties and early sixties, economic underdevelopment was accounted for essentially in terms of 'failings' in the culture, the values, the institutions, and the traditional leadership of the underdeveloped. This view of underdevelopment had wide currency in the corporate world, in the halls of academe, and in the corridors of state power. A soothing explanation indeed, but twenty years later it would appear to be a rather Pharisaic one.

The credibility of this Pharisaic view of economic underdevelopment has been seriously undermined, paradoxically enough by the fact that French Canadians shared the same beliefs and acted upon them. The educational system was completely revamped and modernized. The provincial state took over the leadership from the Church in all spheres of societal life. Catholicism as a set of values and as a set of practices collapsed. There is no social or political stigma in quitting the 'faith' among the elites and the urban working classes.

Stated in other words and in a historical sequence, the inadequacy of the educational system as a causal explanation might have had some credibility in the thirties, forties, and fifties. But by the sixties and the mid-seventies, its explanatory value is more than doubtful.

The subordination of economic rationality to other cultural values as a causal explanation of the limited size and competitiveness of French-Canadian entrepreneurship is equally questionable. It has, indeed, become increasingly evident to all, and alarming to some, that the economic growth of firms has not been achieved by the process of small firms becoming big in a linear fashion, but rather by their integration to large corporations, mostly American.[43] In other words, English-Canadian firms in secondary manufacturing, despite their Protestantism and their supposedly more rational character, could only grow through their integration to, or their absorption by, dominant continental corporations.

Finally, although the number of 'properly educated' Québécois (many of whom have also obligingly dropped their Catholicism) has grown by leaps and bounds, their presence in the Montreal-based large corporate world has not substantially changed. The only remaining reason for their small penetration in the corporate world becomes their Frenchness, not in an ethnic or racial sense, but as a technical flaw. This language barrier would easily account for their low entry rate as well as for their low mobility rate once having joined. Nathan Keyfitz has already shown how such a language barrier might limit not only the performance of French Canadians, but also the capacity of Anglophone managers to perceive and promote talent.[44]

It becomes apparent, then, that language has been working as a sorting device in the allocation of people in English and French workplaces. Institutions dependent on the provincial state have become French workplaces while the corporate world has remained an English workplace. Both areas expanded bureaucratically in the post-war period. The French workplace gave rise to new elites in the public and parapublic sectors. These elites were created by the provincial not by the federal state. In fact, the federal state's own record within its own corporations *in Quebec* is not substantially better (definitely not in the case of airline pilots and air-traffic controllers, to name two politically aggressive groups) than that of the corporate world itself. In both cases, perfect bilingualism is the required passport for upward mobility, if not for sheer entry. Within such a context of a rapidly modernizing Quebec, the federal state's language policy was not only politically irrelevant but clearly reactionary. That it led to the progressive alienation of Québécois elites is glaringly obvious. The consequence of prolonged and expanding elite alienation had its electoral outcome on November 15, 1976. On November 16, though stunned, the federal establishment was convinced that the Québécois did not want independence but good government. Undoubtedly, but from which government?

The inertia of the federal state and its irrelevance, in my opinion, can be traced to the basic thrust of the Official Languages Policy. The RCBB's frame of reference precluded it from focusing on the structural changes required to make the Québécois true partners in the Canadian political economy. Its objectives should have been concerned principally with the French majority in Quebec, not with the French minorities outside Quebec. Secondly, it ought to have changed the language 'rules' of the corporate game in Quebec, instead of forcing the uneconomic introduction of TV and radio stations in British Columbia. Its central concern should have been not to try to shore up the collapsing language frontiers upholding vanishing French communities outside Quebec, but to break down the unacceptable language frontiers preventing the expanding Québécois elites from penetrating both the federal state's own corporations and the private corporate world in Quebec. Prophetic in its proclamation of an impending crisis in the legitimacy of the federal state, it provided the state with bad counsel when it cavalierly refused to give serious consideration to the forging of a bilingual Canada on a territorial basis.

At this juncture, one must look at the history of the RCBB. It was well along in its deliberations when it was faced with the explosive fact that, in Quebec, Francophones as a group ranked, in personal income, just above the native peoples and the Italians, but below all twelve other ethnic groups.[45] In fact, public knowledge of these data came about via a press leak. The RCBB, despite this revelation, did not refocus its basic objectives. Instead, it contented itself with pious recommendations to the private corporate sector of Quebec, and with advising the federal state to establish French units within the federal civil service.[46] Exhortations are not substitutes for official state policy.

The RCBB's reasons for not considering a territorial definition of bilingualism for Canada are uncommonly ludicrous. The RCBB would have us believe that North Americans, by contrast with Europeans, are unique in being geographically very mobile. The cultural trait of mobility made it impractical, therefore, seriously to consider territoriality as the organizing principle for bilingualism. If mobility is a cultural trait, rather than a consequence of economic variables, why have Maritimers been going to Ontario but not vice versa? Is it that the culture of the Atlantic provinces has this characteristic to a very high degree and that of Ontario to a much lower degree? That distinguished Canadians should serve such gobble-degook to the Canadian public in order to dismiss a possible basis for forging a bilingual policy is quite bewildering. At best, the RCBB naively accepted the assumptions of what I have called the Pharisaic theory of underdevelopment: that is, the belief that the economic underdevelopment of French Canadians was to be traced to a deficient educational system, the archaic character of its institutions, the lack of entrepreneurship, and the pre-industrial character of the French-Canadian value system. In this view, with the Quiet Revolution in progress, the modernization of Quebec's institutions would automatically create economic development. That would eliminate economic disparities. At worst, the RCBB fantasized that the urgent crisis in national unity it had itself proclaimed could be solved without any drastic changes in the rules of the game of the Canadian political economy. The urgent political crisis was reduced to the psychological dimension of political alienation that increased bilingualism of federal civil servants was supposed to remedy.

CANADA'S BILINGUAL POLICY AND ITS CONTINUING
AMBIGUITIES: THE CASE OF THE CORPORATE WORLD
AND IMMIGRANTS TO QUEBEC

Since it had refused to adopt a territorial bilingual policy, the RCBB could not logically proclaim that the federal state's language policy's main objective should be to make Quebec French in all societal functions, including the language of the workplace.

The corporate world and multinational corporations may be faulted for many things, but they cannot be faulted for not implementing what is not the official policy of the Canadian state. Furthermore, no matter what the objective contradictions of corporate capitalism in its multinational expression may be, failing to handle different languages efficiently is not one of them. Multinational corporations need the benevolent cooperation of sovereign nation-states far too much not to conform to an official state policy, especially if it is proclaimed to be fundamental to the political unity of the state and is not detrimental to their corporate interests.

The American multinationals, in the particular instance we are concerned with, only followed the historical practice that had been initiated by the Anglo-Canadian and British corporate world years before the massive American entry into the Canadian corporate scene. The ratio of British ethnics in Quebec has been declining for more than a century.[47] If the Anglophone proportion of the population in the greater metropolitan area of Montreal has been able to maintain itself, it has been by the absorption and integration of immigrants.[48] The leverage for such integration was the workplace on the one hand, and the locally autonomous, locally financed, and locally managed institutions on the other. I have described elsewhere this pattern of mutually satisfying self-segregated institutions,[49] which gave rise to MacLennan's poetic expression of the two solitudes. The two solitudes was a tacit agreement between two elites: the English merchant class of Montreal, and the Catholic clergy in Quebec. Both elites had an interest in this agreement. The economic hegemony of the merchant class ceased to be politically threatened (as it had been in the troubles of 1837).[50] And the clergy was guaranteed a century of social and political dominance over its flock. With Confederation, the political implementation of this agreement was formalized and enacted. In order to facilitate industrial capitalism from sea to sea, the federal state was given exclusive control over those areas vital for an enterprise which required the free flow of capital, labour, and products. The enabling political structure was to be the federal government, which was given jurisdiction over the areas crucial to 'national' questions: money and banking, defence, transportation, etc. The provinces were given jurisdiction over 'local' matters: health, education, and welfare, etc. In terms of nineteenth-century economics, these areas were unimportant and undeveloped. And, in social fact, they were, in Quebec, the undisputed domain of the Church which could thus minister to its flock, as well as ensure that it remained French and Catholic.

The economic hegemony of the English merchant class in Quebec was politically maintained from the time of the conquest. 'Responsible government,' the rallying cry of the Patriotes in 1837, was a political threat. Lord Durham correctly reported that what he had observed was 'two nations warring within the bosom of the same state.' Confederation constituted a solution to all 'parties' concerned. By introducing 'responsible government' once the English became a majority, by locating in the central government the political jurisdictions required for industrial capitalism, it ensured for the English merchant class of Quebec a twofold guarantee: first, that it would no longer be threatened by the local political institutions; second, that it would be able to participate fully in the developing industrial capitalism and maintain its economic supremacy in Quebec.

For the Church, formalizing the provincial competence in local affairs of health, education, and welfare meant that since these services were organized, financed, and managed at the community level, its social and political power was legally enshrined. Within such a framework, it becomes clear that both parties to the agreement needed a 'weak' provincial state. Finally, to ensure the institutional autonomy of the English in Quebec, Protestant education as a constitutional right was enshrined in the statutes of Confederation.

That, in a nutshell, is the social contract underlying the Canadian Confederation of 1867. It worked smoothly until the 1960s. The breakdown in its effectiveness coincides with the 'modernization' of Quebec. The breakdown in its legitimacy coincides with the collapse of the social and political power of one of its parties: the Catholic hierarchy of Quebec.

This social contract underlying Confederation also formed the basis of accommodation and the institutional division of labour in Quebec. The surplus population of the French Catholics would become the unskilled and semi-skilled labour force of industrial capitalism. Anglo-Canadian and British capital would control the technical and managerial part of these enterprises, recruiting Anglophones across the Dominion and in England, and, later, absorbing immigrants in its ranks. The Catholic church's legitimacy would no longer be challenged by the Crown. Further attempts to assimilate French Canadians would stop. The trade-off for the preservation of language and religion was the complete institutional and educational autonomy of the English, and exclusion from partnership in the industrial capitalist enterprise. Put more bluntly, the trade-off was between religion and language and economic subordination or underdevelopment.

In this perspective, the oft-quoted exhortation of Monseigneur Paquet takes on a new meaning. He preached that French Canadians had a more noble mission than the material things of life, which were best left to the English Protestants. This has been universally interpreted, within the pharisaic view of economic underdevelopment, as one of the 'causes' of the economic retardation of French Canadians. It was claimed, as a consequence, that the Church was one of the causes of the economic underdevelopment of French Canadians.* Pierre Elliott Trudeau, in the

*The Catholic church, now politically irrelevant, has been maligned not only by the right in the fashion just described but as vehemently by the left which describes it as being in direct collusion with the capitalists to prevent the rise of class-consciousness within the

decade before the Quiet Revolution, was the main spokesman for the intellectuals who faulted the Catholic church of Quebec specifically for that reason.[51] It would seem, paradoxically, that the much-maligned Monseigneur Paquet understood the social contract underlying Confederation better than the professor of constitutional law who was to become Prime Minister of Canada.

Yet the Prime Minister of Canada, in his earlier days, came dangerously close to understanding it when, commenting on English-Canadian nationalism, he wrote the following:

Throughout this period [1763–1940], Canadians of British origin would have considered it an indignity to be in any inferior position. So they invented all kinds of stratagems by which democracy was made to mean government by the minority ...

Generations passed. Hopes of assimilating the French Canadians dimmed to a flicker (although right up to 1948, immigration laws continued to favour immigrants from the British Isles over those from France). But English-speaking Canadians have never given up their condescending attitude to their French-speaking fellows, even to this day.

At Ottawa and in provinces other than ours, this nationalism could wear the pious mask of democracy. Because, as English-speaking Canadians became proportionately more numerous, they took to hiding their intolerance behind acts

---

proletariat. This is an exaggeration. The Church needed no direct collusion. The Church's ambivalence toward industrial capitalism came from knowledge of what happened to the urban proletariat in the second industrial revolution in Europe: specifically the de-christianization of the masses. That it wanted to avoid this in Quebec is understandable enough. That this fear made it accept the social contract underlying Confederation is probable. The secularization of the masses in Europe coincided with and to some extent was a consequence of the separation of Church and State and the consequent secularization of education. It could therefore not entertain such a separation. In social fact, with the jurisdictional division of competences within Confederation, with education being the exclusive jurisdiction of the provincial state, such a separation was avoided. The Church's gingerly approach to international trade-unionism must be understood within the same context. True enough – Church property was not confiscated as it was in France during the French Revolution. Instead, its social and political power was preserved for another century (1867–1967). Its downfall coincided with the growth and power of the provincial state in the fields of health, education, and welfare. The provincial state replaced the Church with – much to the Church's credit – no significant opposition. The challenge to the social contract underlying Confederation had no leverage until both the substitution of the provincial state for the Church took place and the jurisdictional competence of the provincial state in health, education, and welfare became an area of economic growth and gave rise to new elites.

of majority rule; that was how they quashed bilingualism in the Manitoba legislature, violated rights acquired by separate schools in various provinces, savagely imposed conscription in 1917, and broke a solemn promise in 1942 ...

In Quebec, 'where they had the money if not the numbers, our Anglo-Canadian fellow-citizens have often yielded to the temptation of using without restraint the means at their command.' This was how, in politics, Anglo-Canadian nationalism took on the form of what André Laurendeau has so admirably named the 'cannibal-king theory' (*théorie du roi-nègre*). Economically, this nationalism has been expressed essentially in treating the French Canadian as *un cochon de payant* [*sic*].* Sometimes, magnanimously, they would go as far as putting a few straw men on boards of directors. These men invariably had two things in common: first, they were never bright enough or strong enough to rise to the top, and second, they were always sufficiently 'representative' to grovel for the cannibal-king's favours and flatter the vanity of their fellow-tribesmen. Finally, in social and cultural matters, Anglo-Canadian nationalism has expressed itself quite simply by disdain. Generation after generation of Anglo-Saxons have lived in Quebec without getting around to learning three sentences of French. When these insular people insist, with much gravity, that their jaws and ears aren't made for it and can't adapt themselves to French, what they really want to get across to you is that they will not sully these organs, and their small minds, by submitting them to a barbarous idiom.[52]

The refusal to learn French was not, as Trudeau implies, a product of English-Canadian arrogance and disdain, but went to the core of the social contract implicit in Confederation. That social contract involved a language frontier and this latter could only be enforced by Anglophone unilingualism. 'Pelletier has pointed out that, having preached – through *Cité Libre* – systematic scepticism in the face of established dogmatism, and having practised it as regards most of our traditional institutions, we should hardly be surprised if a new generation should turn it against one of the establishments we ourselves have spared: the Canadian state.'[53]

While Trudeau admits that this statement has some validity at the psychological level, he fails to see its political relevance. Its political relevance hits at the core of the social contract implicit in Confederation. Having been instrumental in destroying the social and political power of one of the parties to Confederation – *viz*: the Church – that hindered the development of modernization in Quebec, he is now in the uncomfortable

*In the original French text the word is 'paysan.'

position of having to defend the Act of Confederation itself and the other party to the social contract against the very forces of secularized modernization he himself helped unleash.

The case of the immigrants: a structural analysis
Since it is the federal state, and not the multinational private corporate sector, which is at fault for refusing to define as a state policy that all sectors of societal life in Quebec should become French, the immigrants in Quebec can hardly be blamed for integrating into the economic system and wanting to learn the language of that system. Here again, one sees clearly that the ambiguous situation of immigrants in Quebec is as much the consequence of the language policy of the federal government as of the social and political pressures of the Québécois majority.

The thorny issue involving immigrants in Quebec centres on the fact that roughly 80 per cent of them integrate into the English institutional system and insist on choosing the English school system.[54] Given the structure of the political economy of Quebec, it is not difficult to demonstrate that this choice is a rational one.

I have already pointed out that the Anglophone proportion of the population in Quebec has been more or less constant over the last century because of the absorption of immigrants, since the proportion of Anglophones of British ethnic origin has been decreasing continually over the same period. I have also pointed out how the bureaucratic expansion in the corporate world more or less coincided with the bureaucratic expansion of state-dependent institutions, with the former remaining an English workplace and the latter becoming an expanding French workplace which helped to absorb the new middle class.

This structural context provides a framework within which to analyse the immigrant question in modern Quebec. The great wave of immigration in Quebec covered roughly the two decades immediately following the Second World War.[55] Skilled immigrants moved directly into the white-collar and lower-managerial ranks of the corporate sector and into the professional and semi-professional ranks of the Anglophone parapublic sector: education, welfare, and health institutions. The unskilled immigrants became the clientele of these parapublic institutions, since without them, these institutions, rather than expanding, would have shrunk.

The private corporate sector, as an English workplace, could not have maintained itself without a fully developed Anglophone parapublic sector. Without it, it could not have attracted the 'managerial pool' of

English-speaking Canadians (or Americans) to staff the expanding corporate bureaucracy. Without the absorption of immigrants, the Anglophone parapublic sector would have collapsed.

The immigrant rationality

Immigrants in Quebec had no dilemma until language became a political issue. And language did not become a political issue in Quebec until the Québécois new middle class needed further outlets, outlets blocked by the language frontier.

While the political function of immigrants in the political economy of Quebec was to ensure the institutional autonomy and the economic hegemony of the English in Quebec, thus enabling the continuation of the social contract implicit in Confederation, these were not, obviously, their conscious motives. Consciously, immigrants to Quebec, as everywhere else in the world, were seeking to better their economic opportunities. In the case of the post-war skilled and professionally trained immigrants, the war-ravaged economies of Europe made it difficult if not impossible for them to find the same opportunities in their countries as could be found in Canada. Unskilled immigrants, a self-selected group from economically underdeveloped regions within their national homeland, were immigrating to Canada, in Quebec as elsewhere, in the hopes of avoiding the urban proletariat fate or *lumpenproletariat* fate awaiting them in Naples, Rome, Athens, or Lisbon. For the majority of these, the hopes of the adults were unfulfilled; but the hope that their children will escape the proletarian fate by education is strongly kept alive.

In the case of skilled and professionally trained immigrants, integration in the English workplace, where they were needed, was smooth and instant. They came already equipped with a working knowledge of English, and their children could proceed through the educational system from primary school to university without hindrance. Their career fate was and is linked to the fate of the Anglophone workplace and the Anglophone parapublic institutional sector. This is true for two reasons: first, the corporate workplace needed external reinforcement to remain English; second, the French public and parapublic sector was being built from scratch and was not short of manpower.

Unskilled immigrants choose the English school system for their children first of all in order to ensure upward mobility for their children in Quebec and Canada, in the corporate world or the Anglophone institutional system. Failing that, they seek scope for geographical mobility through acquired fluency in English in order to have access, without handicap, to the whole Canadian labour market.

Old and new myths
The foregoing structural analysis enables us to account for much of the political debate around language in contemporary Quebec. It also enables us to cut through some of the old and new myths abounding within it.

The first myth to explode is the one vehicled by the RCBB: that Quebec is the model for the treatment of minorities.[56] The ethnic minorities in Quebec, as a consequence of the modernization of Quebec, are caught in a dilemma not of their making; but they are the first to be victimized by the required changes in the political economy of Quebec. Their victimization is as much the consequence of the outmoded institutional bilingualism of the federal state as it is of the pressures of the Québécois majority – who correctly perceive the institutional autonomy of the Anglophones as a vestige of colonialism traceable to the social contract of Confederation ensuring Anglophone economic dominance.

The second posture which merits attack is the self-righteous stance of the Anglophones in defence of the immigrants' right to an English education under the new slogan of the 'rights of parents' to choose the educational system of their choice. The fact of the matter is that the immigrants bear the brunt of the conflict between the French majority and the English minority in Quebec. Economic rationality forces the immigrants to attach themselves to the English system in order to avoid the economic status of the Québécois. Furthermore, their integration in the French public and parapublic sector is more than problematic, given the fact that there is a native manpower surplus in that sector. The Anglophones need the immigrants in order to maintain the viability of their autonomous institutional system. Self-interest lurks dangerously close below the surface of altruism.

The so-called 'rights of parents' to choose the educational system they want for their children takes on a special meaning within this context. This is a new myth highly conducive to political mobilization and with broad appeal. Its validity, however, is more than doubtful when it is seen both in relation to the practice of nation-states and, in the present instance, to an analysis of the BNA Act.

The American as well as the French Revolution proclaimed the separation of Church and State. In those countries where this separation was realized, the educational system became dependent on the State, not the Church. As a consequence, the state educational system, in law if not always in fact, was non-religious. In such countries, however, religious schools are not formally prohibited by law; they are only denied state funds. Any set of parents, therefore, on religious or language or any other grounds, may found schools with the understanding that they are not entitled to state funds and the provision that the state has the monopoly on degree granting and the setting of examinations. Such parallel systems of education often exist and are, naturally enough, private and expensive.

In Canada, a formal separation of Church and State was never proclaimed in the Constitution. In practice, however, the public-school system was in fact Protestant in all provinces except Quebec, where the Constitution, while giving exclusive jurisdiction to the provinces, specifically spelled out that, in the Province of Quebec, the province was obliged to provide a Protestant education as part of the public-school system. Never was this constitutional provision prefaced by a declaration of the 'rights of parents' to choose. Religion, not language, was guaranteed in the constitutional provision, and in Quebec only.[57] Constitutionally, therefore, the immigrants have a right to a Protestant education in Quebec, not an English one. This holds true even for the Anglophones in Quebec.

That this battle-cry of the 'rights of parents' should suddenly be resorted to in a modernized Quebec is surprising to the Québécois, since it has an old familiar ring. It was the principle that used to be called into play by the Church in the old dispensation to combat both the 'Welfare State' and compulsory education, or its extension. The clerical view of the time was that children belonged to their parents first, then to the Church, which was charged with their eternal salvation, and only last to the State. This was the rationalization for opposing family allowances, old-age pensions, and compulsory education to the age of sixteen – all initiatives taken by the State, financed by the collectivity, and threatening to the social dominance of the Church. In the forties and fifties, when such debates were carried on within the Quebec intelligentsia, with the clerico-nationalists upholding this view and the modernizing liberal democrats rejecting it, the unanimous stance of the Anglophone intelligentsia and its media was one of condescension toward the 'medieval' and 'backward' character of the Quebec Church. That present-day editorials about the current school debate in the written and electronic Anglophone press should still regard this as axiomatic only illustrates that 'backward myths' can be transformed into 'philosophical principles' according to the dictates of self-interest. If parents' rights were paramount in choosing the language of education, immigrants could insist on a public-school system entirely in Greek, Italian, or Russian.

The only possible grounds for claiming an English as opposed to a Protestant education must be found in the Official Languages Act of recent vintage, not in the so-called rights of parents. I have argued all along, however, that the Official Languages Act complicates rather than resolves the current crisis in the legitimacy of the Canadian state. Furthermore, given the constitutional division of jurisdiction within the BNA Act, and of jurisprudence in the case of the Manitoba and Ontario school questions, any such federal intervention in a province's jurisdiction would be clearly *ultra vires*.

The final myth to be exploded by this structural analysis has to do with the so-called xenophobic character of the Québécois. The Québécois are neither more nor less xenophobic than English Canadians. Such cultural stereotypes –with no validation from the analysis of social structures, or, more precisely, from the analysis of the political economy of social structures – are scientifically meaningless and can only serve political legitimations, which is precisely what they are used for. If such cultural traits did exist, we would have to marvel at how much more xenophile are the English in Montreal than the English in metropolitan Toronto.

By and large, people's political culture is grounded in their material conditions and the political economy that shapes them. Their political socialization is a function of their political dependences. In that respect, the immigrants who integrate in the French workplace reflect the political culture of that workplace. Similarly those who integrate into the English workplace reflect its political culture. This is equally true of the Québécois themselves. The political culture of the Québécois integrated with the Anglophone corporate world reflects that political culture, and is in sharp contrast to the political culture of the elites that were created by the provincial state. In the case of the former, federalism is sacred and Quebec independence is anathema. In the case of the latter, Quebec independence is a legitimate option and federalism as presently constituted is a framework in need of major revision.

CONCLUSION: THE PRICE OF NATIONAL UNITY

This essay has argued that the political discontent of Quebec is rooted in and a consequence of the modernization of Quebec. The provincial state created new elites in the public and parapublic domains of health, education, and welfare. The new middle classes that emerged as a consequence of this institution-building process are confined to the public sector, and, because of their language, are practically unrepresented in the ranks of the large private corporations.

While the federal state, through the RCBB and the consequent Official Languages Act, proclaimed a state of crisis in national unity, it failed to address itself to the core of the issue: the economic underdevelopment of Quebec and the Québécois. In its recommendations, it refused seriously to consider territoriality as a basis of its bilingual policies, and instead produced an institutional bilingual policy, setting forth antiquated institutional arrangements in Quebec as the model for French-English relations in Canada. Concerned with attempting to shore up crumbling language frontiers for the French communities outside Quebec, it failed to address itself to the unacceptable language frontiers in the political economy of Quebec.

The federal state has, ever since, followed a language policy that can only be described as a political irritation for English Canada which is entirely politically irrelevant to a modernizing Quebec.

There is a price for a new political consensus in Canada. And certain groups will have to pay this price. Those two unfortunate groups are the French outside Quebec and the English in Quebec.

And what, short of military coercion, is needed for Canada to survive? A new social contract will have to be negotiated. For this to happen, the unequal union, in Stanley Ryerson's apt characterization of the Act of Confederation, will have to be renegotiated. This renegotiation will have to facilitate the full participation of the Québécois in their political economy. For this to happen, basic changes in the rules of the economic game as historically elaborated will have to be implemented. These basic alterations will probably have to deal, not only with Quebec, but also with the regional underdevelopment of the Atlantic provinces and the monopolization of economic growth by the 'golden triangle' to the detriment of western industrialization.

Whether the Canadian people can respond to the challenge of the reshaping of the Canadian state is far from certain at present. Until now, in fact, very few, and least of all our current crop of political leaders, have recognized its absolute necessity.

NOTES

Originally published in D. Glenday, H. Guindon, and A. Turowetz, eds, *Modernization and the Canadian State* (Toronto, 1978)

1 Pierre Elliott Trudeau, *The Asbestos Strike* (Toronto, 1974)
2 Gérard Dion and Louis O'Neill, *Deux prêtres dénoncent l'immoralité politique dans la province de Québec* (Montreal, 1956)
3 L'association des professeurs de l'Université de Montréal, *L'université dit non aux Jésuites* (Montreal, 1961)
4 Hubert Guindon, 'Social Unrest, Social Class, and Quebec's Bureaucratic Revolution,' *Queen's Quarterly*, 71 (Summer 1964), 150–62 [this volume, 27–37]
5 Ibid., 155 [this volume, 30–1]
6 Marcel Rioux, *Quebec in Question* (Toronto, 1971), Chapter 4: 63–72
7 Rapport du groupe de travail sur l'urbanisation, *L'urbanisation au Québec* (Quebec, 1976), Chapter 10
8 Ibid. Annexes du rapport du groupe de travail sur l'urbanisation, Marc-André Lessard, 'La Qualité de vie et les quartiers urbains,' 22. This quotation is translated by myself.
9 Hubert Guindon, 'Two Cultures: An Essay on Nationalism, Class and Ethnic Tension,' in R.H. Leach, ed., *Contemporary Canada* (Durham, NC, 1967), 56–9 [this volume, 52–5]
10 John D. Jackson, 'Institutionalized Conflict: The Franco-Ontarian Case,' in G. Gold and M.A. Tremblay, eds., *Communities and Culture in French Canada* (Toronto, 1973)
11 Guindon, 'Social Unrest, Social Class, and Quebec's Bureaucratic Revolution,' 153 [this volume, 29]. See also Dale Posgate and Kenneth McRoberts, *Quebec: Social Change and Political Crisis* (Toronto, 1976), Chapter 7: 131–6.
12 Ibid., Posgate and McRoberts, Chapter 6: 111–18
13 Daniel Drache, ed., *Quebec, Only the Beginning: The Manifestos of the Common Front* (Toronto, 1972)
14 *Report of the Royal Commission on Bilingualism and Biculturalism* (RCBB) (Ottawa, 1965), Preliminary Report, Books I, II, III, and IV
15 Ibid., Preliminary Report, Chapter 7: 125
16 CATCA strike vote, 15 June 1976; strike begun 20 June 1976; and ended 28 June 1976 (Canadian News Facts, 1976)
17 Otto Lang accepted 'settlement' by airworkers, 28 June 1976 (Canadian News Facts, 1976)
18 Pierre Elliott Trudeau, TV address, 23 June 1976 (Canadian News Facts, 1976)
19 *The Montreal Star*, 25–8 June 1976
20 *Le Devoir*, 26 August 1961 to 24 July 1963, about forty-eight editorials in all
21 *Le Devoir*, 26 August 1961, editorial page
22 *Report of the* RCBB, Book III, Chapter 9

23 Ibid., Book III, Chapters 9 and 10
24 Ibid., Book I, Chapter 4
25 Joseph T. Thorson, B.C. jurist and author of *Wanted: a Single Canada* (Toronto, 1973)
26 Leonard C. Jones, former mayor of Moncton, N.B., presently federal MP for Moncton (Independent), elected despite rejection by Stanfield from PC party
27 Raymond Lémieux, leader of the Francophone side in the St Leonard school dispute
28 Posgate and McRoberts, *Quebec: Social Change and Political Crisis*, 141–2
29 Ibid., 141
30 Ibid., 142
31 Commissioner of Official Languages, *Annual Report for 1975*, 31 March 1976 (Canadian News Facts, 1976)
32 Ibid.
33 *Report of the* RCBB, Book I, Recommendations
34 *The Montreal Star*, 10 April 1973
35 *Report of the* RCBB, Book I, Chapter 4: 88
36 Much of this section is based on the unheralded work of Richard J. Joy, *Languages in Conflict*, The Carleton Library, No. 61 (Toronto, 1972).
37 Ibid., Chapter 4
38 Ibid., 43
39 *Report of the* RCBB, Book I, Chapter 1: 6
40 Ibid., Book III, Chapter 5: 80. See also John Porter, *The Vertical Mosaic: An Analysis of Social Class and Power in Canada* (Toronto, 1975), 95–7.
41 Norman W. Taylor, 'The French-Canadian Industrial Entrepreneur and His Social Environment,' *French-Canadian Society*, Vol. 1 (Toronto, 1964), 271–95
42 Porter, *The Vertical Mosaic*, 287–90
43 Wallace Clement, *The Canadian Corporate Elite: An Analysis of Economic Power* (Toronto, 1975), Chapter 3: 92–3
44 Nathan Keyfitz, 'Canadians and Canadiens,' *Queen's Quarterly*, 70 (Winter 1963), 171–4
45 *Report of the* RCBB, Book III, 23
46 Ibid., Book III, Recommendations, 558–62
47 Joy, *Languages in Conflict*, Chapters 15–17: 91–109
48 Ibid., Table 21, p. 48, and Table 26, p. 59
49 Guindon, 'Social Unrest, Social Class, and Quebec's Bureaucratic Revolution,' 157 [this volume, 33]
50 Stanley Ryerson, *Unequal Union: Confederation and the Roots of Conflict in the Canadas 1815–1873* (Toronto, 1973), Chapter 19: 358–61

51 Pierre Elliott Trudeau, *Federalism and the French Canadians* (Toronto, 1968)
52 Ibid., 162–3
53 Ibid., 172–3
54 Joy, *Languages in Conflict*, Chapter 9: 57–63
55 *Report of the* RCBB, Book IV, Chapter 1
56 Ibid., Book I, Chapter 4: 87–90
57 British North America Act, Article 93

The crown, the Catholic church, and the French-Canadian people: the historical roots of Quebec nationalism

The title of this essay seemed both pretentious and portentous. It evokes conflict and drama as well as commitment and utopia. It calls for re-examination of the past, anxiety about the present, and contradictory hopes for the future. It is a sensitive topic, which can quickly transform the cool, detached social scientist into the emotionally charged citizen. It unnerves business men who normally take pride in the fiercely competitive world they claim to live in, but, contrary to form in this case, declare themselves panic-stricken and cry out for stability, peace, and quiet. It arouses the citizenry from the daily boredom of the business of making a living. It delights the media since public-affairs programs finally have a chance for good ratings. It terrifies politicians who thrive on public adulation in exchange for forged consensus. Finally, it annoys comedians since it strips from them a lot of material that their audiences no longer find funny. Yet humour is not only the last fortress of sanity but very often the first condition of objectivity.

Rather than discussing nationalism and the nation-state in the abstract, I address these concepts in a situated manner: the case of Quebec society in the Canadian polity. Rather than making a critique of the theories that give shape to sociology, I will refer to them as the analysis of the Quebec condition warrants. Rather than attempting a historical overview of the development of capitalism, imperialism, and the fate of the nation-state, I will refer to the larger historical context only when it seems to bear importantly on the issues at hand.

About the larger picture I candidly admit that my mentor is the late Hannah Arendt. Her book *The Origins of Totalitarianism*[1] constitutes, in my mind, the undiscussed classic in the whole area of imperialism and the demise of the nation-state. Written immediately after the Second World

War, it has relevance for the seventies that surpasses that of anything I have read. While her contribution to social science has been acknowledged in broad intellectual circles, her impact on sociology proper has been minimal, if not non-existent. Yet, this book is, in my opinion, the definitive statement on the sociology of the nation-state.

The fact that her focus was on the sociology of the nation-state – its birth, its short reign, and its demise – may be one reason for the work's marginal impact. Sociology, especially in North America, was interested in nation-building, which takes for granted the political structures of the state, rather than in an analysis of the conflicts between state and society.

In the case of the United States, the lack of a feudal past, the fact that sociology was born well after the Civil War had been settled by force of arms, the fact that it took root in the Midwest where history meant the future not the past and that it took shape at the height of massive immigration and new settlements can partially account not only for the lack of concern for the topic but equally for the consequent lack of insight on it.

Canadian sociology, although it was born later and within a 'political economy' approach, did not blossom as an academic discipline until after the Second World War. By that time, Canada was entering a phase of accelerated urbanization involving both its own rural population and a massive influx of immigrants. As a consequence, nation-building rather than the sociology of the nation-state was equally the typical focus of Canadian sociology.

By the seventies, however, sociology in Canada faced a very different set of circumstances from those that still obtained in the United States. What little concern there exists in American sociology with the sociology of the nation-state does not find its origins in the internal dynamics of American society but rather in the external relations the United States, as a superpower, entertains with the developed and developing nations of the world. Mainstream sociology, traditionally unconcerned with foreign relations, is, as a consequence, only slightly affected and influenced by external relations.

In the case of Canada, however, concern for the sociology of the nation-state is a function of internal political tensions. The centrality of these issues in the political and economic arenas of the country is forcing most social-science disciplines, including sociology, to address themselves to sets of questions that they never had anticipated, and upon which very little expertise could be brought to bear from traditional training. The questions have to do with the nature, the history, and the ideology of the Canadian state, with the nature of the Canadian political economy, with the links between political and economic élites within the context of a continental economy, and with the adequacy of national policies. In short, the very legitimacy of the state, as now constituted, is being challenged. As a consequence, a new form of scholarship is taking shape in Canadian sociology, feeding into the national debate.

There are three major facets to the national debate in Canada. The first deals with the political economy of Canada and the United States. George Grant, a philosopher, was the first to provide the vocabulary for the debate. In a celebrated book, *Lament for a Nation*, he accused the economic élites of Canada of having sacrificed the Canadian national interest to their own class interests by becoming the branch-plant managers of the continental economy. C.D. Howe and the Liberal party of Canada were the brokers of the transaction. Since this initial statement was made, economic historians and a few sociologists have begun to draw a clearer and sharper picture of the relationship Canadian capitalism has with the Canadian state, on the one hand, and with the continental economy, on the other.

A second facet, commonly referred to under the rubric of regionalism, is related to economic development and underdevelopment within Canada. Increasingly it is argued that the economic development of Central Canada (the 'golden triangle' of Montreal-Ottawa-Toronto) facilitated by the federal state is done at the cost of regional underdevelopment of the Maritimes and the lack of diversified industrial development in Western Canada.

The third facet of the national debate concerns the relationships between Quebec and the Canadian state. The election of the Parti Québécois in Quebec was an event that attracted world-wide interest. It constitutes a challenge to the legitimacy of the Canadian state. This essay focuses upon this aspect of the national debate. My primary concern is to take a certain distance from the present, and to focus historically on the relationships between the federal state, the Catholic church, and French Canadians as a people. Both institutions have been under attack: the Catholic church with the Quiet Revolution, and the federal state with the development of the independence movement in Quebec. Ironically enough, if any institutions seemed as solid as the Rock of Gibraltar in this country, until the sixties they were the two. The demise of the Church and the challenge to the Crown are the themes of this essay.

Canada, we are officially, though inaccurately, told, started in 1867. While we celebrated its centennial with great fanfare, its birth passed relatively unnoticed, with no burst of popular rejoicing. It was an event that the people learned about, but in which they did not participate. While we envy ideals of the Declaration of Independence, proclaiming the right to life, liberty, and the pursuit of happiness, or those of the French Revolution, proclaiming *liberté, égalité, et fraternité*, no such stirring ideals animated the British North America Act. How come?

The absence of popular rejoicing and of stirring principles is usually explained by some reference to the fact that the Fathers of Confederation were realists and pragmatists. Perhaps there was no cause for rejoicing, no stirring principles to be found. In France and the United States, the rejoicing and the stirring principles were related to a sudden break from an undesirable past. In Canada, continuity, more than discontinuity, characterized Confederation.

A break with an undesirable past was attempted: rebels challenged the undemocratic rule of the Family Compact in Upper Canada and the Château Clique in Lower Canada. The attempts failed and were militarily suppressed. The Canadian word for attempts to break from an undesirable past on the basis of a stirring principle is 'troubles'; hence, 'the troubles of 1837.' The historical roots of the political agreement between the Catholic church of Quebec and the British Crown in Canada were shaped by the unexpected facts already alluded to: a Catholic church thanking God for a Protestant rule (even only as a lesser evil) and a Protestant Crown granting property rights to a papist church (for a greater good).

The Church in Quebec proclaimed itself the embodiment of the conquered nation – and loyal to the alien state. That claim was honoured by the British Crown as well as by the French-Canadian people. When, in the mid-1830s, national sentiment fed by doctrines of responsible government and emerging concepts of democracy erupted in an armed attempt to change the structure of the state, the Catholic hierarchy sided with the Crown, not with the rebels it proceeded to excommunicate. This loyalty to the Crown did not mean that the Church was antinational but that it was against democracy as a political principle, the very principle that was underlying the national uprising.

If the rebellion in Lower Canada was motivated by national sentiment as well as political principle, in Upper Canada only the latter was at stake. Behind the political principle in both cases was a form of class conflict: conflict over control of the state. Stanley Ryerson, more than a decade ago, and Reginald Whitaker, in a brilliant recent essay, both analysed this conflict between emerging industrial entrepreneurs and indebted independent farmers, on the one hand, and a mercantilist and financial family compact,[2] on the other.

If the Church rejected democracy as a matter of philosophical principle, the English merchant class in Montreal opposed it as a matter of economic self-interest, given democracy's political consequence at the time. Politically privileged, threatened by responsible government, thoroughly committed to the sanctity of private property, the English merchants, none the less, did not hesitate to destroy public property when they rioted and burned the parliament buildings in 1849, after Parliament had voted funds to help the rebellions' *patriotes* get back on their farming feet.

No one has more brilliantly castigated the political Pharisaism of the Montreal anglophone establishment than the former prime minister of Canada, Pierre Elliott Trudeau, admittedly in his academic, rather than political, incarnation. They only became converted to responsible government once the English were a majority in the country, he seethingly and accurately stated. They remained insensitive to minority rights when those rights were suppressed in Manitoba and in Ontario. They refuse to sully their organs by learning French.

What Trudeau failed to understand was that it was not English arrogance, as he suggests, but the whole Burkean philosophy that permeated the politics of British colonialism that can explain this behaviour. As Whitaker argued, the Burkean view of society and state was in direct opposition to the ideals of the French Revolution. In fact, Edmund Burke's conservatism was a mixture of total commitment to the market economy and to existing social hierarchies. He alerted British opinion to the dangers of the egalitarian and democratic tendencies of the French Revolution. In Whitaker's words: 'The colonial administrators came to Canada armed with a mission to build a conservative, un-American and undemocratic society in the northern half of the continent … market liberalism and anti-democratic conservatism … served early colonial Canada as a blueprint for the nature of the society to be created.'[3]

For the purpose of my argument, where Whitaker stops, Hannah Arendt takes over to shed light on Burke's view on race. The French Revolution proclaimed *liberté, égalité, et fraternité* as 'the Rights of Man.' Benjamin Disraeli, an assimilated Jew, following in Burke's political philosophy, found 'something better than the Rights of Men in the Rights of Englishmen.'[4] Burke's main argument against the 'abstract principles' of the French Revolution is as follows: 'It has been the uniform policy of our constitution to claim and assert our liberties, as an *entailed inheritance* derived to us from our forefathers, and to be transmitted to our posterity;

as an estate specially belonging to the people of this kingdom, without any reference whatever to any other more general or prior right.'[5]

Arendt drew out the implications of Burke's argument:

The concept of inheritance, applied to the very nature of liberty, has been the ideological basis from which English nationalism received its curious touch of race-feeling ever since the French Revolution. Formulated by a middle-class writer, it simplified the direct acceptance of the feudal concept of liberty as the sum total of privileges inherited together with title and land. Without encroaching upon the rights of the privileged class within the English nation, Burke enlarged the principle of these privileged to include the whole English people, establishing them as a kind of nobility among nations. Hence he drew his contempt for those who claimed their franchise as the rights of men, rights which he saw fit to claim only as the 'rights of Englishmen'.[6]

Within the context of such a political philosophy, for a Burkean English community, the height of arrogance is not, as Trudeau suggests, the refusal of the English Canadian to learn French in Quebec, but the claim by the French to the rights of Englishmen. Extending this claim to French minorities in other provinces becomes the height of irrelevance, and beyond comprehension.

The Catholic church's opposition to democracy on principle and the Crown's refusal to extend the rights of Englishmen to the French, therefore, become the key to understanding the political interaction and co-operation between the two until Confederation.

ON THE DIFFERENCE BETWEEN EMPIRE AND IMPERIALISM

Far from being far-fetched, as modern-day readers might think, the concept of the rights of Englishmen as an 'entailed inheritance' without reference to any other more general or prior right was the political principle upon which the British Commonwealth was built.

Empire-building such as the Romans did is not to be confused with imperialism. In the case of the former, military conquest was followed by the imposition of the Roman legal system on the conquered peoples. In the case of the latter, the conqueror rules by decree rather than implanting the system of law of the empire. Arendt is worth hearing at length on this process: 'Instead of conquering and imposing their own law upon foreign peoples, the English colonists settled on newly won territory in the four corners of the world and remained members of the same British nation.'[7]

That left the 'problem' of the conquered peoples. Arendt exposed the British response, and in the process quotes Selwyn James in *South of the Congo*:

The British tried to escape the dangerous inconsistency inherent in the nation's attempt at empire building by leaving the conquered peoples to their own devices as far as culture, religion and law were concerned, by staying aloof and refraining from spreading British law and culture. This did not prevent the natives from developing national consciousness and from clamoring for sovereignty and independence – though it may have retarded the process somewhat. But it has strengthened tremendously the new imperialist consciousness of a fundamental, and not just a temporary, superiority of man over man, of the 'higher' over the 'lower' breeds. This in turn exacerbated the subject peoples' fight for freedom and blinded them to the unquestionable benefits of British rule. From the very aloofness of their administrators who, 'despite their genuine respect for the natives as a people, and in some cases even their love for them ... almost to a man, do not believe that they are or ever will be capable of governing themselves without supervision,' the 'natives' could not but conclude that they were being excluded and separated from the rest of mankind forever. (10)[8]

The 'aloofness' is reflected in the institutional structures. As Arendt notes, 'in contrast to true imperial structures, where the institutions of the mother country are in various ways integrated into the empire, it is characteristic of imperialism that national institutions remain separate from the colonial administration although they are allowed to exercise control.'[9] Arendt goes on to quote Robert Livingston Schuyler in a footnote that, 'the principle of "colonial freedom" ... cherished by all liberal British statesmen after the American Revolution, was held valid only insofar as the colony was "formed of the British people or ... such admixture of the British population as to make it safe to introduce representative institutions."'[10]

These extended quotes from Hannah Arendt help us make more sense out of the history of the Canadian state than any reading of our national historians. It accounts for the two solitudes of Hugh MacLennan – intended not accidental, cherished not deplored. It accounts for the timing of the introduction of responsible government in the colony. Finally, it sheds light on the nature of Confederation.

THE SOCIAL CONTRACT OF CONFEDERATION
WITHIN THE CONTEXT OF WESTERN IMPERIALISM

On Confederation, there is agreement on little else than that it was a compromise. What kind of compromise, between whom, and for what purposes are crucial questions, especially now that its very legitimacy is under attack.

The Union of the Canadas, paradoxically enough and short-lived as it was, was the closest the state structure of Canada ever got to being binational. Its short duration was not so much a result of its unwieldy character as of its obsolescence, given profound changes taking place in England and the Continent on the verge of imperialism.

Mercantilism was giving way to industrial capitalism in England and the Continent. 'Imperialism,' says Hannah Arendt, 'must be considered the first stage in the political rule of the bourgeoisie rather than the last stage of capitalism.'[11] In her view imperialism and the consequent demise of the nation-state were brought about by the existence of superfluous capital that could not be reinvested profitably within the narrow confines of the nation-state. The export of capital was necessary if it were not to remain idle. The law of capitalism is one of continuous growth.

Contrary to widespread opinion, she claims that the bourgeoisie was not interested in the nation-state after the overthrow of feudalism. The nation-state had to have recourse to Jewish bankers to finance its growing needs.[12] The bourgeoisie became interested in the nation-state only when it needed state power, the state means of violence to protect foreign investments abroad. Attempts to export capital 'without expansion and political control resulted in an unparalleled orgy of swindles, financial scandals and stock-market speculation.'[13] The Panama Scandal in France, which wiped out the savings of small-middle–class people, and the Grundungsschwindel in Germany and Austria became classic examples. The bourgeoisie became interested in the state in order to use its power to stabilize and protect its foreign investment.[14]

This usurpation of the state by the bourgeoisie for its own ends had the conseqeuence of committing the nation-state to political expansion for the benefit of the bourgeoisie. Imperialist interest became defined as the national interest. Imperialism, for Hannah Arendt, was the export not only of superfluous wealth but also of superfluous people. This, she characterizes as the alliance between mob and capital:

Older than superfluous wealth, was another by-product of capitalist production: the human debris that every crisis, following invariably upon each period of industrial growth, eliminated permanently from producing society. Men who had become permanently idle were as superfluous to the community as the owners of superfluous wealth. That they were an actual menace to society had been recognized throughout the nineteenth century and their export had helped to populate the dominions of Canada and Australia as well as the United States. The new fact in the imperialist era is that these two superfluous forces, superfluous capital and superfluous working power, joined hands and left the country together. The concept of expansion, the export of government power and annexation of every territory in which nationals had invested either their wealth or their work, seemed the only alternative to increasing losses in wealth and population. Imperialism and the idea of unlimited expansion seemed to offer a permanent remedy for a permanent evil.[15]

Arendt's argument, then, is that while unlimited expansion was and probably still is a requirement of capitalism, the exportation of state power brought about the demise of the nation-state. Indeed, 'when imperialism entered the scene of politics with the scramble for Africa in the eighties, it was promoted by businessmen, opposed fiercely by the governments in power, and welcomed by a surprisingly large section of the educated classes,'[16] who wanted 'new and ever-growing fields for the honourable and profitable employment of their sons.'[17] This, then, was the European context at the time, and shortly after the birth, of Confederation.

One consoling feature from this analysis of the birth of Western imperialism concerns foreign investment. Under a constant propaganda barrage, emanating from the boards of trade and chambers of commerce, that we should be ever so grateful for and mindful not to discourage foreign investment, it is rather refreshing to learn that, at least sometimes, it comes here because it couldn't stay at home. More seriously, it helps us to make sense of the Marshall plan after the Second World War, as well as British foreign investment, not only in Canada, one of its dominions after 1867, but equally in the United States after their revolutionary access to independence. This augurs well, despite the vehement denials, for the probability of investment even in an independent Quebec. Capital, it would seem, moves for reasons of its own, not for reasons of state.

The scandals that racked this country with the construction of the national railway system illustrate that the Fathers of Confederation were not only astonished bystanders during European follies, but could equal them.

What are the main links that one can make between the birth of Confederation and the context of Western imperialism in the last decades of the nineteenth century?

First, it becomes clear how the forging of a nation-state from sea to sea out of the former British colonies would make economic sense to the English bourgeoisie. The transition from mercantilism to industrial capitalism in Canada would require considerable amounts of capital, and so would constitute a convenient outlet for superfluous British capital. Furthermore, exporting state power would be unnecessary since that power was already in the hands of Englishmen who perceived themselves as a part of the British nation, the British empire.

The British abandonment of protection in favour of free trade would not, after all, spell the downfall of the Château Clique or the Family Compact with the move from the status of colony to nation. As pointed out by Whitaker, after the political unification of the colonies, politicians could turn to the serious business of nation-building with the National Policy. Canada could then 'openly [break] with British free-trade dogma under a protectionist national development plan which saw the sponsorship of an east-west economy linked by a national railway, industrialization being protected by tariffs, with a captive market in the western prairie hinterland which would provide foreign exchange through wheat exports.'[18] Under Macdonald's tariff stewardship, the empire of development was to be private enterprise, but 'private enterprise at public expense,'[19] or, if you prefer, in Frank Underhill's phrase: government of the people, by lawyers, for big business. Sir John A. Macdonald's preference for a unitary state had to be abandoned for the federal principle in order to accommodate the Catholic church of Quebec. The British North America Act is a perfect example of Arendt's previously quoted description of the British model of empire-building. The provinces were given jurisdiction over local matters, such as health, education, and welfare, while national matters, such as money and banking, defence, and international trade, were located at the level of the federal government. These political arrangements were the compromise of Confederation that satisfied the French Catholic church, the English establishment of Montreal, and the nation-builders from Upper Canada. An 'aloof' colonial structure was forged.

The threat to the economic hegemony of the English merchant class of Montreal that the claim for responsible government in Lower Canada had represented would now be structurally eliminated in Confederation. Since industrial capitalism required the free flow of capital, products, and labour within an enlarged and unified state, the proper jurisdiction for overall economic development would be located at the level of the federal government where, in the new circumstances, the democratic principle equally ensured, henceforth, the rights of Englishmen.

With the economy and economic development secured at the right level of government, the local matters of religion, education, and culture were allocated to the provinces. This meant in social fact, in Quebec, to the Catholic church since these matters were territorially organized as an extension of the Catholic parish. To alleviate any fears of the English in Quebec, a special constitutional provision was made to establish the right to a public Protestant educational system in Catholic Quebec.

By consenting to this new state structure, the Catholic church of Quebec was equally responsible for its enforcement and its acceptance by French Canadians. This it did – in a very loyal manner – until its demise as the institution embodying the French-Canadian nation. Retrospectively, it is now clear that what was revolutionary about the Quiet Revolution was the liquidation of the Catholic church as the embodiment of the French nation in Canada. Paradoxical as it may seem, the crisis in the legitimacy of the Canadian state is a direct consequence of the demise of the social, political, and moral power of the Catholic church in Quebec.

THE CHURCH AS THE EMBODIMENT OF THE NATION

It takes little courage to kick dead horses. Never has this maxim been better illustrated than in the case of the Catholic church since its demise in Quebec society during the last decade. If verbal crucifixion produces purification, it can now indeed be called the Holy Roman Catholic church. What was new was not that the Quebec church was under attack, but that it was attacked from within the nation it embodied.

Historically, the blind hatred it evoked among the Orange Lodges of Upper Canada was such a commonplace ritual that it eventually produced public boredom. That this hatred was national as well as religious was a tacit acknowledgment of the Catholic church's claim to represent the French-Canadian nation. When the Catholic bishop of London, Ontario, spearheaded the movement to abolish French separate schools in Ontario, in collusion with the Orange Lodges (thereby creating wounds within the Catholic clergy of Ontario that have never fully healed), he was not so much challenging the propriety of the Church's assumption of the French-Canadian nation as signifying that the French nation would stop at the Ontario border. When the British Crown upheld this move to curtail French schools in Ontario, it doomed forever the possible claim by the federal state to be above nations. The political tragedy of Pierre Elliott Trudeau has essentially been that, while he successfully destroyed the national mission that the Church in Quebec had claimed, he was unable to wrest the federal state from being the embodiment of the English nation.

The full assumption of the nation by the Church in Quebec was, paradoxically enough, the consequence of its support of the Crown's suppression of the national uprising of the *patriotes* in 1837.

As Marcel Rioux brilliantly outlined, there ensued a period of conservative nationalism that lasted a full century.[20] The Church's custody of the nation permeated all spheres of societal life: from politics to culture, from education to welfare. Its tutelage of the nation eventually included trade-unionism when members of its flock became proletarians at the turn of the last century.

If the Church consented to the suppression of the *patriotes*, it was because they were imbued with ideas contrary to the blueprint of the social order it espoused. The French Revolution was anathema to the Church as well as to British Toryism. What the French Revolution proclaimed besides the rights of man was the separation of Church and State, and the confiscation of Church property. Distancing the State from the Church was the essence of French liberalism. English liberalism, in contrast, proclaimed the priority of private enterprise over the state as the embodiment of the national interest. When L'Institut Canadien began expounding French liberal views within the left wing of the Liberal party, the Church promptly excommunicated the members, and they were quietly but efficiently eliminated from the Liberal party by Sir Wilfrid Laurier when he became its national leader. Later, he was widely acclaimed for his impromptu rebuke of Cardinal Merry del Val who, as an official envoy of Leo XIII, admonished the Catholic Québécois to be wary of the modernist heresies of liberalism. Liberalism in Canada, Laurier reminded the papal envoy, was of the British not the French variety. Indeed, political heresy was not to take root in the body politic of Quebec until the 1950s when modernism would eventually successfully challenge the Church's embodiment of the nation.

By proclaiming 'la langue gardienne de la foi,' the Church was emphasizing its primacy as the custodian of the nation; by declaring that French Canadians had a more noble mission than the accumulation of wealth (an activity best left to the English Protestants), the Church was living up to the social contract of Confederation to which it had consented. We can see, then, that the two solitudes, so often deplored by well-meaning people, far from being an unfortunate accident, were a planned outcome basic to the very birth of the Canadian state as embodied in the Act of Confederation. They became the basic principle of social organization until the sixties in Quebec and were insisted upon and enforced by the Catholic church. But this should not blind us to the fact that this political arrangement dovetailed nicely with the British model of colonialism and indirect rule.

The Catholic church in Quebec should be and will eventually be judged on the basis of its having opted for national survival as against economic growth at the expense of the former. Currently these are not the grounds upon which judgment is passed.

On the right, the Church has been accused of being the cause of the economic underdevelopment of the French-Canadian nation, either because of the inadequacy of its educational institutions in an industrial world or because of its transmission of a value system that did not sufficiently promote entrepreneurship. On the left, it has been accused of being an accomplice in exploiting the French-Canadian working class. Both accusations are exaggerated and miss the point.

The right-wing attack mistakenly assumes that Canadian entrepreneurship and the growth of a national capitalist bourgeoisie in Canada developed outside the context of the state. Quite the contrary, the Canadian state, the move from colony to nation, created a national bourgeoisie in Canada, and that was clearly intended to be a bourgoisie of English gentlemen. The national bourgeoisie in Canada was a direct creation of the Canadian state, not of the Anglican church, which remained, then as now, content to give it its blessing. Why the Catholic church of Quebec would have been in a position to create a bourgeoisie then or later, even had it wanted to, is a measure of conservative mystification still popular in this country.

Some left-thinkers miss the target for no other reason than that the *patriote* uprising was not a proletarian uprising, since the French-Canadian proletariat barely existed; nor was it an uprising of a class of agricultural workers, since the latter did not exist, and never has existed, in Quebec society. It was an uprising of petit-bourgeois professionals and small independent farmers. Furthermore, is it not asking too much of the Catholic church to expect it to have been the vanguard of the working class even before Marx and Engels had written *The Communist Manifesto*?

No one can quarrel with the statement that building a British North America was what Confederation was about. It involved many things: collapsing former independent colonies into a single state; claiming sovereignty over lands that had previously been ruled by private enterprise (a neo-conservative's utopia); claiming jurisdiction over territories that had not really been settled. It involved building uneconomical railways from sea to sea with a massive influx of foreign (British) portfolio capital guaranteed by the new state. It involved the industrial development of southern Ontario where, it would seem, the troubles of 1837 eventually paid off. What the building of North America did not involve were the French Canadians as a people in any part of the action. Therein lies the congenital weakness of the Canadian state. This exclusion was deliberately planned, and the Catholic church of Quebec was its victim not its accomplice. Therein lies the historical root of the economic underdevelopment of the Québécois. Still worse, it set the pattern for the ethnic division of labour in Quebec up to the present day. 'La grande noirceur,' so much associated with the ideological backwardness of the Church, can much more convincingly be related to the 'unequal union' that Confederation successfully achieved.

The concession in the BNA Act to the French people was to stop short of a unitary state and create a federal one. The creation of provinces and the limited political franchise, as well as the areas of jurisdiction they were allocated, reflect the political culture of the British empire previously described by Hannah Arendt. 'The British,' it is worth repeating, 'tried to escape the dangerous inconsistency inherent in the nation's attempt at empire building by leaving the conquered peoples to their own devices as far as culture, religion and law were concerned.' Local matters, this was called. It is, therefore, in a context of a politically marginalized people that the stewardship of the nation by the Church must be assessed. While it does not come out unscathed, it is by no means a record to be ashamed of.

The Catholic church did not believe in democracy. But, for that matter, neither did the Anglican church or any other. It was against modernism. While that struggle was indeed a losing one, who, on second thought, now that it has triumphed, is willing to celebrate it unconditionally? The Church's ideological backwardness, bitterly attacked in the fifties, centred on its ambivalence towards industrial society, its conservative stance on state social welfare, its resolute neutrality on labour relations. But, to my amazement, the source of moral indignation among the intelligentsia in the fifties has become its conventional wisdom in the eighties. The ecological movement focuses on the negative impact of industrialization; Canadian Reaganomics focuses on the undesirability of social welfare; the new entrepreneurs celebrated by the neo-classical economists dream of a world unfettered by labour unions and are, temporarily at least, in the ascendancy. The triumphant conservative mood of the eighties either means that the ideological stance of the Catholic church was not so backward after all or that backwardness has become very popular. I tend to think the latter to be the case.

As custodian of the nation, within the constitutional strait-jacket imposed on the French people in Canada, the Church managed to instil a pride in one's difference and distinctiveness, a passion to survive as a people, an attachment to language and culture in spite of economic poverty, and a deep commitment to traditional Catholicism, which kept alive warranted undertones of political distrust of the Canadian state.

The Church did not confine itself to teaching. It also acted. Unable to shape urban industrial life, it aggressively settled the countryside. Parishes were multiplied, thereby facilitating the geographical occupation by the French people of the unpopulated areas of Quebec. A nation needs territory. The Church gave the French a territorial basis. Settlements sprung up in Lac St Jean, la Gaspésie, L'Abitibi, and eventually the Eastern Townships, an English bastion created after the American Revolution. As the number of French settlers increased in the Townships, there developed among some segments of the English settled there a growing conviction that there was an organized conspiracy by the Catholic church to 'take over' the Townships. Aileen Ross, a distinguished sociologist from McGill, proffered a more reasonable explanation. For her, the increasing settlement of francophones was the consequence not only of the surplus rural population in Quebec, but also of the fact that the English were moving up and out of farming. Intentional or not, organized or haphazard, the fact still remains that the Church was building a homeland for the French people.

With its flock excluded from the impending industrial capitalism, distrustful of the State, the Church initiated, before Confederation, the development of a rudimentary school system. Monseigneur Bourget, the reactionary archbishop of Montreal, was the main activist in this regard. He induced religious orders in France (where their fortune was politically unpredictable for a whole century after the French Revolution) to settle and open branches in Quebec. He laid the foundations for what would become an architectural bench-mark typically found in every urban and fully developed rural parish: a complex of fieldstone buildings, including the church, the *presbytère*, the school and convent, all located at the centre of community life. With the institution of the provinces, this educational infrastructure spread over the national territory. The Church set up its own system of secondary education called classical colleges. The Church established, as part of its own self-defined mandate, a network of charitable institutions ranging from hospitals to orphanages, hospices for the aged to asylums for the mentally ill. In short, the Church established an institutional system through which the French as a people could cope with the human life-cycle in their own way and in their own distinctive cultural style.

The basic national legacy of the Church was nurturing the development of a few basic economic institutions. The Caisses Populaires Desjardins, a deservedly celebrated success story, started as a desperate attempt, under most dire economic conditions, to create a financial institution whose foremost commitment was service to the French people. Having no access to foreign capital, tolerated but not encouraged by the Canadian state, it painstakingly struggled to tap the savings, meagre as they were, of an impoverished peasantry and a growing urban proletariat, unobtrusively and with perseverance. I was told that when the Desjardins movement first capped the $100 million mark in capital, plans to celebrate this landmark were scuttled lest the response of the large Canadian banks be to curtail their continued growth through lobbying and legislation.

In the field of agriculture, the Church relentlessly preached the virtues of co-operatives – for a long time with mixed success. Here again, eventually it paid off with the gradual development of La Co-opérative Fédérée which competed successfully with foreign agro-business. As their scale increased, both the Desjardins movement and the agricultural co-operative were criticized for taking on the features of their competitors. No one, however, has accused them of being antinational.

Briefly stated, if in the field of agriculture and financial-savings institutions a growing share of the market has come under French-Canadian control, it is thanks to the pioneering steps taken by the Church more than half a century ago. It is not thanks to the Crown.

The national stewardship of the Church was, therefore, not ineffective because it was ideologically conservative. It maintained a traditional antimodernist world-view and a protective mantle over its politically submissive, socially insulated, and economically subordinated flock. It silenced its internal dissenters, but it equally resisted the attempted encroachments of the English-controlled state. The Church's distrust of a state bent on assimilation or subordination led it to resist the former, to celebrate the rural life over the urban industrial, and to erect the double barrier of language and religion as a social frontier that would secure 'la survivance.' In need of a religious 'motif' to legitimize its becoming custodian of the nation, the Church boldly proclaimed 'la langue gardienne de la foi.'

A century later, after the Second World War, this custodial strategy came strongly under attack from very diverse quarters of the French-Canadian intelligentsia. Trudeau saw in this 'clerico-nationalism' major obstacles to democracy. Marcel Rioux described the whole century as 'la grande noirceur' and championed the 'laicisation' of the social institutions. Michel Brunet castigated the antiquated myth of 'l'agriculturisme' and denounced the Church's 'anti-étatisme' as no longer helping but rather harming national economic development. Trudeau's liberal democracy, Rioux's socialism, and Brunet's nationalism (as diverse as the political paths along which their respective ideologies would eventually lead them) share a common impatience in bringing about a 'modern' society that would take shape with the Quiet Revolution.

Their shared impatience was politically effective, and a modern Quebec was indeed born – though it would fall short of their preferred outcomes. Trudeau, for whom any form of nationalism inevitably leads to national socialism, would see the end of clericalism but not of Quebec nationalism – which would live to haunt him. Rioux's version of a secularized society was to become real, but his dream of a socialist society has not come to pass. Brunet's vision of a rejuvenated nationalism through an interventionist state would materialize, but his unspoken hopes for a fully fledged sovereign state would be thwarted.

While the Quiet Revolution symbolized modernity, it also, unexpectedly, modernized and rejuvenated the national movement. Its modernization spelled the end of its embodiment by the Church. Its rejuvenation signalled its imminent involvement in mass-society party politics. Welcomed and acclaimed developments when they occurred, time would eventually show that they also carried serious liabilities for the national movement. The Church would cool towards a secularized national movement. A political party, one would eventually discover, is perhaps not the best of vehicles to lead the national movement to its primary goal.

NOTES

The Hawthorn lecture, delivered at the Canadian Sociology and Anthropology Association meeting, June 1978. Revised for publication in this volume, in 1987, at St Benoît du Lac

1 Hannah Arendt, *The Origins of Totalitarianism*. Part Two: *Imperialism* (New York, 1951, 1968)
2 Reg Whitaker, 'Images of the State in Canada,' in Leo Panitch, ed., *The Canadian State: Political Economy and Political Power* (Toronto, 1977), 28–68
3 Ibid, 35–6
4 Sir James Stephen, quoted in Arendt, *Origins of Totalitarianism*, 55
5 Edmund Burke, quoted in ibid, 56

6 Ibid
7 Ibid, 8
8 Ibid, 10
9 Ibid, 11
10 Ibid, 11–12
11 Ibid, 18
12 Ibid, 15
13 Ibid, 29
14 Ibid
15 Ibid, 30
16 Ibid, 27
17 J.S. Hobson, quoted in ibid
18 Whitaker, 'Images of the State in Canada,' 45
19 Ibid, 43
20 Marcel Rioux, *Quebec in Question* (Toronto, 1971)

The referendum: the lessons of defeat

Two weeks before the referendum on 20 May 1980, sensing that the outcome was already settled, there was among the 'partisans' of the 'oui,' and I was one of them, a faint hope that, contrary to the polls, people would burn their bridges and plunge into the unknown adventure of an unchartered future. On the other side, after a slow start, a systematic exploitation of the fears of the vulnerable and the privileged, a rather motley alliance, their forces gathered momentum because of an unforeseen affront to housewives that led to the now well-known result. With a bit of malice not devoid of insight, one could say that the fearful, including the very vulnerable and the very privileged, outnumber the others three to two, a social fact with political consequences but of little solace for those who would wish a more solid consensual foundation for a state. The referendum is finally over; the crisis of the Canadian state continues.

Joyless victories, though not uncommon, are a puzzle to me. Tops in this category in Canadian politics was the victory of Jean Drapeau in 1970 when all his political opposition was wiped out. Drapeau and his cohort, in dark business suits, looked on the TV screen like village notables speaking at a wake. While the Verdun auditorium did not look like the site of a wake, it did look disorganized and unprepared for the media. When Radio-Canada announced the victory of the 'non,' the auditorium was nearly empty and the cheering was not on cue, uncoordinated, and mechanical. Dozens of Canadian flags were flaunted but not a single fleur-de-lys was to be seen. 'Mon non est québécois' did not include the flag of Quebec. This oversight was corrected a half-hour or so later when a huge flag consisting of fleur-de-lys sewn to a maple leaf was waved on the screen. Subtlety was not the order of the day.

Why the Verdun auditorium was empty at the moment of victory while the Paul Sauvé Arena was filled to the rafters at the moment of defeat calls for an explanation. It was not that the 'non' forces expected defeat while the 'oui' forces expected victory. Could it not be a result of the nature of the alliance behind the 'non' vote? The vulnerable, one could speculate, couldn't get there because, for many, it was dangerously close to their bedtime. The privileged, one may be quite sure, hadn't finished dinner, and anyway, most of them would not know how to get to Verdun.

A further contrast of importance lies in the difference in the interaction between the crowd and the podium in both instances. Aware of the final outcome, filled with a common emotion of unrequited wish-fulfilment, the crowd at Paul Sauvé greets its dejected leader with an outburst of sympathy; it consoles him. In Verdun, when the notables reach the victory podium what the viewers first witness is the discrete withdrawal of Jean Chrétien, after an impulsive gesture towards the microphone, to make way for Claude Ryan, who saw to it that no one else would address the crowd while the media were present. What a shame, since his speech was boring, sermonizing and distasteful to look at, with his index finger constantly flailing in our faces. A shame also since it was a distortion of history; everybody in the auditorium and the viewing audience knew full well that Chrétien and the Feds had won the day for him. Ineffectual in the campaign, Claude Ryan comes out cheap in victory. Common sadness for a dream postponed, on the one hand, shared sighs of relief from an apprehended nightmare on the other – these were the dominant crowd moods on the evening of the joyless victory.

THE PROCESS OF DEFEAT: EYEING THE POLLS

More interesting than the social composition of the 'oui' and 'non' votes is the strategy common to both camps, one that, in a sense, contained the ultimate result. That strategy consisted in playing up to the polls, whose results had been common knowledge in political circles for the previous three years or so. Faced with a fourfold choice – renewed federalism, sovereignty-association, independence, and the status quo – Quebec voters overwhelmingly chose the first, by a clear majority chose the second, and decidedly rejected the third and fourth.

The referendum campaign embodied this common strategy. The first phase takes place at the Quebec National Assembly. In the debate on the question, the 'oui' forces make an articulated attack on the status quo. It is convincing and by all accounts gives the 'oui' forces a decided edge. Claude Ryan, by continuously stating that the question is dishonest, attempts to convince the audience that the PQ is masking its true aim: independence. Ryan wanted to reduce the issue to independence versus federalism. He fails.

The obvious collapse of Ryan's efforts brings the Quebec Feds into the forefront of the action. Realizing that the 'oui' forces had the edge, they decide to counteract it by Trudeau's solemn pledge that a 'no' vote would mean 'yes' to renewed federalism. The contest then effectively becomes a choice between the first two alternatives: renewed federalism and sovereignty-association. Ten days before the vote, people's minds are made up, and a visible climate of saturation and frustration permeates the atmosphere and conversations. People would like to have the vote over with. Although it was a very short campagin, because people had become emotionally drained, they felt it was interminable. Finally, on the twentieth of May, the polls were validated: the older, the strongly Catholic, and the less-educated Québécois joined with the immigrants, the Jews, and the anglophones to produce the 60–40 result.

THE LESSON OF DEFEAT: THE OVERINSTITUTIONALIZATION OF THE NATIONAL MOVEMENT

Two lessons can be gleaned from this outcome. Both of them have to do with the overinstitutionalization of the national movement since the Parti Québécois took office. A movement capitalizes on the unrest that it spreads. Institutions, on the contrary, adapt to their environment as constituted. As a movement succeeds, its legitimacy as well as its membership and resources increases; its degree of conflict with things as they are decreases. This process of increasing accommodation is called, in sociological jargon, the institutionalization of a movement. The claim made here is that the Parti Québécois overinstitutionalized its embodiment of the national movement.

Political marketing in lieu of political mobilization
Polls and surveys have become, since the late fifties, the basic technology of marketing in a consumer society. By the mid-sixties, they equally became the basic tool of the political market. What they promise to their customers is their capacity to predict consumer preferences. Playing up to the consumers' preferences, which are taken as a given, becomes the central ingredient of strategy.

Political mobilization, in contrast, takes for granted that the 'consumer' preferences, as given at any specific time, must be changed through political action. Rather than playing up to consumer preferences, it intends to transform them.

The first clue that the Parti Québécois chose political marketing rather than political mobilization as a basic strategy is to be found in the embarrassment surrounding the use of the word 'independence.' For a year or more prior to the referendum, the suspense centred around what the nature of the question would be. That such suspense could be created around this matter by the media was itself a product of the polls, since 'independence' came in a poor third in the surveys' multiple-choice question. The poll-oriented strategy so permeated political planning that the word 'independence' itself became suspect and was downplayed. During the whole campaign, only one heavyweight of the Parti Québécois, Jacques Parizeau, dared to say: what's so wrong with independence? Ambivalence towards independence has besieged the Parti Québécois ever since its victory of 15 November 1976. The party itself came to believe that it was elected in spite of, rather than because of, its commitment to political independence. The indecision concerning the date and the question gave an impression not only of hesitation but even of regret that a referendum had to be called. Such posturing had the effect, as I shall presently argue, not of mollifying its opponents but of bewildering its supporters. In any event, polls and pollsters to the contrary notwithstanding, I, for one, do not believe that Quebec will or should achieve independence 'à la cachette.' That approach has now been proven ineffective; furthermore, it was, all along, unbecoming.

That 'independence' as a goal could be so muted says a lot about the overinstitutionalization of the national movement in the hands of the Parti Québécois. To realize it, one need only think back to 1960 when the first movements for political independence were born. Had 'playing up to the polls' been the political strategy of its leaders then, the movements would, of course, have been stillborn. While it may be true that political independence may still frighten a majority of the electorate, it is equally true that political independence, nothing short of it, has the power to stir and mobilize a subordinated people.

The 'reassurance' strategy and its political boomerang
The Parti Québécois, after having enacted Bill 101, embarked on a reassurance strategy that may have established its credibility as a 'good government,' but that equally cast doubt on its commitment to achieve political independence. This strategy had a twofold negative consequence: it demobilized its supporters and mobilized, without fear of

consequences, its political opponents: the corporate establishment, the Conseil du Patronat, and, as previously mentioned, the immigrants, the Jews, and the anglophones.

There is one lesson to be clearly drawn from the referendum's outcome. No matter how reassuring, reasonable, understanding, and accommodating the Parti Québécois may be in office, as long as it is striving, even vaguely, for an eventual kind of sovereignty in even a distant, indeterminate future, it will make no more inroads politically than it has so far achieved into the ranks of its monolithic opposition groups. No matter how democratic it is, in fact, it will be suspect of Fascist tendencies; no matter how committed it is to liberal democracy, including private property, it will be suspected of socialist tendencies by the corporate establishment. No matter how gradual the implementation of its language policy, it will be resisted systematically, inch by inch, case by case, through inertia, passive resistance, and sporadic mobilization. That is one solid fact with which a critical reappraisal of its political action should start.

The demobilization of its own supporters may not be as clearly discernible but is of equal importance. The reassurance strategy gives the impression that time is on your side, that independence will be inevitably reached with little or no social agitation. The political movement is superseded by a political organization, a political machine that operates more like a sales staff of a business organization that is set in motion on cue and uses communications 'techniques' rather than a model of constant presence and interaction. The reassurance strategy and the well-structured organization equally contribute to the impression of automatic, inevitable, and painless attainment of the political objective. This has now been proven to be an illusion. A business-like organization is no substitute for a mass movement nor is 'communications technology' one for sustained grass-roots interaction.

So far I have argued that the overinstitutionalization of the national movement in the hands of the Parti Québécois is traceable to its strategy of political marketing rather than political mobilization, and to its political reassurance strategy that demobilized its own forces and enabled its monolithic opposition to mobilize, in leisurely fashion, without apprehension. What alternative strategies are there available for the future?

The positive lesson of the referendum is that it has clarified whom, among the Québécois, the national movement must still reach. The energy of the movement should be harnessed to bridge the gap of fear, not by word or arguments, nor by policy promises or political platforms, but by a presence, continuous and sustained in their midst; a presence that listens to them, that befriends them, that lends them their arms, their pens, and their lesiure; a presence that helps them cope with the concrete problems of their daily lives. One fears not one's friends, and come election time they will not perceive themselves as a target group submitted to a barrage of contradictory propaganda; they will not feel scared and overwhelmed. Let there be, then, a bigger barrage of federal propaganda, let the federal minister of health send them a double cheque, it will be to no avail. They will politely say: 'Non merci, Madame la Ministre.'

The negative lesson of the referendum is that time and energy should not be wasted on the monolithic opposition. The Parti Québécois has been overly sensitive to the criticism of the English media. The *Gazette* should have in Quebec City the same weight that *Le Droit* has in Toronto. Cabinet ministers of the Lévesque government should give the same number of interviews in English to CBC Radio and CTV that the cabinet ministers of the Davis government give in French to Radio-Canada and TVA. State services provided with state funds should be exclusively delivered in the official language, not defensively but aggressively. Compliance with the law should be closely monitored not by bureaucrats but by aroused citizens.

Nation-building should be aggressively pursued within the national territory. The fact that the Canadian state tolerates that the corporate world and the market system may discriminate against the Québécois in their one and only metropolis is more than sufficient grounds for the Quebec government to be completely intolerant of the same situation. That a party committed to sovereignty should be so lenient on this basic issue while it is in office is sufficient to seriously undermine the credibility of its commitment among its own ranks as well as that of its opponents.

The Parti Québécois seems to believe naïvely that legislation with a supporting bureaucratic infrastructure will bring about change. Bureaucracies, by their very nature, can best cope with routinized activity. Unless prodded by a concerned, mobilized citizenry, they will inevitably settle for doing nothing at full pay. And they would be fools to behave otherwise. Should they, indeed, become zealous, they take the risk of being penalized. By acting only when prodded, they avoid such an unpleasant risk. Furthermore, those groups who will feel the sting get organized, mobilize the media, and will bring pressure to bear to deflect, forestall, and defeat the intended purpose. Finally, it is increasingly believed, in academic circles, that regulatory agencies tend to be tamed by those they are supposed to regulate rather than the other way around.

L'Office de la Langue Française might be a good example. To have unenforced legislation may, sometimes, be worse than having none at all since it permits both its supporters and its critics to entertain a common illusion of change contrary to social reality.

In point of fact, the lessons of the last two decades concerning the 'francisation du Québec' bear out the foregoing analysis. The mobilization of the Québécois that altered the whole governmental approach towards language in Quebec City, irrespective of party in power, was triggered by the massive opposition to Bill 63 that would have given the right to immigrants to choose English as the language of instruction for their children in Quebec's public schools. Since the enactment of Bill 101, however, when, symbolically, the 'francisation' of Quebec was to become pervasive, one gets the definite impression that the password became, instead, to tread softly. Such reassurance has been and will continue to be counterproductive.

If Quebec is a nation, and it is, and if Quebec is its territory, and it is, nothing will be gained by soft-pedalling. When corporations move their head offices for these reasons, their departure should not be regretted but be an occasion for rejoicing. Sun Life's departure should not have been resented; it should have been celebrated. The first duty of a party committed to sovereignty is to build the nation on its territory. And the only way to achieve this is to rely on an aroused citizenry not on career bureaucrats. That, the Parti Québécois can still deliver. Instead, it has tried to reassure everyone, with pitiful success. In the process, it, rather than its opponents, was tamed.

A timid people with Hybrid Leaders

A sad observation that must, none the less, be made is that unless a Québécois is uprooted from his own culture, or detaches himself from it, or was marginal to it from birth, he cannot make it to the top in Canada, politically, bureaucratically, or corporately. Politically and bureaucratically, he can make it in Quebec. In the corporate world, he cannot make it even there.

Of the three doves – Trudeau, Pelletier, and Marchand – only the first could maintain himself. Pelletier, once a sensitive journalist, discreetly retreated to a diplomatic post; Marchand, a rough-and-tumble former labour leader, was publicly discredited by the media for a weakness not uncommon among the press, the corporate executive, and politicians who relished his demise. Bureaucratically, it is often stated, as a regrettable fact, that the well-qualified Québécois is hard to attract to and harder to keep in federal public service.

There is a quite simple explanation for all of these amazing facts. It simply has to do, to use the late Christopher Beattie's felicitous phrase, with having to be 'minority men in a majority setting.' For a minority man to be effective in a majority setting, he is required to play down his ethnicity, to be perfectly fluent in the other's language, and to be content with a slower rate of promotion. If he is very ambitious, he should be equally careful about where he lives, what clubs he joins, what schools he attends, and with what group he socializes. Without this proper socialization, and maybe without ever understanding why, he will be perceived as less efficient on the job, a little odd, and lacking in leadership potential; he will lose out on the 'merit principle,' which, in fact, has a built-in network mechanism that ensures that co-optation will triumph over qualification.

It so happens that there are two ways to achieve this 'proper' kind of socialization. The first way is to have been born French outside Quebec. Should you have been so fortunate, the state, the job market, the supermarket, city hall, the school-board, the police station, the local jail, the hospital, and, sometimes, the funeral parlour have all solicitously taught you, from a tender age, how to behave 'properly.' You learned, unless you were content to till a marginal farm, cut wood, or dig for minerals, that the better course of wisdom was to behave like 'minority men in a majority setting.'

Such socialization makes one properly prepared to smoothly enter the public service. As a matter of fact, when the Feds proudly proclaim that the French are now represented in the public service in a ratio nearly equal to their statistical number in the country, they quietly neglect to mention from where they come. The French who are hard to recruit and to keep are the Québécois who have been 'deprived' of such socialization.

Mind you, this did not apply to the English in Quebec, since they could and did live in their 'own' full set of institutions, including all of the above and more (privileged access to the corporate sector) and could therefore easily behave as 'majority men in a minority setting.' Don Johnston, the MP for Westmount, gives us a striking example of this in his same-day rebuttal of the Task Force on Canadian Unity. Proud of his achievement, he had his press interview translated into French and the bilingual version distributed to all his constituents.

Let us listen: 'Positive aspects of this report will be lost on this Quebec community which can only view the recommendations on language as a cowardly policy clothed in platitudes, in eulogies to the goodwill of majorities. Unfortunately history has proved that the latter does not exist in the real world.' A little further on, he continues: 'We are being offered a vision of Canada divided into a unilingual French Quebec and a unilingual English Canada. We are being offered "de facto" separation soon to be followed by "de jure" separation.' Then, a third thrust: 'And our French-speaking citizens are being offered a ghetto where those without the means of obtaining a bilingual education at private schools or outside the province will be condemned to live and work only in French.'

He tops it all with a call for action on two fronts: 'One, we must explain our attitudes very clearly to French-speaking co-citizens in Quebec. Secondly, Ontario holds the key and this message must be taken to the people of Ontario by the English-speaking community of Quebec. We must convince Ontario that a strong, vibrant French-speaking community in Ontario is in the best interests of all Canadians.'

Since then, Trudeau promoted Don Johnston from the back-benches to the presidency of the Treasury Board. One wonders whether the promotion was given in spite of or because of such 'enlightened views.'

Lest some readers not detect the minor flaws in the president of the Treasury Board's logic, let me point out that if, as Mr Johnston claims, history has proved that the goodwill of majorities does not exist in the real world, why should the Québécois want to remain in Canada, where they are a minority?

Second, if a French Quebec in an English Canada constitutes a *de facto* separation to be followed by a *de jure* separation, isn't Mr Johnston a little late in reporting the news? Institutional bilingualism has only existed in Quebec; in the rest of the country *de facto* unilingualism of the state and the market is more than a century old. How come *de jure* separation didn't take place?

What most qualifies Mr Johnston as the 'majority man in a minority setting' par excellence is the lyric heights he reaches when he bemoans the tragic fate of the Québécois 'condemned to live and work only in French.'

Regarding his call for action, Mr Johnston need not worry about his first 'front': the Québécois fully understand his and his community's attitudes. On his second front, the Ontario front, I unfortunately cannot be as reassuring: Bill Davis can be good but, in my book, only God performs miracles ... Such statesmanship on the part of the new blood in Trudeau's cabinet augurs well indeed for the prospect of renewed federalism. It makes one fondly remember Warren Allmand.

If the first route to be properly socialized as a 'minority man in a majority setting' is to properly choose one's geographical location, the second route, less achievable, is to properly choose one's parents, plus one condition. It involves being born of a mixed French-English marriage and the condition is: that both cultural identities be kept alive. While mixed marriages of this kind are not a rare event, seldom is the specified condition met outside Quebec. Ethnic hybrids in a social context of ethnic tension often become personally distressed, torn and bewildered, because the polarizing public conflict brings to the surface normally repressed and unresolved personal anxiety concerning their identity. In less troubled times, hybrids, because of their double marginality, inevitably acquire the learned capacity to operate with considerable skill as 'minority men in a majority setting' since theirs is a permanent condition. In times of public crises, however, for those in positions of leadership, ambivalence can lead to rather erratic behaviour. We can sympathize with them but not to the point of condoning their behaviour.

A painful example of this was to be found in the crisis brought about, on the one hand, by the proclamation by the Canadian Air-Traffic Controller's Association and the Canadian Airline Pilots' Association that French constituted a threat to air safety, and, on the other hand, by the massive mobilization across English Canada on their behalf. Trudeau's first action was to pre-empt prime-time television to proclaim solemnly that this defiance constituted the greatest crisis Canada had ever faced. Then, a few days later, we witness a complete about-face: he packs his bags, goes to Bermuda, and invests Otto Lang with the full powers to settle the whole issue without further consultation. Otto Lang, naturally, promptly surrendered to all of their demands, including that the issue be the object of a free vote in Parliament. A more dramatic example of hybrid ambivalence would be hard to imagine. Marchand, the leader of the Quebec caucus, a troubled 'minority man in a majority setting,' resigns in protest from the cabinet but without rocking the boat, which is 'proper' behaviour. The Québécois are, indeed, a timid people with hybrid leaders.

THE DIM FUTURE OF RENEWED FEDERALISM

If sovereignty-association was doomed by the referendum's outcome, renewed federalism's future strikes me as equally glum. The expression, as everyone knows, is a pollster's tool to quantify people's feelings. Its one handicap, and it is a major one, is that it has no political content. Because of its great popularity, it jumped into the public discourse of political leaders straight from the pollsters' magic box.

It was solemnly pledged by Trudeau when it became obvious that the 'oui' forces were gaining ground after their vigorous, extensive, convincing, and scathing attack on the status quo in Quebec's National Assembly. What exactly did Trudeau promise? Exactly nothing. Since the referendum, it has become abundantly clear that Trudeau's foremost concern is to hastily strike the iron while it's hot. This effectively guarantees that no new content can be introduced.

Within this post-referendum context, my preceding comments on 'minority men in a majority setting' and on the ambivalence of hybrid leaders in times of ethnic tension take on added political meaning. How can Trudeau, who could not meet the challenge of CATCA and CALPA to the official language policy, a policy endorsed by all parties in Parliament, be expected to make the substantive changes needed to fit the glaring changes required in Quebec's political economy? Instead, for a starter, he proposed, in his declaration of principle, to fashion Canada in his own image: 'We, the people of Canada ... born of a meeting of the English and French presence ...' Freud must be snickering.

If Trudeau cannot be trusted to bring about the needed reforms, can the seventy-four Liberal MPs from Quebec be expected to provide substitute leadership? Hardly so. Except for Don Johnston and a few others, they are all, indeed, 'minority people in a majority setting,' properly socialized and, if not, efficiently neutralized. Furthermore, should they believe barely 25 per cent of the fear propaganda they so enthusiastically spread, they will obviously settle for very little, if not for nothing. Finally, their record can only be reassuring for Trudeau since, when he deserted the helm in the time of crisis, they were content to keep their hurt mostly to themselves.

The needed changes are glaringly blatant. Any passing stranger becomes aware of them in a day. Any adult living in Montreal, be he a Québécois, a Greek, an Italian, a Jew, or an anglophone, knows what they are. He may fear them, fight for or against them, resent them or yearn for them, or want to ignore them; no matter, he knows what they are. Even Mr Don Johnston knows what they are. Even Trudeau and the seventy-four Liberals, who never speak about them, know what they are. The fact of the matter is quite simply that, unless forced to, the Liberals will not push for them. And the reason for that is equally quite simple: because implementing them means to disturb and upset. Politicians are in the business of getting re-elected and reaping gratitude, not abuse. The only way to have politicians muster political courage is to infuse them with it through massive doses of social unrest, orderly but unremitting, peaceful but unrelenting.

The Canadian state was born barely a decade before the imperialist scramble to the four corners of the world by the Western European countries. Imperialism in this country took the form of wilful subordination of the French in their homeland. The Canadian state was a party to this in its very infancy. In 1980, it is still a party to the same contradiction, and the will to keep things that way is still very much alive.

When the issue of the French nation comes up for discussion, Trudeau becomes a Jesuit. He borrows from his erstwhile enemies of the fifties their whole arsenal of scholastic casuistry. Trudeau knows full well that the political intentions and consequences of the schools question in Manitoba, Nova Scotia, and Ontario were to define geographically, once and for all, the territorial limits of the French nation in Canada. The British North America Act, Trudeau seems to forget, was so called not only for the benefit of the Americans, but also for the benefit of the French Canadians, who had committed, thirty years before, not an apprehended but a real insurrection. Had the contemporaneous insurrection in Upper Canada, which was even more ruthlessly squashed, been successful, one could have a retrospective dream: that a common bond, forever binding the two nations of Upper and Lower Canada, based on a common cherished memory of a shared dramatic break from an undesirable past, could have provided us with our very own motto of 'liberty, equality, fraternity.' It would not have had the same meaning here as in France, since, in our case, it would have symbolized not the relationships between 'citoyens' of the same state, but the bond between two nations sharing a common state: *dans la liberté, dans l'égalité, et dans la fraternité.* Unfortunately for Mr Trudeau, and still more so for us, he is by his office, in a direct line of succession, the embodiment of the Château Clique and the Family Compact. I can understand that he can't do anything about it, but I can't forgive him for not trying. That dream was not to be and so we stand, more than a hundred years later, in the festering quagmire of the politics of despair that has beclouded the political atmosphere of this land for more than a decade.

Let me promptly descend from these heights of Johnstonian lyricism and categorically state that I refuse to believe that the beaver is a Canadian symbol; it has to be the ostrich. Trudeau would have us believe that the territorial boundaries that were politically settled and sealed more than eighty years ago are no longer real, or if still so, can still be changed. This is not only empirically untrue, it is politically irresponsible, and a gratuitous insult to the French outside Quebec who know better every single day of their lives.

The time has come to define the limits of the English nation in Quebec. The process will have to be the same: unpleasant and not particularly tasteful. What was it? An aroused citizenry, mobilized and led by socially respected persons and organizations, including the Roman Catholic archbishop of London, Ontario, pressures the state to enact the appropriate legislation and jealously 'stands on guard' ever after. The same need, the same recipe: true Canadian pragmatism. Let the Canadian state, which was a party to the first such operation, be a party to the second, and the chances for its survival will dramatically increase.

It would be unbecoming not to bring into this scenario the contribution of the other Canadians. The immigrants and the Jews in Quebec cannot escape the feeling that they are pawns in a French-English conflict, and they duly resent the status. But with their incontinent mobilization, instead of discrete withdrawal from a historical conflict in which they had no part, the least one can say is that, since the referendum, they have become willing pawns. During the weeks preceding the referendum, the federal immigration courts were mass-producing citizens so that they could directly enter the polling booths. Such indecent haste will not, over the long run, stop the course of history. The immigrants should not be blamed for this, nor should they be praised for it, nor should they be rewarded for it. If short-sightedness characterizes the leaders of the country, and it does, one should not fault its fearful new citizens for not being far-sighted.

The referendum has settled nothing. The referendum, plus the nature of the current constitutional discussions, clearly indicates that the short route to a political solution of the Canadian political crisis is out of the question. It will be the long route. And the burden will fall, as it probably should, on the Québécois, since independence or sovereignty-association earned by a simple nose-count could not be a highly cherished victory.

The task ahead will be arduous and unpleasant. The methods will involve breaking with the narrow electoralist parameters that have failed. It will require the determination of an English bulldog. It will be a long and tortuous journey. We may even have to endure a Ryan government, but if the will is there, and I think it is, if the work is done and I think it will be, it will eventually come about. It might leave bittersweet memories for those it will have inconvenienced. But what have our memories been if not bittersweet?

NOTE

Originally published in an abridged version as 'The Referendum: Another Decade of Apprehended Political Instability,' in *Canadian Forum*, LX, no. 707 (March 1981)

Quebec and the Canadian Question

A century and a half ago, after the Rebellion of 1837, Lord Durham observed in his famous report that when he looked for the cause of the unrest, he found, to his astonishment, 'two nations warring in the bosom of the same state.' He proposed a simple remedy: 'I believe that tranquility can only be restored by subjecting the province [of Quebec] to the vigorous rule of an English majority.'

Were he to return today, Lord Durham would no doubt be astonished to learn that, despite the application of his proposed remedy, his initial observation holds true. Quebec and English Canada still seem to be 'two nations warring in the bosom of the same state.' Today the viability of Canada as a political entity remains in question. And for the Québécois it is *the* question, the distinctively *Canadian* question.

How are we to understand Quebec and its place (or lack thereof) in Canada? For most English Canadians, the rise of the separatists in Quebec has been inexplicable. Quebec, that quiescent paragon of rural provincialism, has suddenly been transformed into a seat of rabid nationalists intent on the dismemberment of Canada.

If this change seems inexplicable, it is because it does not fit the political stereotypes and cultural myths that English Canadians long used to interpret Quebec as an archaic, traditional society. Ruled by an autocratic clergy fiercely possessive of its own powers and opposed to democracy, modernization, or social progress, Quebec, it was said, was a rural backwater of poverty, illiteracy, and political despotism.

This political/cultural vision of the French in Canada did not emanate from bigoted Orangemen. Strangely enough, it was the conceptual framework of the politically liberal anglophone academics of the 1950s, and it was shared and disseminated by the 'progressive' French-Canadian intellectuals in and around *Cité Libre* magazine, who then lived in Montreal and went on in the 1960s and 1970s to work mainly in Ottawa. (That move may seem particularly surprising, but it was theoretically predictable. Minorities are often known to internalize the majority's view of themselves, and when people from a minority want to chart a career in the majority setting, it is a necessary precondition that they adopt the common mindset.)

Political fairy tales are always with us, and only belatedly do we become aware of them. It is, therefore, easier to spot distortions of social reality in the older ones than in the current ones. How are we to understand what has really been going on in Quebec these past few decades? What processes have made the Canadian question so urgent for the Québécois?

I have argued elsewhere ['The Modernization of Quebec and the Legitimacy of the Canadian State'] that the delegitimation of the Canadian state in the eyes of the Québécois is a consequence of the modernization of Quebec, which took off with the provincial government's massive intervention in the areas of health, education, and welfare. In this chapter I explore this issue at somewhat greater length and disentangle some of the separate threads in the modernization process. This necessitates distinguishing between the processes of government involvement, secularization, and political alienation.

The modernization of Quebec was heralded by the beginnings of large-scale government involvement in the structure of Quebec society in the early 1960s – a process now called the Quiet Revolution – and by the overthrow of the Union Nationale party, which had held provincial power. The secularization process became visible six or seven years later, as a massive dropout rate among priests and nuns became noticeable. Finally, political alienation became clear in the late 1960s, as the independence movement took shape: the Mouvement Souveraineté-association, the precursor of the Parti Québécois, was created.

THE QUIET REVOLUTION

Antecedents: social unrest in the 1950s
The modernization of Quebec is popularly described as beginning with the Quiet Revolution, as if it had sprung full-blown from the traditional society preceding it. That, of course, is nonsense. The Quiet Revolution was preceded by a decade of unrest, during which more and more Québécois came to question their society and its capacity to meet their needs.

Labour unrest

The designation of a single event as the beginning of any social change is always arbitrary. Nevertheless, a logical starting point for this history is the strike of the asbestos miners in 1949, a highly symbolic event. Quebec's asbestos mines, largely American-owned, were virtually closed down by this strike involving some 5,000 workers, who were mainly seeking better job conditions. Their unions were affiliated with the Canadian Catholic Confederation of Labour (the predecessor of the Confédération des syndicats nationaux or CNTU), which until this time had stressed cooperation with management; they received backing from many other Quebec unions, which put aside their history of internecine quarrels and came together to support the asbestos workers. The dispute became particularly bloody, partly because of the goon-squad tactics of the police, who were under orders from the ruling Union Nationale party to aid management and break the strike.

The strike rapidly became much more than a labour dispute. It signalled a questioning of the whole internal political and social order of Quebec society. For many years, the institutional Church had backed the political regime of Maurice Duplessis and the Union Nationale. Now two bishops openly broke with the Church, instituting collections in the parish churches of their dioceses in support of the workers. (One of them, Archbishop Charbonneau of Montreal, was eventually forced to resign his see as a consequence.) Equally significant, the intelligentsia of Quebec, who normally did not choose sides in labour disputes, mainly supported the workers.

The whole event was deeply revealing of the kinds of changes that were beginning to occur in Quebec. Here was an American corporation (at that time we did not have the word 'multinational' to describe it) with English-speaking managers and French-speaking workers who were contracting asbestosis. In retrospect, it seems amazing that under such circumstances it was Maurice Duplessis, not the Johns-Manville Corporation, and the provincial police, not the anglophone management, who became the scapegoats and villains in the political unrest that grew out of this prolonged strike.

The world of the arts

This unrest spread during the 1950s, through the social, political, and cultural institutions of Quebec's traditional society. The world of the fine arts was ready for it. In 1948, Paul-Emile Borduas, an influential painter, lost his teaching position for writing a manifesto, Le Refus Global, that called for artists to reject the ideological hegemony exercised by the institutional Church, and to demand total freedom of expression. Although Borduas subsequently went into self-imposed exile, his message left its imprint.

Social welfare

Unrest also developed in the area of what is now called social welfare (it was then still called charity). New professionals, such as social workers, were beginning to emerge and become critical of Church control over the welfare institutions and the lack of professional qualifications of many who cared for the socially disadvantaged, the economically deprived, and the mentally disturbed. This growing dissatisfaction with the traditional ways of organizing social activities was an echo from the area of labour, where a growing critique of paternalism foreshadowed a push toward unionization and formalized collective bargaining as the normal way of organizing work.

Education

It was in the area of education that the loudest demands for change were heard. During the mid-1950s, a teaching brother anonymously published a series of letters, collected as *Les Insolences du Frère Untel* (in translation, *The Impertinences of Brother Anonymous*), which satirically decried the education system, at the time almost entirely controlled and run by the Church. The articles, which were very funny, attracted broad attention within the middle class, partly because the author castigated the atrocious distortions of his students' spoken and written French, coining the term *joual* (a colloquial pronunciation of *cheval*) to refer to their language. That lower-class French could be spoofed meant that a middle class had been sufficiently developed to constitute a willing audience for such humour. These educated Québécois were equally ready to read the satirical criticism of the 'yearly pilgrimage' to Quebec City that was undertaken by each school board in order to have its budget approved. Such mockery was a way of demanding new, more professional bureaucratic structures to handle educational needs.

By the end of the 1950s, educational concerns had shifted to the universities. Three law students of the Université de Montréal staged a sit-in in Premier Duplessis's waiting-room, with the well-publicized purpose of achieving a statutory grant system for the universities – in other words, more automatic transfer of public money to institutions of higher learning. Once again, case-by-case administration was being criticized.

In retrospect, another episode can be seen to herald the secularization of Quebec's public institutions. In reaction to a request by the Jesuits to obtain a charter to start a new French university in Montreal, the newly formed Association des Professeurs de l'Université de Montréal published a booklet entitled *L'Université dit Non aux Jésuites*. The Jesuits failed to obtain the charter.

Health care
Health institutions were also an object of social dissatisfaction. The costs of health care, which were rising fast, were borne exclusively by the patients of their kin. A twofold demand was emerging: increased involvement of the state in funding and, as a consequence, secularization of health-care institutions. In the meantime, lay people were increasingly questioning the selflessness of the religious orders that oversaw the administration of these institutions.

The end of the decade
Toward the end of the decade, two events occurred that foreshadowed two political developments: the impending demise of the Duplessis regime, and the eventual rise of the independence movement.

In the first, two priests, Fathers Dion and O'Neill, castigated the political immorality of the Union Nationale party – Duplessis's political vehicle – in a clerical periodical, *Ad Usum Sacerdotum*. The article was leaked and widely publicized and acclaimed. The fact that the charge of immorality was made by clerics who were neither parish priests nor bishops but university professors may have been significant. Certainly, they received no official rebuke. Only the bishop of rural Gaspé made a faint – and inconsequential – rebuttal. Thus, the decade that had begun with the toppling of an archbishop from his see for his expression of sympathies for the workers in a strike declared illegal by the Duplessis regime, ended with a formal, direct attack on the political immorality of that regime – an attack that went unchallenged and its authors unpenalized.

The first ripple of the independence movement, like that of the Quiet Revolution, surfaced in a labour dispute. In 1959, producers at Radio-Canada, the French network of the CBC, tried to start a trade union. The management objected that producers were managers and therefore could not be granted certification as a union. The producers went on a strike that lasted for more than two months and galvanized public attention. Once again, amazingly, the villains of the tale were not the francophone bureaucrats of Radio-Canada but the Canadian Parliament, not the minister responsible for the operation of the CBC, but Confederation itself. The asbestos strike had signalled the questioning of the internal socio-political regime of Quebec society. A decade later, the Radio-Canada strike began the eventual questioning of the external political and economic constraints on the development of Quebec society.

Agents: the emerging middle classes
The evolution of the social unrest of the 1950s in the fields of labour, welfare, education, politics, and communications raises the question of who, sociologically speaking, was politically restive and why. The reception given *Les Insolences du Frère Untel* was one indication among many of the existence of a new middle class; in Quebec's increasingly differentiated society, it was this group that felt, articulated, and progressively disseminated social unrest.

The massive urbanization that had accompanied the Second World War and immediate post-war period in Quebec had put pressure on the traditional institutions that dealt with education, health care, and welfare. The new demographic conditions required a radical and sudden increase in the scale of these institutions, which, in turn, transformed their nature. New, expensive technologies and increasingly specialized expertise required large-scale organizations in order to service a greatly expanded clientele with up-to-date levels of service. These public and para-public institutions became a major and growing labour market for members of the new middle classes: in contrast to the self-employed petite bourgeoisie of tradition, they were salaried professionals and semiprofessionals developing their careers in large-scale bureaucratic organizations. In the eyes of this new middle class, Quebec institutions urgently required state money if they were to grow and thus modernize Quebec society. And the Duplessis regime was so slow to respond as to be proclaimed reactionary.

When the priorities of the new middle class became the priorities of the state, the Quiet Revolution was officially under way. This happened after Duplessis's death, when Paul Sauvé became premier in 1950. He had been in office barely three months before sudden death ended his term; it was seen as a terrible and personal loss by the whole of Quebec society. Since he had had no time to implement any changes, the deep sense of bereavement was a consequence of his promise of change (*désormais* – 'henceforth'), which had included three solemnly declared intentions:
1. To provide statutory grants to universities.

2. To establish a royal commission to study the feasibility of free hospitalization.
3. To revise the pay scale for the civil service.

All three promises were soon met, if not by Sauvé's Union Nationale, then by the Liberals, who won the following election on the slogan 'It's time for a change.'

Certainly, many of the new Québécois middle class had a sincere commitment to the ideology represented by these goals. But simple sociological analysis shows that the modernization of health and education met the requirements of their career interests, as well as the needs of social progress. Statutory per capita grants to universities and per diem subsidies for hospital beds meant that state money now flowed automatically from the public treasury into educational and health institutions. These institutions were therefore able to plan rapid development. The statutory grants were politically popular because they provided free services to hospital patients as well as subsidized education for university students; they were also, especially in their design, an inducement for institutional growth. At universities, for instance, no limits were set on the number of students – money flowed from the province simply on a head count: the effect was to induce these institutions to increase their student enrolments rapidly. With such growth, access was secured for more and more people, thereby democratizing the educational system. Simultaneously, moreover, as resources soared, these institutions could attract an increasingly qualified (and increasingly specialized) staff and reward them accordingly. Full-time careers in these institutions, once very scarce for the laity, became plentiful, and soon the introduction of the practice of tenure meant that they also became, in the universities, lifetime careers.

That the Quiet Revolution meant social progress is beyond question. It achieved increased accessibility and democratization of education, as well as improvements in the quality and accessibility of health care. It meant greater financial and bureaucratic participation by the state and rapid growth of public and para-public institutions, as well as the growth of new elites. That it also involved the secularization of Quebec society was neither so clearly foreseen nor, probably, intended. Unanticipated consequences of periods of rapid change are, however, the norm rather than the exception.

THE SECULARIZATION OF QUEBEC SOCIETY

Secularization is frequently associated with modernization in sociological literature. But the links between the two are usually far from clear and far from convincing. At the theoretical level, 'secularization' is generally defined in terms of the shrinking importance of magic and religion, as a result of the expansion of science and the scientific method. The narrowing sphere of the sacred corresponds to the expansion of knowledge, at the expense of faith and myth. Yet to conceive of secularization as a fading of myths rather than an emergence of new ones is to miss the point. Moreover, this idealistic view of secularization fails to take account of how the process takes shape and how it unfolds historically.

If the theoretical perspective on secularization is often rooted in epistemology (theories of knowledge), the popular perspective is usually put more crudely in institutional terms of ignorance and education, as a byproduct of increased (mass) education. People erroneously assume that the world of knowledge and the world of meaning are the same thing. In fact, education has or should have something to do with knowledge, while secularization has to do with the world of meaning, quite another matter indeed.

Secularization is a question of politics, not epistemology. Historically, secularization started with the separation of the Church from the State, with constitutional proclamations in France and the United States, not of a churchless society, but of a churchless state. In the case of France, this proclamation was made at the time of the Revolution to formalize the break with a feudal past. In the United States, the American Revolution needed to distance the state from an official religion (and therefore from all religions), in order to proclaim freedom of religion and accommodate the denominational pluralism of the citizens.

No such political imperatives ever existed in Britain or its dominion of Canada, where a break from feudalism never occurred (although the evolution of capitalism did) and where freedom of religion became politically tolerated and practised, not constitutionally proclaimed. Yet one can argue quite correctly that secularization took place in the 19th and 20th centuries in both Britain and English Canada. The process was the institutional consequence of the break from Roman Catholicism.

The term 'institutional secularization' refers to the process by which institutions initiated, staffed, or managed by clerics came under lay control. In the 16th and 17th centuries, when the Protestant churches broke from Roman Catholicism, whole societies were deprived of the organizational structure of the religious orders whose missions were to aid the poor, to tend the sick, and to provide education (to the extent that it had been developed). Thus new institutions had to be organized on a community basis under the aegis of the Protestant churches, with increased lay participation through voluntary associations. For these structural reasons, the process of institutional secularization took place much earlier in Protestant countries than in Catholic countries. By the 19th century, voluntary associations were well established in Protestant countries and gradual secularization of institutions was taking place. Higher education in Ontario, for example, followed this pattern. Although denominational rivalry long ensured considerable religious homogeneity among the clients and the administrators of institutions (and will probably continue to do so for some time in many places), effective and legal control by the laity, through non-profit organizations, has become firmly rooted in the social structure of Protestant countries.

In contrast, the secularization of social institutions in most Catholic countries did not take place until after the middle of the 20th century.[1] In fact, both the number of religious orders and their membership increased dramatically during the 19th and early 20th centuries in Catholic countries; the Church became progressively more involved in social institutions during that period of transition when the poor, the sick, and the ignorant, as Everett C. Hughes once put it, no longer belonged to their kin and did not yet belong to the state.

This brief historical outline sets the stage for the analysis of the secularization of Quebec, which, it must be remembered, was – and still is – a Catholic society. We will address three issues: the secularization of institutions, the massive dropout from the ranks of the clergy during the mid-1960s, and finally the substantial drop in religious practice.

The social institutions
As the Quiet Revolution swept Quebec, the Church had neither the human nor the financial resources necessary to develop the educational and health-care institutions required to meet social needs as defined by the new middle classes. These needs were broadly defined indeed: nothing short of universal access to free education up to the university level, and heavy subsidies thereafter; free hospitalization for all citizens; and (later in the 1960s) free medical care. When the State accepted such a mandate, it sealed the fate of the Church in the whole area of social institutions. Such massive and rapid investment of public money required the development of a public bureaucracy to act on behalf of the public will (at least theoretically). Neither the Church as an institution nor the traditional community elites could be the agents of this institutional development. New elites – trained in everything from accounting to engineering, from

personnel to industrial relations, from purchasing to architectural design – would swell the ranks of the new middle classes in the ever-growing public bureaucracies.

Although massive growth of public institutions took place during the 1960s, the traditional institutions had already felt great demands during the 1950s. Increasing enrolments had put pressure, for instance, on the traditional *collèges*, the institutions that had offered elite youths secondary and undergraduate education from a classical curriculum. (This *cours classique* was generally the only francophone education available beyond the elementary level.) As the number of students rose, these institutions, once staffed almost exclusively by clerics, had to begin hiring lay teachers, who cost much more than clerics. Yet state subsidies amounted to very little – some $15,000 a year per institution. The same pattern was observable in health care. In brief, the demand for education and health care was outstripping the supply. The costs of expanding the existing facilities were essentially borne by their clients and, to a real but undocumented extent, by the Church – most of whose patrimony, one can assume, was spent in this transitional period of growth preceding the financial and administrative takeover by the State and its emerging professional bureaucrats.

Once the state decided to modernize and expand the educational system by the use of incentives, the secularization of the education system was greatly accelerated. This acceleration had nothing to do, as is commonly assumed, with a growing loss of religious belief or decrease in religiosity. Rather, it came from simple economic calculation at the community level. As long as the costs of education were borne locally, through taxes raised from local pockets, it made local economic sense to have clerical teachers, who cost much less than lay teachers because they lived communally and frugally and were low-level consumers. However, once the provincial government bore an overwhelming share of the costs of education, it quickly dawned on local business people (who made up most local school boards) that it made much more sense – if not to the total local community, at least to its merchants – to seek lay people with the highest possible qualifications. Not only were their salaries highly subsidized; they were big spenders with an assured income. In contrast to nuns and priests, lay teachers paid taxes and got married. Everyone – the hairdresser, the car dealer, the real-estate agent, and the insurance salesperson – could expect some share of the action. When principle and self-interest so neatly coincided, no wonder institutional change was both swift and harmonious.

While communities were securing immediate economic advantage, however, their control over local institutions was being sapped. Whether community elites were aware of this erosion or felt it was a fair tradeoff, the fact is that bureaucratic centralization soon eclipsed the importance of the community. Norms as well as subsidies started to come from outside. Since loyalty is most often a function of dependence, the loyalty of the teaching staff belonged no longer to the school board but to the professional association, which bargained with government for working conditions and salary. In the process, school boards came to represent the government more than the community.

Similar analyses could be made in the realm of social welfare. The voluntary agencies that had traditionally been organized, staffed, and managed by the Church in local communities were now to be organized by lay professionals employed by state agencies.

This massive modernization initiated by the growing state bureaucracies was far from unique to Quebec society. It was common to all industrially developed countries, in fact. What was unique to Quebec (and to similar Catholic societies elsewhere in North America) is that the sudden, rapid secularization of social institutions was mostly conflict-free.

The exodus of clergy
During the late 1960s and the early 1970s, Quebec, like English Canada, the United States, and some European countries, quite suddenly saw a new phenomenon: priests and nuns left their vocations in droves. Part of the process may be explained by ideological changes within the Catholic church and part by the fact that the Vatican increasingly facilitated the release of individuals from their clerical vows. Equally facilitating these 'defections' in Quebec was the fact that, contrary to the situation before the Quiet Revolution, priests or nuns who left orders could now quite easily find a place for themselves within the social structure. No longer were former clerics – especially priests – viewed as having committed spiritual treason by leaving the sacred calling; no longer could a defector cope only by either leaving the society or concealing his or her previous occupation. Suddenly, with the change in the social order, ex-priests could (and did) enter the growing ranks of the public and semipublic bureaucracies. The change was so thorough and so pervasive that priests who taught religion at the Université de Montréal, which holds a pontifical charter, were able, because of tenure, to keep their positions after quitting the ranks of the clergy and celibacy. Such a situation would have been inconceivable less than a decade earlier.

Paradoxically, the same reasons that had prompted men and women to enter the clergy in remarkable numbers in the none-too-distant past could also explain the sudden, massive exodus. Without doubting the selflessness and sincere motives of those who became priests, brothers, or nuns, one can argue that, in social terms, joining the clergy of Quebec had certainly not involved downward social mobility. For women, it had meant an assurance of comfortable, if austere, living quarters and an escape from the burden of large families and domestic chores, while gaining access to socially esteemed occupations in teaching and nursing. The lifestyle of nuns, although basically other-worldly, certainly matched and often surpassed the conditions under which most married women from the same social backgrounds could expect to live. The social distance that nuns maintained from the civil society was compensated by the deference given them by the laity. The majesty of their convents contrasted with the urban tenements their married sisters occupied. Deprived of the privileges of married life, they were equally spared its burdens; on balance, entering a convent was not – and was not perceived as – an irrational decision.

For men, joining the clergy, regular or secular,[2] meant entering a career that could lead to important institutional positions. In the secular clergy, the career paths mainly involved pastoral duties in the urban and rural parishes of a geographically circumscribed diocese. A young man began as a curate, receiving only a very low stipend beyond room and board, but could fully expect to become a parish pastor some day. Promotions, based primarily on seniority, would lead as parish priest from a small, possibly rural, parish to a large urban parish. As he moved from small to large parish, his income rose substantially because it was a function of both the wealth and the size of his parish. The 'good income' years made a relatively secure retirement possible.

For the regular clergy, the career patterns varied according to the kinds of institutions run by the order – from novitiates for the training of future priests to colleges and sometimes universities, as well as shrines, publications, and social agencies involved with cooperatives or credit and trade unions. A man could aspire to positions of leadership, public recognition, and gratitude as his career reached its apex.

Quebec had long had a relatively high percentage of people who chose to follow these patterns. More or less simultaneously with the Quiet Revolution, decisions to enter the religious life suddenly shrank to a trickle, and defections increased dramatically, especially among younger nuns and priests – those who were beginning, not terminating, their careers. The shrinking role of the Church in the newly emerged social order was certainly a key factor. The Church, which had previously offered both full career patterns and social esteem, could now promise neither. One can also say that the Catholic hierarchy unwittingly helped to curtail the potential of clerical careers. Bureaucratic centralization of resources and decision-making, which became hallmarks of the new social organization, did not spare the Church itself. The career patterns of the secular clergy were drastically altered. Parish priests were suddenly transformed into functionaries on a fixed salary – and a low one at that. Any surplus resources were centralized by the bishop, who was, so the rationale went, in the best position to assess the needs of the various parishes and distribute the resources. Bureaucratically unimpeachable, this doctrine led to measures that sapped the morale of the secular clergy by suddenly eliminating the traditional pattern of rewards. Worse, parish priests and their curates realized that a priest who joined the ranks of the rapidly growing para-public institutions as a salaried professional made more than four times their income, was exempt from pastoral duties, could live in a private apartment, and, as a learned man of science, was more visible, better known, and socially esteemed in both the lay and the clerical worlds.

The decrease in religious practice
'Tradition,' Everett Hughes once pointed out in conversation, 'is sacred only so long as it is useful.' If tradition involves a mix of the sacred and the utilitarian, it follows that the first people to question its sacred character will be those for whom tradition is no longer useful. And indeed in mid-20th century Quebec, it was the intelligentsia and the new middle classes – whose careers and interests were no longer served by the traditional culture, institutions, or leadership – who first challenged the legitimacy of all three.

For traditional Quebec society, including the elites, visible religious practices were interwoven with almost every part of life. Many of these folkways all but disappeared over a very short time. For example, people had been accustomed to locate themselves by referring to the parish in which they resided; this custom rapidly disappeared as the majority of people no longer knew the names or the general locations of parish churches.

It would not be misleading to say that most of the population drifted into secularization through inattention. For the majority, estrangement from religious practice developed as a result of the Church's growing irrelevance in meeting their everyday needs. Schools were no longer linked to the Catholic parish; teachers were more apt to be lay than clerical; hospitals and clinics were professionally administered by specialists who lived far from where they worked, and neither knew nor cared to know about their clients in other than a professional capacity. The secularization of charity in the professionally operated agencies of the state left the Church not only with a shrinking role but also with half-empty buildings whose material upkeep became increasingly dependent on the continuing popularity of bingo.

The falloff was evident both in the important decisions of life and in the minutiae of daily living. Stanley Ryerson has observed in conversation how deeply Quebec society has changed: nowadays, people no longer doff their hats or cross themselves when passing in front of a church. When what was commonplace has become bizarre, when automatic, unreflecting, customary behaviour becomes unusual over a very short time, one suspects that deep changes separate the present from the immediate past. In every respect except calendar time, centuries – not decades – separate the Quebec of the 1980s from the Quebec of the 1950s.

No longer visible, now basically silent, the Church, once a dominant institution in social and collective life, withdrew to service the spiritual and private needs of those still seeking its counsel. As its political clout faded, the voice of its critics became louder. The political liberals and conservatives maintain that the Church was, in large measure, responsible for the economic underdevelopment of Quebec, because it did not impart to its flock the 'right' values, those that inspire entrepreneurial leadership and economic success. Under its leadership, they argue, Quebec's institutions failed to adapt to the requirements of a modern industrial society. The Marxists, on the other hand, take the Church to task for having collaborated with the anglophone bourgeoisie in exploiting its flock, the working class. Both charges are ideologically inspired distortions. The Church, however, no longer answers its critics. Is this a dignified silence, or the sign of its collapse as an institution?

THE CANADIAN QUESTION

By the late 1970s, a modern and secular social order had indeed emerged in Quebec society. Quebec had put its internal house in order, in line with other developed societies. In spite of this – maybe because of this – Quebec remained politically restive. It was readying itself to challenge the legitimacy of another sacred institution: the Canadian state. The internal issue of Church and society having been resolved, the external issue of state and society rose to the top of the political agenda. For Quebec society that was *the* Canadian question.

A lament for two nations

Seldom, if ever, do a conquered people give their consent to a conquering state. Conquered subjects' loyalty to the state is always suspect. This is so true that loyalty oaths are routinely administered to and taken by future civil servants. In times of crisis in national unity, these forgotten oaths become instruments of social control for those who fear for the state's security. The point is raised here not to underscore the vulnerability of those fragile freedoms known as civil liberties, but rather to call attention to the historically enduring price of political domination. Both those who created the state and those who are subject to it are forever condemned to wishful thinking: the first, to the dream of national unity, the latter, to the dream of national independence.

Those who dream of national unity are also forced to lament the absence of a commonly agreed-on history. In Canada in the 1960s, the Royal Commission on Bilingualism and Biculturalism went to great lengths and considerable expense to document this great gap. (On second thought, the commission might have realized it owed its very existence to that regrettable fact.)

Commonly agreed-on history presupposes a common celebration of either a glorious past or a common victory over an undesirable past. France can claim both; Britain can claim the first; the United States, the latter; and Canada neither. The cruelty of this observation is mitigated by the fact that political consensus can also be built on shared visions of the future. Such visions, however, must be based on the correction of history, not its denial. 'Unhyphenated Canadianism' is a mirage based on the confusion of individual biography with group history. All immigrants have a biographical break with a past in which the country of origin somehow, to some degree, became undesirable – often because of denied opportunity or political persecution; the country of adoption, by the mere fact of receiving the immigrants, symbolizes a land of opportunity or a refuge from oppression, both of which are good reasons for thanksgiving. In contrast, the French and the English in Canada are burdened with historical continuity. In both cases, the breaking with the biographical past creates not a new citizen but a marginal one. And while marginal people may invent myths and create new visions, a new political order without group consent remains beyond reach.

A political order is a symbolically mediated structure. In other words, the state, to be legitimate, must rely on the substantial – not just formal – consent of the governed. Formal consent can be engineered by manipulation, trickery, propaganda, publicity, and deception, or it can be claimed on the basis of sufficient numbers alone. Shared consent, however, requires shared meanings, shared myths. The French and the English in Canada may have a common fate, but they share no political myths. The closest they have come was the belief that Canada was a partnership between the French and the English, an idea formalized in the compact theory of Confederation, which presents dualism as central to the nature of the state. John Porter spoke of 'charter groups' – while admitting the junior status of one of them. Stanley Ryerson called Confederation an 'unequal union.' Lester Pearson, in striking the Royal Commission on Bilingualism and Biculturalism, spoke of the 'two founding races.' The commission, sensitive to the connotations that might be evoked by the word 'race,' preferred to speak of 'two societies and two cultures.' Pierre Trudeau watered the concept down still further, referring to two language communities (as though language without culture can be the basis of community) and many cultures. One need say no more to illustrate either the inability to define what Canada is or the incapacity of words to cover up an embarrassing social and political reality.

The last person to speak candidly about the social and political reality of Canada in unambiguous, well-established English words was Lord Durham, in his description of 'two nations warring in the bosom of the same state.' As mentioned at the beginning of this chapter, he recommended the subjugation of the French to the vigorous rule of the British, advice that was heeded but that did not succeed. Before Confederation, following this advice required thwarting democratic principles. With Confederation, those principles ensured political domination of the French nation.

Ever after, the word 'nation' to describe the French fact in Canada was banned from the political vocabulary of Canadian academics and politicians. To make credible this semantic confusion, it became customary to refer not to the Canadian *state* but to the Canadian *nation* – creating unity not politically but semantically.

Such obfuscation obviously requires education. Denying reality rather than assuming it is characteristic of Canadian politicians, not of ordinary Canadian citizens. On leaving or entering Quebec, Québécois and non-Québécois alike quickly perceive the reality of cultural and social differences. Some people are dumbstruck by the differences. Others are paranoid about them. Both types of reaction testify to the reality of social and cultural boundaries. The fact that this dual reality cannot find a political expression in the Canadian political system constitutes its basic vulnerability.

The compact (or dualist) theory of Confederation, the myth that so many French Canadians clung to so that they could symbolically legitimate a dignified commitment to the Canadian state, suffered an ignominious death with the patriation of the Constitution in 1982; one partner, they discovered, could force patriation without the consent of the other. That the death blow was struck by a prime minister who was himself partly French-Canadian made it no less lethal; that it involved political trickery transformed the constitutional process from grand ritual into tragic farce, making the final demise of illusion seem unreal and senseless. Rumour has it that Prime Minister Trudeau's ruthlessness in patriating the Constitution was motivated by his frantic determination to secure a niche for himself in Canadian history. Secure a niche he did indeed: whether it will be an enviable one is quite another matter.

The destruction of dualism as a shared myth through the forcible patriation of the Constitution constitutes a proof by political action, rather than national argument, of a doctrine close to Trudeau's heart: that Quebec is a province *comme les autres*. In other words, Quebec is not the homeland of a people, it is merely a region of the country, one region among ten.

In legal fiction, Quebec has become a province *comme les autres*; in social reality it has not. It also is different economically; only in the province of Quebec is the economy controlled by a minority who differ socially, culturally, and ethnically from the inhabitants. This social and historical fact has arisen partly because of the Canadian state. Therein lies its tainted legitimacy. Therein, too, lies the reason it gave birth to the dream of national independence among its subjects in Quebec.

The unreachable dream
The dream of national independence in Quebec society took root when the 'partnership' between French and English in the Canadian state was still a dominant theme in the political rhetoric. In effect, it was the suspicion that English Canadians did not in fact share this political myth that gave rise to the political alienation of the intelligentsia in Quebec society.

While the 1950s were ushered in by the strike in the asbestos mines, the 1960s were opened by the strike at Radio-Canada. Both events heralded basic changes in the sociopolitical order. The asbestos strike led to the

Quiet Revolution a decade later. The Radio-Canada strike led, some 15 years later, to the election of the Parti Québécois. With the Quiet Revolution sprang up a modernized and secularized society, founded by the state and managed by bureaucratically employed professionals. With the independence movement was born an enduring, credible challenge to the legitimacy of an externally imposed political order.

As already stated, both strikes at first glance seem paradoxical. The asbestos strike involved a multinational corporation with English-Canadian management and French workers, but it led to a questioning of the Duplessis regime and the social power of the Church. The strike at Radio-Canada involved a conflict between producers and management within the exclusively French network of the CBC but ended by being defined in ethnic terms. Neither interpretation is really paradoxical. The contradiction between objective fact and social response would be real enough in normal times, but in times of social unrest and of heightened tension it is not unusual for an event to be invested with meanings that transcend what actually happens. The discrepancy signals the major redefinitions of historical situations that precede a challenge of a political order.

The strike at Radio-Canada, unlike many strikes, directly affected the intelligentsia and initiated their political alienation. Soon they scrutinized the federal government's institutions to ascertain the amount and level of participation of francophones within them. They found this participation appallingly low, giving substance to the emerging conviction that the Canadian state is 'theirs, not ours.' Moreover, as the Royal Commission on Bilingualism and Biculturalism eventually substantiated, the few francophones who did work in these institutions had to check their mother tongue at the door. At the Montreal Harbour Board, for example, bilingual civil servants received a routine memo from their francophone boss: 'Since everybody in the department is bilingual, all reports must be written in English.' It made perfect administrative sense internally. Externally, when leaked to the press, it made no political sense, except as an example of Lord Durham's 'vigorous British rule.'

The memo was quoted in the first of a series of editorials by André Laurendeau, the prestigious editor of Le Devoir. Some months later Prime Minister Lester Pearson struck the Royal Commission on Bilingualism and Biculturalism. Noble men filled with good intentions and alarmed by the strains threatening the state, the commissioners came forth with recommendations that perpetuated, rather than eliminated, those strains. By refusing to recommend a language regime based on territory, which would have ensured the francophone majority in Quebec access in their own language to the large corporate sector of Montreal, they proclaimed Quebec the model for the treatment of 'minorities' and urged the rest of Canada to follow suit toward their French minorities. In effect, they recommended leaving Quebec untouched, in terms of language policy, and adopting measures they thought would ensure the viability of French communities outside Quebec.

This viability could not be ensured, however, since postal services and radio and television programming in French were no replacement for a vanishing economic base. Furthermore, they could not convince the politically restive Québécois that Quebec was a model, since within that 'model' they had to choose between a public-sector career in French or a private-sector career in English. If Quebec was to be a province *comme les autres*, as Trudeau insisted, it seemed elementary to correct that strange discrepancy. More skilled in provocation than in integration, Prime Minister Trudeau dismissed the terms of reference of the Royal Commission on Bilingualism and Biculturalism and proclaimed Canada to be bilingual and multicultural. While the proclamation pleased those citizens who were neither French nor English, it certainly did not guarantee any substance to ethnic cultures since they would not be celebrated in their own languages; what it did guarantee was state funds to enable colourful celebrations of official pluralism.

The official bilingualism adopted by the Canadian state was politically irrelevant for the modernizing Québécois majority and politically resented in most of English-speaking Canada. In Western Canada it smacked of privilege, since the few French Canadians living there were fully bilingual but now able to get federally funded French-language radio and television, not to mention bilingual labels on their cornflakes, while the overwhelming majority of neo-Canadians could not receive such services in their cultural languages. The reasons of state clashed with the logic of community, and the reasons of state prevailed, pitting the ethnic Canadians against the French Canadians. The very same result was achieved in Quebec by the failure of the senior government to act, leading, in 1974, the junior government under Robert Bourassa – no wild-eyed separatist but a tame Liberal – to introduce Bill 22, *la loi sur la langue officielle*. Replacing a 1969 act that had the same intent but was less comprehensive, Bill 22 announced that French was the language of the workplace and of government services. It also restricted anglophone education to children who demonstrated a prior knowledge of the English language. Thus, although the new law was loudly denounced by the anglophone media, one of its most immediate effects was to alienate from the Liberal party many of Quebec's new Canadians, who resented having to learn not one but two languages to qualify for effective citizenship.

The vocal opposition to Bill 22 in English-speaking Quebec was disseminated throughout the rest of Canada, leading the Canadian Air-Traffic Controllers' Association to challenge, in 1976, the federal official language policy. Specifically, the air controllers, fearful of eventual bilingual requirements, struck to protest the use of French by francophone pilots when talking to francophone controllers; safety in the air was threatened, the union's public statements suggested, unless both parties had to use English at all times. Until now, implementation of the federal bilingual policy had been passively resisted, as the successive annual reports of the Commissioner of Official Languages ritually attested to. The CATCA strike was, however, an official challenge by a special-interest group. Trudeau responded by solemnly proclaiming in a television address that this challenge constituted a major threat to national unity, packed his bags, went off to Bermuda, and left the whole matter in the hands of Transport Minister Otto Lang – who promptly surrendered to the demands of CATCA.

Only months later, provincial elections brought to power, to the consternation of English Canadians, the Parti Québécois, whose announced goals included the peaceful attainment of independence for Quebec. One of its first actions was to complete the francization of Quebec that Bourassa had begun. It enacted Bill 101, *la charte de la langue française*, which makes French the normal language of work, education, and public life in Quebec. Basically, its authors considered Ontario the model for the treatment of the other official language. But what is normal in Ontario and elsewhere in Canada is considered by those regions to be outrageous in Quebec.

In response to the election of a 'separatist' government in Quebec, Trudeau struck a Task Force on Canadian Unity, headed by Jean-Luc Pepin and John Robarts. Its report, however, did not take sufficient umbrage at Bill 101 and was not only ignored but swiftly denounced, on the very day of its release, by Don Johnston, MP for Westmount–St Henri, then a Liberal backbencher but soon to be promoted to Trudeau's cabinet. Proud of his interview in the electronic media, Johnston eventually had the transcript translated into French and distributed in both languages to his constituents. In it, he solemnly proclaimed his and his constituents' rejection of the Pepin-Robarts Report. The grounds? First, history teaches us one thing: if you leave a minority at the mercy of a majority, its rights will not be protected. And that is what the Pepin-Robarts Report did.

Second, our French-Canadian compatriots would be 'condemned' to live all their lives only in French, a fate presumably worse than death. If Don Johnston was right about the fate of minorities at the hands of majorities, he made it the duty of every self-respecting Québécois to become an *indépendantiste*. By equating living one's life only in French to a sentence, he clearly shows that taking the role of the others is not an automatic consequence of living in their midst.

The Parti Québécois had won its electoral victory preaching sovereignty-association – political independence for Quebec within an economic union with Canada – but had promised to seek a specific mandate before attempting to negotiate the change with Ottawa. A referendum was announced for May 1980, and the federal Liberals combined with the provincial party to throw enormous amounts of money and advertising into the campaign. The referendum failed – a joyless victory of national unity. English Canadians stopped holding their breath, even when the PQ unexpectedly won another victory at the polls the next year. What the referendum had done was to make the dream of national independence unreachable.

Then Trudeau delivered on his promise of 'renewed federalism'; in 1982 the Constitution was repatriated without Quebec's consent. The PQ resisted federal blandishments to sign, but in its eagerness to retain power, it loosened some requirements of Bill 101 (which even in its original form was felt by some Québécois to give insufficient protection to the French culture and language), and it announced a new, quasi-federalist platform that drove several well-known *indépendantistes* to leave its ranks. Those moves proved too much for the Quebec electorate. Although they had voted overwhelmingly against the Liberals in the federal election of 1984, sweeping the Conservatives to victory, a few months later they voted almost as decisively *for* the provincial Liberals – the party that, after all, had come to power in 1960 under the slogan *maîtres chez nous*.

The outcome of the referendum and the purge of the *indépendantistes* from the Parti Québécois spells not the end of Québec's 'national' movement, but the end of its embodiment by a specific political party. It also means that the strategy to achieve independence will not follow the route of party politics. A return to less institutionalized forms of political mobilization is not to be excluded.

CONCLUSION

This essay ends on a melancholy note of disillusionment with statesmanship and party politics in this country. It does not claim to be non-partisan or dispassionate. It is a plea, a public and desperate one, for the youth of this country to distance themselves from the political culture they are exposed to. It is especially a plea to young English Canadians not to accept either the new demonology on Quebec or the idea that all is returning to 'normal' there, but to resolve to help to bring to birth eventually a state that will truly enjoy the consent of the governed.

NOTES

Originally published in M. Michael Rosenberg, William B. Shaffir, Allan Turowetz, and Morton Weinfeld, eds, *An Introduction to Sociology* (Toronto, 1983)

1 The exception was France, where after the Revolution the state took over the direct organization of education, producing bitter internal conflict that lasted more than a century.

2 Catholic priests may be regular or secular clerics. The regular clerics are those who are members of a particular order, such as the Basilians, the Sulpicians, and the Jesuits, and live under its rule (hence 'regular'); they take vows of celibacy, poverty, and obedience (to the hierarchy of the order). Although an order sometimes accepts the responsibility of running a parish, each views itself as having one or more special mandates, which in Quebec before the 1960s was most often education, health, or some form of social service for active orders. (Some orders are strictly contemplative.)

In contrast, secular clerics take a vow of celibacy, but not of poverty or obedience. They work under the local bishop (whose assignment comes from Rome) and run most parishes, as well as other institutions under direct diocesan control.

All nuns and religious brothers are regular clerics.

The rise and demise of
the Parti Québécois

HISTORY, POLITICAL ACTION, AND SOCIAL SCIENCE

History, one must be reminded, can only be read backwards. The meaning of events only becomes clear well after they have happened. The outcome of events always strays away from the intentions of those who set them in motion. While this may be frustrating for those who wish to shape the future, it is rather reassuring for the rest of us who have to live it. Without this measure of ultimate uncertainty, concerted human action would become pointless. Furthermore, because the outcome of events outwits those who set them in motion, the main protagonists on the political stage are in no better a position to understand history than those of us who stayed in the wings or were purely political spectators. In other words, Mulroney doesn't understand his election better than we do, and Bourassa can only, like you and I, marvel at his political come-back. Paradoxically, it is precisely the unintended consequences of conscious political action that ensure its continued relevance and necessity.

Insight is much closer to hindsight than is commonly suspected and it requires a constant fascination with the recent past much more than an inside knowledge of the short-term political goals of the current establishments. Illuminating the recent past is the most that the social sciences can promise with a measure of competence and confidence and, when achieved, it is no small accomplishment. Making sense of what previously baffled one requires the ability to detach oneself from the political dreams one may espouse. It does not require dropping them, only placing them in abeyance, especially when they seem within reach.

Such caution is no longer necessary, however, since nearly all the dreams that were conceived during the sixties and seventies lie shattered in the eighties. Martin Luther King's dream of racial equality in the United States, Solidarity's dream of political democracy in Poland, the dreams of social equality that kindled socialist movements in Western democracies – all of these dreams and the social forces they generated are so clearly spent and have so totally vanished that they seem to be part of a distant, bygone era. The recent past appears strange and folkloric, not only to the new generations who did not witness it, but also for those who lived it.

THE BAFFLING QUESTION

That history is full of the unpredictable is borne out by the political events in Quebec society since the referendum of 1980. The re-election of the Parti Québécois was a surprise, but nothing compared to what was forthcoming. At the bginning of the, since endemic, economic crisis of the early 1980s, the Parti Québécois proceeded to deliberately initiate a labour conflict with its most committed supporters, namely the public- and parapublic-service employees. Not content to freeze the wages of public servants, it deliberately provoked their disaffection by rolling back their wages, an unprecedented move that was not imitated anywhere else. Why?

The next baffling episode was enacted in 1985: the purge, with René Lévesque's blessing, of the elements within the Parti Québécois unconditionally committed to independence. Subsequently, we witnessed a leadership race so democratic that anyone could join the party and immediately have a direct vote in the choice of the next leader. We witnessed a leadership campaign that, in spite of widespread media attention and regional debates, was received with a gaping yawn of public apathy signalling the fact that no one had any doubts about, or any interest in, the outcome.

The election called by the newly chosen leader, Pierre-Marc Johnson, and the campaign that ensued are noteworthy for only two things. The first is Johnson's personal ego trip, evidenced by the size of his picture in the election posters, and the practical elimination from these of any reference to the Parti Québécois. All candidates running for the Parti Québécois had to have more than half of their election posters capped with a reference, not to the party, but to Johnson. The second event worth noting was the fact that the campaign speeches heralded as containing policy statements, and they were few, were delivered in front of business groups only. Johnson's political reference group was to be as clearly signalled to the electorate as his personal appropriation of the Parti Québécois. He stated bluntly that he was concerned exclusively with the development of wealth and not with its equitable distribution. Johnson's newly publicized ideological convergence with the Montreal Board of Trade was personally as well as politically rooted. That fact does not make it less politically surprising, even though it does make it less sociologically baffling.

The Johnson take-over of the Parti Québécois is not, in itself, an important event. Whose interests he wants to represent is a much more important question. Who would have thought in 1976, with the election of the Parti Québécois to power in Quebec – an event that shocked and panicked the business community – that only ten years later the very same party would so clearly proclaim itself in total harmony with that community? Who would have thought, when the Parti Québécois's political victory created a climate of public euphoria among the Québécois, that a short decade later René Lévesque would be forced out of its leadership? Who would have thought that the youth who were so emotionally committed to the dream of independence would become totally politically apathetic?

Finally, one must ask: does the demise of the Parti Québécois spell the end of the national movement in Quebec? The estrangement from the Parti Québécois of the militants for independence, and the demobilization of the part of the electorate committed to the same goal, raise the question of the continued credibility of the national movement in Quebec. Is the movement politically dead or is it only the death of the politically naïve strategy to achieve it? The demise of the Parti Québécois and the future of the national movement in Quebec form the subject of this essay.

THE SEVENTIES: THE POLITICS OF EXAGGERATION

The seventies were ushered in with the October crisis. The crisis was generated as much by the panic of the uprooted doves as by the romantic revolutionaries of the FLQ. The former, Pierre Elliott Trudeau, Jean Marchand, and Gérard Pelletier, had acceded to the centre of the political stage after having successfully challenged the conservative political regime of Duplessis with the promise of modernization. They were called to Ottawa, however, to contain the burgeoning movement for national independence in Quebec.

The progressive alienation of Quebec from Canadian politics was signalled by the more than cool reception of the queen in Quebec City and the famous St Jean Baptiste parade of 1968, when Trudeau, Drapeau, and the others, in the review stand, were suddenly pelted with various projectiles. Trudeau bravely withstood the affront without flinching but subsequently forayed very sporadically into Quebec, only in very safe territory and only with very friendly company. This is easily understood, since bravery cannot be everyday behaviour, and the brave hero of one day may suffer delayed shock, which is obviously not newsworthy.

The distancing of Trudeau and company increased when they were unable to avert the growth of the independence movement within the ranks of the new middle classes, whose aspirations they formerly represented as critics of the clerico-nationalist regime of Duplessis. They were increasingly defined as outsiders and, increasingly, they behaved in the manner in which they were defined.

Meanwhile they were being outflanked on the left. Those who succeeded them as leaders of, and intellectuals committed to, the labour movement turned to Marx rather than to Lord Acton and the papal encyclicals for guidance. As *Parti Pris* succeeded *Cité Libre*, small groups of middle-class students, mesmerized by the aura surrounding Castro's Cuban revolution and Che Guevara's romantic appeal, formed the FLQ, initiating a symbolic attack on the Canadian state by placing primitive dynamite bombs in Westmount mailboxes, in army depots, and on railway tracks. Fed by Franz Fanon's essays, they daringly broke from their families' political culture and, to their parents' despair, became revolutionaries. Pierre Vallières, who, for a short time, was scheduled to replace Trudeau as the editor of *Cité Libre*, eventually wrote, instead, *The 'White Niggers' of America*. While the book's title was shocking, its contents were not for most Québécois who, unlike Trudeau, would not blame Monseigneur Paquet for our economic ills. Monseigneur Paquet was a prominent theologian at the turn of the century who stated, that we, the French, had Truth (Faith), and that material things were best left to the Protestants. Under Vallières's intellectual leadership, the second wave of the FLQ focused on industrial conflicts to symbolize their self-proclaimed status as the vanguard of the working class. During the late sixties, we witnessed the unforeseen blossoming of the student movement, the political mushrooming of Maoism within it, as well as the official institution of the Company of Young Canadians, with its romantic dream of changing the system by political activism at the neighbourhood level. It is within this climate of adventurism that the last wave of the FLQ stole the show.

Impressed by the political kidnappings of the Tupamaros in Central America, they undertook to imitate them and kidnapped James Cross, the commercial attaché of the British consulate in Montreal. They made world headlines because it was the first time that people had resorted to kidnapping as a tactic to bring about political change in a liberal democratic country of the Western world. We were accustomed to the use of such tactics in Middle Eastern and Latin American countries, perennially and contemptuously referred to as 'banana republics.' But it was unexpected here. And, for that reason, it became an event of world-wide interest.

The FLQ cells that created the October crisis were sociologically astute as well as thoroughly knowledgeable about the role of the media in mass society and the craving for status that ferments within it. This is evidenced by the fact that they chose radio, rather than television or the newspapers, as their vehicle. Since the transistor revolution, radios have become personal possessions that can be carried everywhere. The radio lent itself to compulsive listening patterns of a mass audience by allowing for sudden interruptions of the regular programming with news bulletins about a political kidnapping. The astuteness of the FLQ was further illustrated by the judicious choice of addressing their 'communiqués' to the least prestigious member of the media – precisely, the radio newscaster who reads the news from a telex every hour on the hour. To signal that their choice was not a random one, they equally chose to give their scoops to the radio stations with the lowest ratings. And succeed they did, in generating a pattern of compulsive listening that had everyone emotionally and psychologically exhausted on Monday, having been rivetted to their radios all weekend long. Second, they chose to write their manifesto in street French. This had a shock effect, because the media always laundered street language; all Québécois could see a reflection of themselves, whether they spoke only street French or not. In contrast to the shocking form, the content touched sensitive strings in a people who had been, for a long time, conscious of being on the short end of the stick. Faced with a list of FLQ demands, the one Trudeau and company decided to accept was to publish and televise the manifesto.

Deliberate or unwitting, that decision proved to be a major blunder. In the week that followed, the manifesto's impact on the people of Quebec was impressive. While they overwhelmingly disapproved of the FLQ's methods, they vehemently appoved of their aims. Trudeau and associates had misread the impact of the manifesto. When they saw the politically volatile situation they had helped to create, they panicked. The invocation of the War Measures Act made it a crime to agree with the aims of the FLQ at the very time that the Québécois were coming to endorse those aims. For that matter they still do so, though quietly.

The October crisis was as much the consequence of Trudeau, Pelletier, and Marchand's estrangement from the political constituency they claimed to represent as it was of the romantic revolutionary dreams of no more than a dozen restless young people. Trudeau proclaimed an apprehended insurrection and Marchand, the least uprooted of the three Québécois, genuinely believed a vast conspiracy was afoot. He thereby secured, with the help of Aislin, a place in history, albeit in the annals of famous cartoons.

John Turner, then minister of justice, could not divulge the extent of the apprehended insurrection for reasons of national security. He clearly stated, however, that there was ample reason to invoke the War Measures Act and to militarily occupy the province of Quebec to protect it from what we now know to have been a very small group of poorly organized and resourceless young people. It is remarkable that he has never been held accountable by the citizens of this country.

The War Measures Act produced the summary arrest of nearly 500 people, 435 of whom were later released without charges. Only 16 people were eventually sentenced. Claude Ryan, then editor of Le Devoir, was suspected of attempting to organize 'parallel government' and Frank Scott, the eminent jurist of McGill University, spoke of treason; this shows to what extent the incredible was willingly believed and acted upon. Claude Ryan, the suspect, informed me some time later that a third of the names of persons to be arrested had been struck from the list by the deputy minister of justice for Quebec. The list of those eliminated constituted a real 'who's who' of Quebec society.

Such overreaction could only have been fuelled, some believe, by incredible police misinformation. Others believe that Trudeau deliberately created the crisis in order to eliminate the PQ along with the FLQ. Both could be true. However, the exercise smacked of tactics not associated with a solidly entrenched democracy but rather with governments that rule over a foreign people.

To interpret the FLQ crisis in terms of a ritual of national subjugation might seem far-fetched. It becomes more credible when one realizes the vitriolic nature of the letters to the editors, published in the English press, during the October crisis. No distinctions were being made between the PQ and the FLQ, leading Bryce Mackasey – in one of his nobler moments – to state bravely that he was ready to lay down his life for the distinction!

With the assassination of Pierre Laporte, the FLQ lost all credibility and support among the Québécois. The PQ, however, lost none. Its support, on the contrary, expanded among the Québécois, who chose this fashion to protest the official affront to its dignity and to dismiss the self-appointed, juvenile liberators.

The politics of exaggeration did not stop with the October crisis. Two other sets of events contributed to the progress of the PQ. The first was the issue of collective bargaining in the public sector which led to the common-front strike and the eventual imprisonment of the labour leaders. The other concerned language issues, and was initiated with the passage of Bill 22 by the Bourassa government and was terminated with the air-traffic controllers' successful challenge to the implementation of the Official Languages Act. Both sets of events had a political pay-off for the PQ.

In the euphoric days of the 'Quiet Revolution,' the right to strike was extended to public servants. In the process the government, which in normal collective-bargaining situations is at least officially a neutral third party, assumed an ambiguous status. When it came to deal with its own employees it became an interested party, as well as the final arbiter. Furthermore, with the growth of the public and parapublic sector, it became increasingly important for the government to plan its labour costs. To achieve this, it wanted to negotiate with all its employees in all sectors at the same time and at the same central table. In response, the three major unions created what became known as a common front. Naturally, what could best be achieved among unions, unaccustomed to forming coalitions, was to agree on the minimum to be demanded for those public employees at the very bottom of the wage scale. Wages for workers above this level would be adjusted proportionately. This produced a deadlock in negotiations that would not be broken at the highest levels by either party. As a consequence, an illegal strike took place and the labour leaders were jailed, an unprecedented event in the political annals of Quebec.

The lack of sociological sophistication among the technocrats, who were determined to make their financial forecasting less cumbersome, led them to create a crisis. Yet, the desire for confrontation was not absent from the highest ranks of the labour oligarchy. In the late sixties and early seventies, two of the major unions, the Centrale des Enseignants du Québec and the Confédération des Syndicats Nationaux, wrote manifestos couched in inflammatory, Marxist rhetoric. Marxism, at that time, had not yet conceived of the relative autonomy of the state in capitalist society. The state was, therefore, unquestionably a tool of monopoly capitalism, and hence, necessarily exploitive of its workers. Once again the politics of exaggeration had taken over the course of events with the eventual outcome already mentioned. The Bourassa government suffered, none the less, a loss of legitimacy among the working class which, while it was unprepared for the violent overthrow of the state, felt that jailing labour leaders was an inappropriate method of settling labour disputes.

The language issue flared up in the seventies. Five years after the October crisis and two years after the common-front strike, the Bourassa government brought down Bill 22. Its purpose was to make French the official language of Quebec – a reasonable initiative; even, one could argue, a rather tardy one. It required all professionals to be able to handle French in the exercise of their profession in Quebec – a not unreasonable expectation. While this feature of the bill produced some resentment, what infuriated the English and the immigrants in Quebec was the clear-cut intention of Bill 22: the forcible integration of immigrants into the French public-school system.

For the English, it constituted a clear and present threat to the viability of their institutions. The completeness of their institutions had been artificially maintained, one might say, by the absorption of immigrants. Left to their own numbers, the English could not have maintained that complete set of institutions, which is still theirs, but would have had to share those institutions with the surrounding majority and abide by their rules of the game. The immigrants, however, did not come to Quebec out of a sense of proletarian solidarity but, on the contrary, to avoid the proletarian fate that awaited them in their native countries. Bill 22, in this context, constituted an additional hurdle to overcome in their quest for mobility.

What triggered their emotional mobilization, however, was a feature of Bill 22 that was a clear-cut exaggeration. The children of immigrants, in order to qualify to enter an English school, had to pass a language test. That their children had to be subjected to the pressures inherent in such a situation produced much resentment. The immigrants massively defected from the Liberal party and, thereby, contributed to the Liberal defeat in 1976.

Bill 22 gained a terrible reputation, and widespread refusal to comply with its provisions was prevalent. That included open defiance of the law by the Protestant School Board of Greater Montreal. It was bitterly denounced in the English press, and the old alliance between the English and the Liberal party was shattered while feeble attempts were being made to revive the Union Nationale.

Being the victim of exaggeration does not preclude one from having one's own exaggerations. And that is precisely what happened, a very short time later, when the air-traffic controllers went on strike against the use of French in the air. This constituted an open challenge to the implementation of the Official Languages Act of Canada. The English in Quebec initiated a massive petition supporting the air-traffic controllers, who were, by then, joined by the airline pilots' association. The Québécois majority silently witnessed this exaggeration and, a few short months later, voted the PQ into office.

Past exaggerations that have been sanctioned by custom are sometimes known as acquired rights. That much of this took place in Quebec prior to the activist 1970s has to be underlined. Twenty-five years ago, in Montreal, Bell Telephone operators answered in English first. Immigrant taxi drivers, who could speak only a faltering English and no French, were still issued licences. When they were required, eventually, to pass a bilingual test, *The Gazette* protested this as an immeasurable burden on poor immigrants. In order to be hired by a major Crown corporation a francophone had to be bilingual. Not so for an anglophone. The Task Force on Canadian Unity discovered but did not publicize the fact that, even by the late seventies, 49 per cent of the higher federal civil servants from the province of Quebec were English although the English-speaking people constituted less than 20 per cent of the population. While the underrepresentation of the English in the Quebec civil service is continually harped upon, their preponderance in the corporate world is never mentioned. Playing victim is indeed everyone's preference.

THE PQ YEARS: FROM MOVEMENT TO PARTY POLITICS

In a two-party system, in the best of times, it is difficult to ascertain whether a party was voted into office, or whether the party in power was voted out of office. In times of frustration and exacerbation, which the politics of the early seventies embodied, it becomes even more problematic. In 1976, it would seem a pretty accurate assessment to say that the English and the immigrants voted the Liberals out of office and that the Québécois voted the PQ into office.

The day after the PQ victory, consternation and apprehension, bordering on panic, constituted the mood of English-speaking Quebec. Panic was strongest among the small- and medium-sized English and Jewish firms. The multinational corporations were stunned to find themselves in the unusual situation of knowing no one in the new political cabinet. Panic was unnecessary, however, since their managerial personnel were in touch then, as before, with the provincial bureaucrats and could, therefore, establish lines of communication.

The PQ was sternly reminded by the English media that it was elected for the purpose of good government not for the purpose of achieving independence. The PQ itself created the ambiguity clouding the meaning of its victory. 'L'étapisme,' or the promise to hold a referendum prior to any movement towards achieving independence, shrouded the meaning of its mandate. Had the PQ been elected because of this promise or would it have been elected anyway? Maurice Pinard, McGill University sociologist, told me shortly after the election that his data showed they would have been elected anyway.

The PQ's hesitation and embarrassment surrounding the referendum issue, it has since become clear, was not basically a question of strategy and tactics. It indicated a deep cleavage within the leadership of the party itself that dated back to its very formation by the fusion of the radical Rassemblement pour l'Indépendence Nationale (RIN) with the more moderate Mouvement Souveraineté-Association. It can, indeed, be assumed that all the indecision about the date of the referendum and the nature of the question to be asked was a function of the inner tension within the party.

This ambivalence was best characterized by René Lévesque himself, whose bolt from the Liberal party was inspired as much by pique as by principle. The very name given to his political offspring, Mouvement Souveraineté-Association, can be read as meaning reconfederation as much as independence. The referendum question, itself, carries both connotations and, in his book *Option Québec*, René Lévesque speaks glowingly of the new economic relations to be established between a sovereign Quebec and Canada as 'de nouvelles intimités.' (The first time I became aware that economic relations could be described in sexual terms.) René Lévesque's ambivalence was further evidenced when, for two elections, he deliberately chose to run in a riding where the outcome was very highly determined by a sizeable immigrant vote. Both times he lost. Final evidence of his ambivalence rests upon the hesitation and reservation with which he finally moved on the language issue – where he followed more than he led the party.

That René Lévesque embodied the aspirations of the Québécois was evidenced in defeat as much as in victory. That he equally embodied their hesitations is less well-known and never emphasized. But he did. One of his favourite expressions, 'il ne faut pas charier,' means that one should not go overboard, and he used it as much to characterize the more radical elements of his own party as he did Pierre Bourgault, the leader of the RIN, whom he perceived as reckless, impulsive, and radical. What he sought was sovereignty-association and he always insisted on both elements. At most he sought a reconfederation. That ambiguity is consistent with the unending polls, checking the pulse of public opinion. The polls always indicated that the people's choice, in increasing order of preference, was: the status quo, independence, sovereignty-association, and renewed federalism. The bitter taste of renewed federalism, empty of content at that time, was yet to come.

While René Lévesque could not bring himself to burn his bridges with Canada, he did burn his bridges with the traditional culture of Quebec. He actually embodies the newly secularized society and he shed an old wife to espouse a new one while in office, clearly signalling his distance from the religion of his forefathers, which still forbade such conduct. While divorce is now commonplace in Quebec and far from shocking anymore, it none the less distanced him and his party from the traditional elements in society, who are now out of power, ageing and silent, but who yet retain their right to vote.

While René Lévesque was taking his chances with the outcome of the afterlife, he was prudent about the uncharted course that a proclamation of independence would have created. Those people in Quebec still unwilling to take their chances with the afterlife by dropping the faith of their forefathers felt that he was a reckless leader precisely because of his gamble with the afterlife. The vast majority of the more active and militant members of the PQ had taken their distance from the religious component of the traditional culture. Less worried by the wrath of God than the Queen's army, some elements were pushing to set aside other elements of the tradition. When Lise Payette, during the referendum, heaped scorn on the 'Yvettes,' it generated an issue for the 'non' forces who, prior to that moment, could not get their act together. The momentum of the referendum campaign changed course after that incident. It was, therefore, appropriate that Lise Payette shared centre stage with René Lévesque on the night of the referendum defeat in the Paul Sauvé Arena.

The Lévesque government did go some way towards liberalizing the availability of abortions by refusing to prosecute Dr Morgentaler after three juries had acquitted him. Yet, Lévesque, as leader of the party, refused to endorse policy resolutions emanating from the party congress that would have gone further in the process of liberalization of the abortion laws. As a political man, he rightly sensed that further estrangement would be politically suicidal. Some feminists might say that he drew the line not on divorce, which affected him, but on abortion, which affected women.

Fear of the unknown and the uncharted explains the outcome of the referendum. In any event, the referendum was a handicapped race with a 20 per cent advantage given to the 'non' forces at the start. It was, indeed, a foregone conclusion that the English and the immigrants could decide, and did, whether the French nation should accede to independence or not. It is quite clear to me that only under these conditions could a referendum on this issue have been allowed to take place. François-Albert Angers, an eminent nationalist economist from the Ecole des Hautes Etudes Commerciales, was the only person, true to his loner style, to have raised the issue.

The issue he raised was the following one: Democracy is an internal political principle predicated on the equal status of all citizens who all have the same political franchise. When it comes to international relations, democracy as a principle vaporizes; it is not one nation, one vote – as the purely symbolic importance of United Nations resolutions clearly indicates. Angers stated that since the holding of a referendum could only be based on the principle of national self-determination, it made no sense to give the anglophones and immigrants in Quebec the right to vote on the issue while depriving the French Canadians outside of Quebec of the same right. His logic was unimpeachable but his politics were naïve. He was curtly rebuked with a reference to Fascism. For François-Albert Angers it is not an unusual event to find himself in a situation wherein he is not being heard, but is being rebuffed. For that matter, so did St Jean Baptiste preach in the desert.

The outcome of the referendum, a joyless victory for the 'non' forces, was a bitter defeat for those who were deadly serious about their aspirations for political independence. But we know that this did not mean all of the membership of the PQ. Pierre-Marc Johnson's father wrote a book entitled *Egalité ou Indépendance?* The title suggests that independence is to be used as a threatened alternative rather than as an end in itself. It is indeed a bit odd to present a dream as a threat. But it does make Pierre-Marc Johnson's decision to postpone, indefinitely, the dream of independence, so conceived, much less baffling. What lost all credibility after the referendum was not the dream of independence but the use of independence as a threat.

With the referendum still very much a recent event when the Constitutional Conference was called by Trudeau, René Lévesque and his constitutional adviser, Claude Morin, made the mistake of accepting the invitation to attend and left themselves at a loss for a posture. Taking a hard line would both look incongruous and seem in defiance of the referendum result. Reluctantly they attended, and were then suckered into giving up Quebec's right to veto the patriation in exchange for nothing. Outraged, they left, the victims of political trickery.

Renewed federalism, Trudeau-style, had been revealed. And so it is that the Canadian constitution moved from London to Ottawa. In fact, it came home the same way it was conceived: in stealth, secrecy, wheeling and dealing, and without any popular participation. In academic lingo, this is translated in the oft-repeated dictum that the Fathers of Confederation were not idealists but pragmatists – the implication being that this is the Canadian way. Indeed! In the process the only political myth that provided a modicum of dignity for the French participation in the Canadian state, namely the 'compact theory' of Confederation, went to the dustbin.

The referendum defeat, most people assumed, would lead to the PQ's defeat at the end of its mandate. It was not to be. Partly because of the uninspiring and 'school-marmish' style of Claude Ryan's leadership but perhaps, also, because of a wish to remain the perennial riddle to outsiders, the 'peuple québécois' re-elected the PQ for a second mandate. A consolation prize, one could surmise, but possibly also a signal to Trudeau and the federal Liberals of their discontent with the degradation ritual to which they had been subjected.

Stung to the quick by the degradation ritual Trudeau had inflicted on Quebec at the Constitutional Conference, the Conseil Nationale of the PQ introduced, as a defiant gesture, and over the opposition of its political leader, Article 1 of its program, categorically stating its commitment to independence. Miffed, René Lévesque insisted on a referendum within the PQ, irreverently called the 'Renérendum' by his baffled supporters, that would allow future elections *not* to be fought on the issue of independence. He was granted what he so doggedly insisted upon.

At that very precise moment the PQ leader had decided that the party would no longer lay claim to embody the national movement in Quebec. This only became clear to outsiders like ourselves in 1985 with the purge from the party of those committed to independence as a *goal* rather than as a threat. Paradoxically, René Lévesque, who up until then had systematically avoided the politics of exaggeration, started to indulge in them. What is more baffling is that he indulged at the expense of his own political constituency.

As a result of the squeeze in public finances brought about by the economic crisis of the eighties, not only did the PQ freeze the salaries of public and parapublic employees, the very core of its committed followers, but it rolled back their wages by 20 per cent. In no other public bureaucracy in Canada did a government go to such extremes. This was done in violation of a contract agreement that was still operative. A salary freeze could have been interpreted in pure economic terms; the roll-back has to be explained in political terms, and the only explanation that makes sense is that the leader had opted to disaffiliate his party from the national movement. The alienation and estrangement from the party of the die-hard *indépendantiste* had to be signalled clearly by the leader. A better signal than a wage cut-back is very hard to conceive.

Once the dissociation of the PQ from the national movement is assumed, the political alliance between the PQ and Mulroney's Conservative party becomes credible. In exchange for a political revenge against the federal Liberals, who sheepishly let Trudeau scorn Quebec in the patriation issue, the PQ made an alliance with the Tories, in whose ranks anti-French sentiment is politically entrenched, with the Lyons and the Nielsens embodying the tradition. And Brian Mulroney, 'le p'tit gars de Baie Comeau,' could proclaim that 'national reconciliation' was around the corner and, once again, its content would be the same as renewed federalism: *niente*.

This interpretation assumes that the initial coalition between the RIN and Mouvement Souveraineté-Association (MSA) which gave rise to the PQ could no longer be maintained by the personal charisma of René Lévesque. Indeed, the failure of the referendum and the disastrous results of the Constitutional Conference put the PQ in a political dilemma: it either had to raise the political ante by mobilizing its supporters and entering into confrontational politics with Ottawa or it had to lay aside its national aspirations. René Lévesque, for whom sovereignty and association were inextricably linked, was wary of the uncharted course of events that confrontational politics might entail and chose the course of national abdication.

It, therefore, followed that those who were unwilling to shelve the national question should leave the party and to signal it clearly. Pierre-Marc Johnson, whose ego need for public display is insatiable, was chosen as the dauphin and executor. He promptly tabled the goal of independence, called an election, and was disastrously defeated. He was, none the less, pleased by the results because never before had he gotten such public exposure.

Meanwhile, René Lévesque made a pathetic exit from politics, dumped by his own followers, roasted on television, and sent on his way with an American Express card for a trip around the world. It made me feel I was watching 'The Price Is Right.' And he knew it too, as he melancholically referred, in his acknowledgment of this gift, to the American Express slogan: 'ne partez pas sans elle ... mais partez.' After having failed to deliver the dream he had kindled, René Lévesque surrendered it in the fall of 1985. In two years we witnessed the pitiful exodus from politics of the two major political figures from Quebec. Trudeau, after having done 'la job de bras' for which he had been chosen, left politics, unloved as he wished, in a frantic display of last-minute patronage, cynically giving credence, in his last gestures, to the stereotype of corrupt Quebec political culture to which anglophones so dearly cling. Blaming the victim is nothing new in the Dominion and for Trudeau it was the substance of his political career.

The unexpected change of direction of the PQ requires an explanation. I have already suggested the inner tensions of the party, the ambiguity surrounding the meaning of their victory, the preoccupation with not going overboard. Social-movement theory also suggests that social movements, born of unrest and dissatisfaction with the status quo, are bound, if successful, to become institutionalized over time. The consequences of success are increased membership, increased resources, a need for organization, easy access to membership, increased social respectability, substitution of goals, growth of oligarchy, and attenuation of conflict. It would be easy, indeed, to substantiate these stages in the history of the PQ. Its activist stage, feeding on the indictments of the status quo, is to be found in the RIN where it was much more a movement than a party. With the fusion of the MSA and the RIN, the movement became a political party, and this is a major step in the process of institutionalization. It means that the movement accepts the political rules of the game in order to get into office. Once elected, it means its membership has broadened, its resources have increased, and it becomes burdened with the responsibilities of government. This brings the movement into constant interaction not with its political base but with its political opponents – in this case, the business community and the federal bureaucrats. Since, in a liberal democratic state, public funds are spent to a considerable extent in the private economy through contracts and subsidies, the swell in the membership can, and will, be motivated by normal profit motive rather than ideological commitment. As the bridges between the state and the corporate world get built, as the gulf between the PQ cabinet and the corporate world is bridged, a new configuration of social worlds and common understanding takes shape. Unexpected links get forged and communication networks get established. In the process these foreign worlds become familiar to each other. Finally, once *in* office, *staying* in office becomes at least as important as the goal that motivates the quest in the first place. It is quite clear that by the end of its second mandate the PQ was fully institutionalized, and that the goal of staying in office had superseded the goal of independence. By the time the last lack-lustre leadership race took place, its membership was overwhelmingly composed of yuppies rather than radical nationalists.

The last question to be raised in this essay concerns the consequences for the national movement in Quebec of the demise of the PQ. Many would like to think that it spells the end of the separatist threat. The more naive would even go so far as to think that the Québécois have had a change of heart. More realistically, it can be cogently argued that a political issue cannot be kept in the forefront indefinitely. It either advances or recedes.

The real lesson to be learned from the demise of the PQ is that the aims of the national movement will not be reached by the route of party politics. An incredible dose of political naïvety was necessary to imagine that one can achieve an independent state by taking over part of a political apparatus designed, and controlled, by the state from which one wants to sever ties. Independence is not won by infiltration. The states that achieved independence by ballot-box were states whose masters no longer wished to retain control and preferred to leave them to their own devices. A referendum is a ritual which should symbolize a 'fait accompli' not a political dream.

NOTE

Written for this volume, May 1986, Montreal

The other options of
the national movement in Quebec

Although the referendum defeat and the purge of the *indépendantistes* from the Parti Québécois do not spell the end of the national movement in Quebec, they do close a chapter in its history: namely, the attempt to achieve independence through party politics. The options still open to the national movement in this new context become the topics discussed in this essay.

Parting company with the Parti Québécois is widely perceived as a serious setback, if not a fatal blow, to the national movement in Quebec. I will claim that on closer scrutiny the parting of the ways with party politics is more a blessing than a blow. The first argument has to do with the nature of social movements. We tend to over-celebrate organization. Deep changes are often reached through drift rather than a plotted course. Poets certainly rival organization men in this process and, while meanings spread, they do not spread like merchandise. Commitment more than cash is required; mobilization rather than marketing is effective. Deep changes, Herbert Blumer taught us, are often the outcome of diffuse, general social movements rather than specific and visibly organized ones. 'Black is beautiful' was a revolutionary change in self-concept with manifold meanings that cut across very different and often competing groups and organizations: it evokes deep unspoken feelings that bind people; it speaks to outsiders; it is both a rebuttal and a proclamation. American blacks entered a new era, stood up, took pride in themselves, and claimed their place in America.

'Je me souviens' is also full of meanings that reach deeper in the past and deeper in the soul than 'egalité ou indépendance' or 'souveraineté-association' can convey. It links the past's painful memories and unfulfilled dreams to the broken promises of the uncertain present; it is the unspoken common bond that unites otherwise bitter rivals; it expresses the silent solidarity of a people that transcends the conflicts of current party politics. It is a proclamation of continuity that forever binds the future to the past. Breaking the national movement's ties to party politics can mark a new beginning, the restoration of its freedom. Its energies, released from the narrow parameters of electoral politics, can be devoted to building the nation rather than administering the state.

The second argument deals with the burden of party politics. The mountain of organizational trivia required to create a credible party can easily be underestimated; the power it can wield once elected to office can just as easily be overestimated. In both cases, in or out of office, this political route cannot create the conditions that would accelerate political independence.

By becoming a political party among others, the national movement necessarily forces the other parties to distance themselves from it, in total or partial opposition. Furthermore, it implicitly lays claim to a 'superior calling.' The 'Mon non est québécois' trumpeted by the 'no' forces during the referendum was a response to the implicit disqualification that a 'party embodiment' of the national movement conveyed.

A political party is not the appropriate instrument to achieve independence. How can it challenge the legitimacy of a state when it has to abide by its rules of the game? Everything is geared to secure a majority of votes in a ritualized exercise called an election. Party membership drives, riding associations, party platforms, finance campaigns, media strategy, party congresses, letter mailing, sloganeering, door-to-door canvassing, media mobilization, policy speeches, campaign promises: all this and more are the stock-in-trade of political parties and elections. And to achieve what? The responsibility and, for some, the privilege of administering the state. Party politics are based on interest groups. The pursuit of the superior calling becomes even less possible *after* electoral success. Once in office one is caught up with the responsibilities of day-to-day administration, with crisis management and crisis avoidance on the top of the agenda. The superior calling, in contrast, would require crisis creation. Once in office, in so-called power, can the party be used to change the structure of the state? Clearly not, since the means of violence, the army, escapes its control.

One final argument to welcome the national movement's break from party politics has to do with the artificial polarization created by that form of politics. Historically, reaching back into the nineteenth century, the social group most concerned and frustrated by the English hegemony over economic activity in Montreal was French-Canadian business men. Their frustration led to the establishment of the St Jean Baptiste Society of

Montreal. It was always composed of business-oriented professionals and was a bulwark institution underpinning the national movement, and traditionally supported the Union Nationale. When, despite its opposition, that party, under Jean-Jacques Bertrand, pushed through Bill 63, an antinational bill designed to placate immigrants assimilating to the English, the St Jean Baptiste Society withdrew its support and the Union Nationale withered away.

With the founding of the Parti Québécois, uniting disaffected Liberals and the more radical Rassemblement pour l'Indépendance Nationale (RIN), the national movement entered the arena of mass-society politics. It hit the media. It was enthusiastically received by students and their teachers. It swept the intelligentsia, made inroads in the labour movement and eventually within the civil service. Left out, and uninvolved, was the francophone business community. Finally, the national movement created hysterical fears among all anglophones, which were equally 'hyped' by their media. Since the mid-sixties, and increasingly so since then, elections have become essentially media events, typically without content and issues. Like all fads, however, political fads are short-lived, and what is important is to join on time.

The euphoria of quick success, and the youth and youthful enthusiasm of its most active suporters, gave a false sense of inevitable and facile victory. Don't we always say that 'the youth of today are the leaders of tomorrow'? Yet this is the tritest and most senseless of clichés since (as though we didn't know all along) by the time they lead they will no longer be young – and practically all of them will be among the 'led' of tomorrow. Dreams, as one tries to achieve them, can take on the shape of nightmares. This one was to be spared such labour. When they come so cheap they don't last long. The shallowness of media can easily blur the lines between dream and reality. Media marketing has not affected the fortunes of the Parti Québécois alone. Not only have René Lévesque and Pierre Elliott Trudeau been quickly destroyed by media campaigns. Robert Bourassa and Claude Ryan have also tasted media defeats. John Turner was chastised, and Brian Mulroney, it would appear, gets his come-uppance sooner than expected.

Mass-media politics do not seem to be, therefore, an appropriate vehicle to reach a serious goal such as independence. They tend to cheapen what they carry and are best left to advertise market commodities, the quick fix, and cheap thrills.

The parting of the ways should, therefore, be welcomed. It will eliminate the artificial conflicts between segments of Quebec society, between business men and intellectuals, between different political parties claiming to represent the nation when, at most, they represent interest groups. Other better and deeper means can be counted on to further the cause of the national movement.

What are the options open to the national movement after its divorce from institutionalized party politics? Clearly, they involve extraparliamentary politics. But such politics offer an array of possibilities, some of which can equally be counter-productive. The first option to eliminate is the use of subterranean military force. Guerrilla warfare and terrorism are not politically effective. No more than stalemates can now be achieved, as is clearly evident in Northern Ireland and Lebanon. When such strategies did work, it was because the costs outweighed the benefits to the occupying power. For the costs to outweigh the benefits two conditions are required: great physical distance from the occupiers' home base and sparse settlement of nationals from the occupying country. That is how Israel and Kenya could achieve independence. Neither of these conditions obtains in the case of Quebec. Furthermore, even in such circumstances, the nationals settled there must have a country to which they can retreat. The French could return from Algeria; the English in Rhodesia would emigrate. But the Boers in South Africa have no place to go. It is doubtful if they would be welcomed in Holland; nor is it clear that they would want to go there. Their resistance, as their history shows, can be expected to go on to the finish.

In the case of Quebec, we have the worst geopolitical situation of any of the states already referred to. Nicaragua is in a most enviable situation by contrast. Indeed, the Americans are unable to recruit any real support among Latin American countries to bring down the Sandinista regime. They would have no such trouble enlisting support to keep Quebec in Canada.

Furthermore, an independent Quebec state involves the partition of Canada. Territorial integrity is to a country what bodily integrity is to a person. Geopolitically, total independence for Quebec requires the will to go it alone in the Maritimes and Newfoundland. The latter, I am sure, could be tempted. None of these considerations ever became issues of public debate and discussion during the whole 'electoralist' approach to independence. The common myth shared by both those opposed to sovereignty-association and those in favour was that should the 'oui' forces have won decisively, it would have led automatically to the creation of a sovereign state with association with Canada. That 'myth' would have had a rude awakening very shortly after a victory for the 'oui.' Such naïvety, in a sense, honours us. But it augurs poorly for the kind of sophistication that will be required to inch our way towards sovereignty.

The remaining options will require shunning from the media. The days of mobilization of the masses, which is what the media can help to deliver, are not at hand. Hard work, serious business, has to be attended to before that. The media, by their nature, deal with the ephemeral, the current event. They can quickly report world events because they do not know or care to know what caused them. Nothing is as old for a true media person than last week's news. Shunning the media is the first condition of serious planning. Communications specialists are to modern society what gossipy spinsters were in yester-year's small town, and should be treated the same way. What will be needed are men and women who are tight-lipped, serious and single-minded, strategically located in private organizations and public institutions, able to garner human and material resources and information and to quietly and effectively pursue very specific goals.

The first option is to appropriate the territory, very consciously and systematically. For a century the Church fostered the settlement of the unoccupied territory of the province. The time has come to take full possession of the urban territory of Greater Montreal. Montreal West had a convenant for generations not to sell houses to French Canadians. The Lakeshore, as a string of communities, developed during the post-war period changing small parishes into suburban towns in systematic opposition and resistance to the needed changes in Quebec society. The best way to stop this resistance is to have the present occupiers become minorities in their own communities. The same things are happening to the French community in the Bytown section of Ottawa. Let it be a natural, progressive process and Joan Dougherty, the MLA from the West Island, will lose her seat and her platform.

The second option concerns the development of a national economic basis. Denied access to foreign portfolio capital that set up Confederation and its industrial policy, the Québécois managed to achieve modest capital accumulation the hard way: through savings of peasants and workers in the parishes' Caisses populaires. A few indigenous insurance and trust companies and a few small-scale chartered banks rounded out the institutional framework.

During the fifties, Michel Brunet and other nationalists chided the laissez-faire nature of the provincial state. It argued that the state should intervene in the market-place for the economic development of the Québécois as a nation. While the attempt at state capitalism during the early period of the Quiet Revolution was none too successful, an unmitigated success was achieved in the field of capital accumulation with the establishment of the Quebec Pension Fund and La Caisse de Dépôts et de Placements. A young graduate of L'Ecole des Hautes Etudes Commerciales once described the new situation as public capital searching for ways to become private. The investment policies of the Caisses de Dépôt were, for a time, a source of controversy. The conservatives on its board, and Eric Kierans was among them, wanted to shy away from investments in French-Canadian firms because that would constitute an inappropriate outlet for the savings of the people of Quebec. Economists are obviously not immune from cultural bias. In 1982 its investment decisions prompted the Canadian Pacific Limited to lobby for legislation – the ill-fated Bill S-31 – in the Canadian Parliament to set a limit as to the shares it could own in Canadian corporations. When Québécois capital achieved a position from which it could take over such a British institution as the Canadian Pacific Railway, it was defined as a threat to be politically thwarted. It is ironic that Québécois capital is defined as 'hostile' while American capital is always perceived as 'friendly.' After their election, Bourassa and the Liberal party proceeded to make amends, as expected, by giving Quebecair over to CP Air, which then joined with Alberta capital to create a new 'national' airline. These conflicts, in contrast with those of a hundred years ago, are an outgrowth of surplus rather than of scarcity, which, I suppose, is of some consolation.

The path to be taken, it seems to me, is to channel the investment of Quebec savings increasingly into the economy of Quebec and more particularly of Montreal, its metropolis. One of the paradoxical features of the Caisses de Dépôts et de Placements is that, through its investment practice, it is the single greatest exporter of capital from Quebec. While this may be economically prudent and useful, it should also have as a clear-cut objective to increase francophone control of the economy of Quebec. With the revival of entrepreneurship and the fiscal incentives to promote savings investment in Quebec firms Quebec is becoming, according to Tom Courchene, a prominent right-wing economist from Ontario, the vanguard of economic enlightenment. Be that as it may, the fact of the matter is that Quebec today is in a much better situation to exercise increasing economic control than it ever was in its history. Furthermore, if it has managed to come so far, it is not, as is commonly believed, in spite of the national movement but, quite the contrary, because of it.

The third option open to the national movement concerns the language issue. My argument is quite simple. The legislative route that was taken with the enactment of Bill 101 was important in a symbolic manner. It proclaims that the language of public space in civil society in Quebec is French, and that was and remains necessary. But to leave the enforcement of this legislation to an administrative body through a bureaucratic process is the best way to ensure very little progress. Although the Office de la Langue Française was set up to implement Bill 101 it proceeded in the 'bureaucratic' way. 'State' bureaucrats haggled with 'corporate' bureaucrats in negotiating a bureaucratic 'certificate of francization.' What a 'certificate of francization''s impact on social reality has been, or will be, no one knows but we may assume that the changes are more cosmetic than substantial.

Nothing is more effective as a language 'cop' than the unilingual citizen who feels at home, and who refuses both to speak a language other than his own and to be addressed in a language other than his own. The unilingual person is the most political of individuals when it comes to language enforcement, the most adamant and unyielding, and yet that person need not be politically conscious. Becoming unilingual is a sign of full membership, if not for the immigrant who is 'transitionally' bilingual, then for his offspring who will achieve unilingualism.

The well-intentioned, politically unconscious intolerance of the unilingual citizen dawned on me a few years ago in response to a question I was asked after a talk on Quebec society to a group of Montreal-based civil servants of the secretary of state. One of them, responsible for the Chinese immigrants in Montreal, asked me the following question: Could you explain to me why Chinese immigrants in Montreal, on the whole, neither speak nor understand French or English when they come to their citizenship hearings while the Chinese immigrants in Winnipeg speak and understand English when they come to their citizenship hearings? After a protracted pause, I gave roughly the following answer: For better than two centuries in Montreal, the English on the whole neither spoke nor understood French; the French, in the great majority, neither spoke nor understood English. Not speaking or understanding a language widely used in your midst is, therefore, a 'normal' state of affairs for both the English and the French. It should, then, come as no surprise if neither group is upset at not understanding or being understood by the immigrant Chinese or for that matter any other immigrant group. This kind of 'tolerance' will not be found in any other Canadian city. That was the substance of my answer.

This leads me to raise the following questions: Where is the 'normal' state of affairs to be found – in Winnipeg or in Montreal? Is Winnipeg intolerant or Montreal intolerably tolerant? The answer to me is clear: The intolerable tolerance of the French in Montreal is something that the national movement can mobilize to change. Legislation alone will never achieve it, but a mobilized citizenry that will not tolerate being spoken to in another language and that will not tolerate not to be understood when speaking their own language by other citizens of Montreal will achieve a language revolution swiftly and cheaply.

The advantages of a mobilized citizenry over 'state' bureaucrats are abundantly clear. The latter are few in numbers, work five days a week, are seldom seen, and are very expensive. The former are everywhere to be found, in every walk of life and social setting, seven days a week at no pay. In the first instance, the price exacted from the nonconformist is a paltry fine after long legal battles. In the second the 'deviant' is submitted to unrelenting social discomfort that is psychologically very exacting every time he attempts to resist the new language code of everyday life. In the first instance the Supreme Court of Canada can declare the laws out of line with the constitution. In the second instance the decisions of the Supreme Court will become a dead letter of the law unable to affect the new social reality. When it comes to conflicts between mores and the law, sociology, a most uncertain discipline, is fairly certain that the law, not the mores, is the loser. That applies to all laws, including constitutions. In such an event, the law remains basically unenforced and unenforceable, and its transgression produces neither guilt nor, most of the time, punishment. And when the law does mete out punishment it feeds rather than crushes the mores that it tries to eliminate. Trudeau and his docile Westmount echo Don Johnston have frequently claimed that a French Quebec in an English Canada is tantamount to separatism. Let's test their assumption that Canada cannot accommodate a French Quebec. The potential to do so is there. Defining this third option as a top priority is one of the tasks of the national movement. Another generation should pick it up.

The retreat from party politics is not a blow, but a welcomed change of course for the national movement. The new situation opens up new options and courses of action that can best be carried out away from the glare of the mass media. Rather than attempting another foray into party politics, the energies of the national movement should be devoted to considering and implementing these new courses of action. As, indeed, they once were. And they are not spent. In a quieter, more unified, and mature fashion the dream of nationhood shall live on.

NOTE

Written for this volume, October 1987, St Benoît du Lac

Glossary

Aislin cartoon The famous cartoon by Aislin (Terry Mosher) which illustrates
Jean Marchand's reference to the broad basis of conspiracy with the FLQ by
having Marchand carry all of the Bell Telephone directories of the major cities
in Quebec.

Ancien Régime The name used to refer to the political regime under the absolute
monarchy in France during the centuries before the French Revolution.

Angers, François-Albert (1909–) A distinguished economist and Quebec nationalist who spent his entire career at the Ecole des Hautes Etudes Commerciales, where he had been trained. A conservative economist, who opposed
the basic features of the welfare state such as family allowances and old-age
pensions, he was also a champion of co-operatives, corporatism, and provincial autonomy. One of his books is *Les droits du français au Québec* (1971).

Arendt, Hannah (1906–75) A political-philosopher of German-Jewish descent,
educated in the German philosophical tradition under Husserl, Heidegger,
and Jaspers. She fled Germany when Hitler took power. After a stay in
Paris she made her way, after escaping from Var, a concentration camp in the
Vichy regime, through the Pyrenees and Spain to the United States. She
taught at the New School for Social Research in New York and the University
of Chicago. Her first major publication in English, *The Origins of Totalitarianism* (1951), an account of what led politics in Western society to totalitarianism,
has become a classic.

Asbestos Strike A bitter strike in 1949 against the foreign-owned Canadian Johns-
Manville Company that signalled the birth of political opposition to the
political regime of Premier Maurice Duplessis. After he declared the strike

illegal, the provincial police were brought in and violence erupted. University students sided with the workers and organized help for the strikers. By organizing worker-subsidization through parish church donations Archbishop Charbonneau of Montreal helped the workers to weather the strike, thus incurring the wrath of Premier Duplessis. He was eventually forced to resign his see for 'health' reasons.

Barrette, Antonio He had a brief tenure as Premier of Quebec in 1960, succeeding Paul Sauvé. While Sauvé had succeeded Duplessis without any dissent, Barrette's bid for succession was bitterly contested. His government was defeated after a few months by the Liberals under Jean Lesage. Later John Diefenbaker made him ambassador to Greece.

Beattie, Christopher A very promising sociologist who, before his premature death, produced the best work within the research commissioned by the Royal Commission on Bilingualism and Biculturalism. His still very relevant research was published as *Minority Men in a Majority Setting* (1975).

Bernier, Mgr Paul Before becoming Bishop of Gaspé he was secretary to the Canadian Conference of Bishops. His rebuke of Dion and O'Neill for their 1957 publication 'Le chrétien et les elections' received little attention and had no effect. *See also* Dion.

Bill S-31 Tabled in the senate in November 1982, this bill – 'An Act to Limit Shareholding in Certain Corporations' – died on the order paper when the 1984 election was called. The stated purpose – 'to prevent provincial governments and their agencies from acquiring more than a 10% interest in companies involved in interprovincial transportation' – was aimed in fact at preventing the Caisse de dépôts et de placements from attaining a controlling interest in Canadian Pacific Limited. The bill was denounced by Quebec finance minister Jacques Parizeau, by the Caisse, and by many politicians and senators from Quebec.

Bill 22 Introduced in May 1974 by the Liberal government of Robert Bourassa, this bill proclaimed French the official language of Quebec. It provided incentives for firms to expand use of French in their daily operations, something they had been curiously oblivious to before. It also sought to integrate immigrant children into French schools. The 'language tests' that preschoolers had to pass produced very emotional outbursts among English-speakers. Bill 22 infuriated the anglophones but did not please the francophones, many of whom felt it did not go far enough.

Bill 63 Passed in 1969 by the Union Nationale government headed by Premier Jean-Jacques Bertrand, this bill was introduced by a reluctant minister of education, Jean-Guy Cardinal. It gave the immigrants the right to choose the school system they wanted: English or French. It stirred strong and vocal opposition among the francophones of Quebec. When Bertrand called an election for 24 April 1970, the Union Nationale lost to the Liberals. The Liberals, with 44 per cent of the vote, won 77 seats; the PQ, with 27 per cent of the vote, won 7; the Union Nationale, with 20 per cent of the vote, won 17 seats; and the Ralliement Créditiste, with 12 per cent of the vote, won 12 seats. The 1970 election marks the rise of the Parti Québécois and the eventual demise of the Union Nationale. Bill 63 played an important part in both events.

Brunet, Michel A noted and prolific historian, as concerned with the present as with the past, who taught at the University of Montreal, where he had considerable impact. Although a student of Lionel Groulx he parted company with his mentor when he took issue with the 'messianism, agriculturalism and anti-statism' of traditional nationalism. For that reason he can be considered the founder of 'neo-nationalism' in Quebec.

'Cahiers de Doléances' A political document outlining the grievances of the Estates General for Louis XIV in 1789 just before the French Revolution.

Caouette, Réal (1917–76) For a long time the lone French Canadian elected by the Social Credit to the Canadian parliament. In 1962, however, under his impetus, the Créditiste party sent twenty-six members from the province of Quebec to Ottawa. These results came as a total surprise, except to Peter Regenstreif, a young political scientist who had covered the election. Dismay, disbelief, and a good measure of worry spread in the political and corporate establishment.

Cité Libre A review founded by Pierre Elliott Trudeau and others that expressed the dissent of the emerging middle classes in the fifties. Its main target was what Trudeau labelled 'the clerico-nationalist regime' of Premier Maurice Duplessis, which it characterized as reactionary, corrupt, and undemocratic.

Common Front Strike The three major labour unions in Quebec created a 'common front' in the negotiations with the provincial government for all of the public-sector employees. When their negotiations were unsuccessful they called a general strike in April 1972. Legislation forcing the end of the strike was resisted, and the three labour leaders – Marcel Pepin of the Confédérations des syndicats nationaux (CSN), Louis Laberge of the Fédération des Travailleurs du Québec (FTQ), and Yvon Charbonneau of the Corporation des Enseignants du Québec (CEQ) – were jailed by the Bourassa government. The rift between the labour unions and the Liberal party led them to support the Parti Québécois.

Compact Theory Representing the view that Confederation was a 'pact' between the two founding peoples of Canada, this theory was widely held among French-Canadian constitutionalists, but never acknowledged in similar English-Canadian circles. Lester B. Pearson, in setting the terms of reference of the Royal Commission on Bilingualism and Biculturalism, referred to the 'two founding races.' This dualist conception of Confederation died with the patriation of the Canadian constitution, which Quebec opposed but which was nevertheless 'enforced.'

Company of Young Canadians The CYC was initiated by the federal government of Lester Pearson in 1965. The theory behind its establishment was influenced by the perspective elaborated by Saul Alinsky, an activist sociologist, who observed that the urban poor were disorganized and, because of this, were not part of the political process. Since the political process basically responds to organized pressure groups, he championed, as his basic strategy, the idea that organizing the poor around their needs would have far-reaching consequences for the nature of the society. This was the era of the proliferation of 'citizens' groups,' 'social animation initiatives,' etc. Members of the CYC moved into poor neighbourhoods and attempted to mobilize and organize them.

corvées Represented the labour that peasants or indentured servants had to undertake for seigneurs or the king.

Dion, Rev. Gérard (1912–) A professor at Laval University and long-time director of the School of Industrial Relations of Laval University, he was the co-author, with Father Louis O'Neill, of 'Le chrétien et les elections' (1957), an article in which the political morality of the Union Nationale party under the leadership of Maurice Duplessis was denounced. The article achieved instant notoriety in the press and intellectual circles and constituted a daring attack by two clerics on the premier of the province, an unusual occurrence in those times.

Fanon, Frantz (1925–61) Born in Martinique, he studied psychiatry in France, served as a doctor in Algeria during the French-Algerian war, and found himself in sympathy with the rebels. His book *The Wretched of the Earth: The Handbook for the Black Revolution That Is Changing the Shape of the World* (1961) had an impact on the left in Quebec.

Gérin, Léon The first sociologist in Canada. Trained in Paris in the late nineteenth century he did research on a part-time basis when he worked as a federal civil servant. His essays and books have had a considerable impact on the view of French-Canadian society held by social scientists, notably of the Chicago School: the American anthropologist Horace Miner, who published a classic community study, *St. Denis: A French Canadian Parish* (1939), and Everett Hughes, an American sociologist who had considerable influence on some Quebec sociologists. Hughes taught at McGill University in the late 1930s and early 1940s and published a classic monograph, *French Canada in Transition* (1943). Among Gérin's most notable works on French Canada were *Aux sources de notre histoire* and *Le type économique et social des canadiens-français*.

Grant, George (1918–) A distinguished social philosopher from McMaster University. His classic book *Lament for a Nation* (1965) initiated a debate in the 1960s about the anti-national behaviour of Canada's economic élites. His exchanges with Cy Gonick and Gad Horowitz in *Canadian Dimension* gave rise to the expression 'red tory,' the label that became attached to the political stance his book had initiated.

Groulx, Lionel (1878–1967) A priest-historian who had a long teaching career at the University of Montreal. His writings had a great impact on the University of Montreal school of history and on Quebec society. An ardent nationalist, he represents the traditional nationalism, which Pierre Elliott Trudeau labelled 'clerico-nationalism' and attacked during the 1950s.

Holy Alliance Refers to a mystical pact concluded in Paris on 26 September 1815 whose signatories, the kings of Russia, Austria, and Prussia, were committed to mutual assistance every time the power of kings was threatened in Europe by popular movements. It remained a hollow pact shunned by the Englishman Castlereagh who, instead, initiated the Quadruple Alliance between England, Austria, Prussia, and Russia, an alliance particularly sensitive to suppressing any liberal movement in Europe.

Johnson, Daniel (1915–68) A member of Maurice Duplessis's cabinet in the 1950s, he succeeded Antonio Barrette as leader of the Union Nationale after defeating Jean-Jacques Bertrand in a leadership convention. He became premier of Quebec in 1966 when the Union Nationale unseated Jean Lesage's liberal government, marking the end, according to some, of the Quiet Revolution. His book, *Egalité ou Indépendance* (1965), set forth his positions on federal-provincial relations. He died in office. *See* Pierre-Marc Johnson.

Johnson, Pierre-Marc Son of a former premier, Daniel Johnson, he succeeded René Lévesque as leader of the Parti Québécois in 1985. Another son of the former premier, Daniel Johnson Jr, is the current minister of trade and commerce in Robert Bourassa's Liberal government. Pierre-Marc Johnson, under criticism from the *indépendantistes* in his party, in a surprise move, resigned as leader of the Parti Québécois and member of the National Assembly just after René Lévesque's funeral in November 1987 after he had become the object of public criticism by some MPs in his own party.

Kierans, Eric (1914–) A well-known economist and maverick politician whose Canadian nationalism and economic conservatism brought him academic respect and political misfortune. Professor of finance at McGill University, in 1960 he became president of the Montreal and Canadian stock exchanges. While he held this position he took to the hustings to attack the Créditistes after they had won twenty-six seats in Quebec in 1962. He entered the Quebec National Assembly in 1963 and joined the Lesage cabinet as minister of revenue and then of health. In 1966 he thwarted René Lévesque's bid for the presidency of the Quebec Liberal Federation, which he then headed until 1968. That year he became a member of the House of Commons and post-master general in the Trudeau cabinet. He resigned in 1971 and returned to teach economics at McGill. In 1979 he was appointed to the board of the Caisse de Dépôt et de Placements. He resigned from this board in May 1980 because he disagreed with the investment policies of the Caisse. He now lives in Halifax.

Lamontagne, Maurice (1917–83) One of the first Harvard-trained economists who, under the sponsorship of Father Georges-Henri Lévesque, OP, dean of the new social science faculty of Laval University, developed the department of economics. His book, *Le Fédéralisme Canadien* (1954), which emphasized the need of a strong central government to ensure economic stability, stirred controversy in Quebec nationalist circles. He became a cabinet minister in the government of Prime Minister Lester Pearson. His political influence waned as P.E. Trudeau's waxed. He was appointed to the senate in 1967.

Lesage, Jean (1912–80) A lawyer, Lesage entered the field of federal politics in the cabinet of Liberal prime minister Louis St Laurent. Later he became leader of the Quebec provincial Liberal party. In 1960 he defeated Antonio Barrette, who had become premier after Paul Sauvé's death. While Sauvé heralded the Quiet Revolution, Lesage is referred to as its father since it was under his tenure as premier that the reforms it ushered in were implemented. His party was defeated in 1966 by Daniel Johnson, who had become by then the leader of the Union Nationale. Many social analysts, especially in Marxist circles, date the end of the Quiet Revolution with the defeat in 1966 of the Liberal government of Jean Lesage. The same people labelled the subsequent years the 'quiet repression.'

Lévesque, René (1922–87) Initially a journalist and an American war correspondent during the Second World War, he subsequently became a highly popular TV journalist on world affairs as host of Radio Canada's 'Point de Mire.' He became politicized with the Radio-Canada strike in the late fifties. He joined the Liberal party and the cabinet of Premier Jean Lesage. He was, among other things, minister of natural resources and spearheaded the movement to nationalize the private power companies that still existed. During the 1962 election, in which this was the major issue, the political slogan 'maître chez nous' caught on and the Liberals were re-elected. Disenchanted with the provincial Liberal party's policies, he bolted the party and formed the Mouvement Souveraineté-Association (MSA). When it coalesced with the

Rassemblement pour l'Indépendance Nationale (RIN), the Ralliement
Nationale, and other smaller independence groups, the Parti Québécois (PQ)
was born. Elected to office in 1976 he led the 'oui' forces in the referendum
on sovereignty-association. Although he lost the referendum in 1980 his party
was re-elected for another term in 1981. He was eventually eased out of
office and was succeeded by Pierre-Marc Johnson. He died in the fall of 1987
and some 60,000 people in Montreal and Quebec paid him a final tribute
when he lay in state.

Mackasey, Bryce (1927–) Once a Liberal member from the Montreal riding of
Verdun and a member of the Trudeau cabinet, he was stunned by the lack of
distinction made by the English Canadians between the FLQ, the terrorist
group that created the October crisis, and the Parti Québécois, a political party
that advocated the independence of Quebec through the democratic
electoral process.

Maoism An ideology adopted by a radical left-wing student movement in the
1960s. China, Mao Zedong and the Chinese cultural revolution were their
references rather than Soviet Marxism, which had become suspect. The split in
the left gave rise in the sixties to the expressions 'the Old Left' and 'the
New Left,' the Maoists being the 'far-out' new Left.

Marchand, Jean (1918–) After graduate studies at Laval's Faculty of Social Science
he worked in the labour movement and became a prominent leader in the
Confédération des Travailleurs Catholiques du Canada (CTCC), later renamed
the Confédération des Syndicats Nationaux (CSN). He was a minister in the
Trudeau cabinet, from which he resigned over the Canadian Air-Traffic
Controllers' strike. He eventually became a senator.

MacLennan, Hugh (1907–) A distinguished Canadian novelist and essayist
whose novel *Two Solitudes* (1945), a story of French-English relations in
Montreal, was critically acclaimed.

Merry del Val, Cardinal A papal emissary sent on a mission by Pope Leo XIII in
1897 to warn the Catholics of Quebec of the dangers of 'modernism,'
including 'liberalism.'

Metternich, Clements Von (1773–1859) Minister of foreign affairs and chancellor
of Austria for nearly forty years. After Napoleon's defeat he restored
Austria's influence over Germany and Italy. Conservative and counter-
revolutionary, his power waned and, with the revolution of 1848, he was
forced to flee to Holland.

MSA *See* René Lévesque.

October crisis Refers to the kidnapping of James Cross, the British commercial
attaché in Montreal, by a cell of the Front de Libération de Québec (FLQ) on
5 October 1970. About a week later, on 10 October, Pierre Laporte, the

minister of labour in the Liberal government of Robert Bourassa, was kidnapped. On 16 October, the Trudeau government invoked the War
Measures Act. A round-up of 436 people by the police was set in motion. None
of them was released until after the crisis was over. On 17 October Pierre
Laporte was executed. Cross was found and released in early December in
exchange for the safe conduct to Cuba of the FLQ cell that captured him.

Parti Pris A Marxist periodical, which in the early 1960s represented for the
youth of that decade what *Cité Libre* had represented to the restive part of
the intelligentsia in the fifties.

Parti Québécois Formed in 1968 with the merger of René Lévesque's Mouvement
Souveraineté-Association, the Rassemblement pour l'Indépendance
Nationale (RIN), then led by Pierre Bourgault, and the Ralliement National,
an offshoot of the Créditiste party. The Parti Québécois won the general
election in the province of Quebec on 15 November 1976.

Payette, Lise In the 1976 election, after having left her popular 'talk show' on
Radio-Canada, she was elected as PQ member of the Quebec National
Assembly. She joined the cabinet and pushed through the 'no-fault'
automobile insurance plan. Initially resisted, it has become a 'model' not yet
implemented in most other Canadian provinces. In the referendum
campaign she is charged with having made a political blunder by scorning the
'Yvettes' – The 'Yvetes' referred to women as stereotyped portrayal of
women found in school textbooks – and referring to Claude Ryan's wife as an
Yvette. This 'gaffe' helped crystallize support for the 'non' forces of the
referendum, which, after this event, developed the momentum they had been
lacking. Lise Payette did not stand for re-election, and returned to television as a writer of popular serial programs.

Pelletier, Gérard (1919–) One of the so-called three 'doves,' the others being
Pierre Elliott Trudeau and Jean Marchand. They became involved in federal
politics both to enhance the quality of francophone representation in federal
politics and to thwart the development of the independence movement in
Quebec. All three had roots in the Catholic Action movements of the late
1940s. Pelletier, who had become editor of *La Presse*, Montreal's major daily
newspaper, was a well-recognized and esteemed 'progressive' intellectual in
the post–Second World War period. He was secretary of state in the
Trudeau government. He left politics for diplomatic assignments in the late
1970s.

Renérendum A colloquial expression that gained currency when René Lévesque
insisted upon an internal referendum in the Parti Québécois because he
disagreed with the party's national convention resolution of December 1981.
At that convention the delegates stripped any reference to association in

the first article of its program, defining independence as the goal of the party, in retaliation for the unilateral patriation of the constitution against the expressed dissent of Quebec. The write-in referendum gave in to René Lévesque's wishes: 95 per cent of those who participated confirmed his position.

RIN *See* René Lévesque.

Rioux, Marcel A well-respected anthropologist at the University of Montreal. A politically committed intellectual who espoused separatism and socialism, Rioux wrote *Quebec in Question* (1971), a book that received both academic and political attention.

Royal Commission on Bilingualism and Biculturalism A commission struck by Prime Minister Lester Pearson in 1963. It was co-chaired by Davidson Dunton, who had headed the Canadian Broadcasting Corporation (CBC) and was then president of Carleton University, and by André Laurendeau, who was director and editorialist of *Le Devoir* of Montreal. It was often referred to as the 'Bi Bi Commission,' and more sarcastically as the 'Bye-Bye Commission.' Its five-volume report was issued in 1967.

Royal Commission on the National Development in the Arts, Letters, and Sciences This commission was struck in 1949 and chaired by Vincent Massey, later governor general of Canada. Father Georges-Henri Lévesque, OP, a Dominican priest who had founded and was the first dean of the social science faculty of Laval University, was the prominent Quebec member of the commission. It became known as the Massey-Lévesque Commission, and its report led to the establishment of the Canada Council.

St Jean Baptiste Parade Held on 24 June, the day of the patron saint of French Canadians, this traditional ritual event with floats and bands was witnessed by hundreds of thousands of Montrealers every year. In the parade of 1968, members of the Rassemblement pour l'Indépendance Nationale (RIN) joined the parade and created an incident. Prime Minister Trudeau stayed in the review stand while many others, including Mayor Jean Drapeau, fled for cover. The traditional parade has since been cancelled.

St Jean Baptiste Society Founded by Ludger Duvernay in the nineteenth century to protect and promote the economic and national interests of French Canadians.

Sauvé, Paul (1907–60) Succeeded Premier Maurice Duplessis as leader of the Union Nationale and premier of Quebec in autumn 1959, after Duplessis's sudden death. He had been called 'le Dauphin' because it was widely and rightly assumed he would succeed Duplessis. He had earned the respect of the new middle class and the intellectuals opposed to the Duplessis regime even though he had been a member of the Duplessis cabinet. It was widely known in these circles that Paul Sauvé disagreed with the autocratic nature of the Duplessis regime. He wanted to bring in reforms and had in fact announced some before his sudden death three months after taking office.

Scott, Frank (1899–1985) An eminent professor of law at McGill University and expert on constitutional law. He described the attempt by Claude Ryan, then editor of *Le Devoir*, to discuss the establishment of a government of national unity during the October crisis in 1970 as treasonous. Such a coalition would apparently have included the opposition party as well as the major leaders of institutions such as trade unions and municipalities.

Spicer, Keith A fluently bilingual political science professor at York University who was appointed the first commissioner of the Official Languages Act and, as such, was charged with making an annual report to parliament on the progress or lack of progress in the implementation of the Official Languages Act.

Tocqueville, Alexis de (1805–59) A nineteenth-century French political essayist and politician whose *Democracy in America 1835–1840* has become a classic. In 1856 he published *The Ancient Regime and the Revolution*.

Tupamaros The name given to Uruguayan revolutionaries whose political action consisted of kidnapping diplomats and executives of multinational companies and extracting ransom money for their release or the release from prison of their comrades. Political terrorism and financial extortion to fund such activities became fashionable, feared by most, admired by some.

Vallières, Pierre With Charles Gagnon, the theorist of the Front de Libération du Québec when it started to attack the symbols of capitalist oppression rather than those of purely political subjugation of Quebec. They were arrested in New York when they went to protest the plight of Quebec at the United Nations. While in jail Vallières wrote *Nègres blancs d'Amérique: autobiographie précoce d'un 'terroriste' Québécois* (1968). They were extradited and tried for inciting to violence but were acquitted in jury trials.

Yvettes See Lise Payette.